D0858304

Electroshock:
Its Brain-Disabling Effects

Peter Roger Breggin, M.D., is in the private practice of psychiatry in Bethesda, Maryland. He is the founder and executive director of the Center for the Study of Psychiatry, a nonprofit research and educational institute formed to examine the impact of psychiatry upon individual well-being, personal freedom, and civil liberty. Its board of directors includes psychiatrists, psychologists, lawyers, and congressmen concerned with psychiatric reform.

Dr. Breggin was graduated with honors from Harvard College in 1958 and from the Case Western Reserve University School of Medicine in 1962. He completed his psychiatric training at the State University of New York, Upstate Medical Center, in Syracuse, and at the Massachusetts Mental Health Center in Boston, where he was also a teaching fellow at Harvard Medical School. He has been a full-time consultant to the National Institute of Mental Health.

Dr. Breggin has written many professional and lay articles dealing with scientific, ethical, legal, and political issues in psychiatry. He has previously published three books, including a novel, *The Crazy from the Sane* (Lyle Stuart, 1971), which deals with ethical and political issues in psychiatry. His forthcoming book, *The Psychology of Freedom* (Prometheus Books, in press, 1980), presents a philosophy and psychology of life based on free will, personal freedom, and the capacity to reason and to love.

Electroshock:
Its Brain-Disabling Effects

Peter Roger Breggin, M.D.

Springer Publishing Company
New York

**For my wife and best friend,
Phyllis Lundy Breggin**

Selections from *One Hundred Years of Psychiatry* by Emil Kraepelin (New York: Citadel Press, 1962) and from *Shock Treatment Is Not Good for Your Brain* by J. Friedberg (San Francisco: Glide Publications, 1976) are reprinted with permission.

Copyright © 1979 by Peter Roger Breggin

Springer Publishing Company, Inc.
200 Park Avenue South
New York, N.Y. 10003

79 80 81 82 83 / 10 9 8 7 6 5 4 3 2 1

Library of Congress Cataloging in Publication Data

Breggin, Peter Roger, 1936-
  Electroshock, its brain-disabling effects.

  Bibliography: p.
  Includes index.
  1. Brain damage. 2. Electric shock therapy—
Complications and sequelae. 3. Electric shock—
Physiological effect. I. Title. [DNLM: 1. Shock
therapy, Electric—Adverse effects. 2. Brain damage,
Chronic—Etiology. WM412 B833e]
RC386.2.B73   616.8'912   79-15223
ISBN 0-8261-2710-X
ISBN 0-8261-2711-8 pbk.

Printed in the United States of America

Contents

Preface

This is the first systematic compilation and analysis of the medical literature pertaining to severe or permanent brain damage and mental dysfunction caused by electroconvulsive therapy. It is also the first time that the principle of brain-disabling therapy in psychiatry has been fully elaborated. Of course I take sole responsibility for my ideas and for examining each of the several hundred articles in this review, but I also wish to acknowledge a several-year-long flow of moral support, constructive criticism, and information from many friends and resources.

Among those who read the manuscript at various stages and gave me special help were Robert Grimm, a consummate neurologist, and Leonard Frank, a devoted advocate of the rights of psychiatric inmates. I want to give credit to John Friedberg, who during his neurology residency became the first physician in the history of medicine to risk his career by making *public* criticism of electroshock treatment. His example helped inspire me to finish this work. Because of the efforts of individuals like Friedberg, Grimm, Frank, and two other friends, Lee Coleman and Thomas Szasz, the public and the profession alike are now showing renewed concern about the dangers of electroconvulsive treatment. I also want to acknowledge Ursula Springer for having the courage to publish this book, and for coining the phrase "brain-disabling therapy."

As a psychiatrist in private practice, I have not had the advantage of help from a university, from research assistants, or from students. Without the existence of the National Library of Medicine, which stands but two blocks from my home and office, I could not have carried on this work. I want to thank Howard Drew of the National Library of Medicine for his good-hearted assistance over several years, and, indeed, I want to thank the entire staff for their uncommon pleasantness and helpfulness during the many hundreds of hours I have spent in their company. I also want to thank Jean Jones and the staff of the American Psychiatric Association Museum Library for their help with special requests, and my typist, Donna Aspinall, for her excellent and enthusiastic work. And though she has had no direct connection with this book, I want to mention *Boston Globe* reporter Jean Dietz, whose brave and honest reporting of the psychosurgery and electroshock controversies has encouraged me and stimulated a healthy public response. Reporter Robert Trotter also wrote many important pieces on psychosurgery for *Science News* and other periodicals.

As in everything else I have done since we first met, no one and no resource has been as important as my wife, Phyllis Lundy Breggin, who has helped me find everything from my misplaced note cards to a more mature style of presenting the material. She has assisted me in the library, edited several drafts of the manuscript, and made many good suggestions on style and content.

I want to say a few words to those people who have been subjected to electroconvulsive therapy. While there can be no doubt that the treatment frequently causes great harm, it is possible that many individuals escape with little or no bad aftereffects. Most important, experiences with personal friends have shown me that even individuals who feel they have been harmed by the treatment can nonetheless live fully responsible, worthwhile, and happy lives.

I also want to address myself to those physicians who may find themselves confronted with a difficult moral choice. I know of at least three medical doctors including John Friedberg whose careers were seriously harmed when psychiatrists retaliated against them for criticizing electroconvulsive therapy. I did not have the courage to risk my own nascent career by refusing to give electroconvulsive therapy during my hospital training. I have regretted that cowardice for more than a decade. I hope this book will provide physicians with sufficient theoretical and scientific support to enable them to oppose the treatment without placing themselves in such jeopardy.

My concluding wish is for this book to encourage beginning professionals in every field to look beyond "expert opinion" and beyond "the authorities" to discover the facts for themselves and to develop theories and principles consistent with their own rational perceptions of reality. When individuals in psychiatry and elsewhere turn to reason, research, and experience rather than to experts and authorities, treatments such as electroconvulsive therapy will die of their own irrationality.

P.R.B.

Electroshock:
Its Brain-Disabling Effects

1

Major Issues in Electroconvulsive Therapy

Electroconvulsive therapy (ECT) and electroshock therapy (EST) are synonyms for a psychiatric treatment in which electricity is applied to the head and passed through the brain for the production of a grand mal, or generalized convulsion. ECT is often called shock treatment or convulsive treatment, although these are general terms that can also be applied to related psychiatric interventions. More recently, in order to dispel the threatening connotations of words like "shock" and "convulsion," it has been renamed electrotherapy by its advocates.

Electroconvulsive therapy, or ECT, was invented by Bini and Cerletti in Italy in 1938 (Bini, 1938) and was first used in the United States in May 1940 (Pulver, 1961). It quickly won wide acceptance among psychiatrists, and by 1943 tens of thousands of patients had been treated in the United States alone, and hundreds of articles had been published concerning its effects.

In the beginning ECT was used in large state mental hospitals, often as a method of subduing and controlling large numbers of difficult, uncooperative, or unruly patients. It also was widely considered to be a treatment for schizophrenia. In more recent years its more conservative advocates have limited its use to severe psychotic depressions; but it continues to be used for a wide variety of other purposes. Those psychiatrists who favor the treatment are in general agreement that it greatly benefits individuals suffering from psychotic depressions and that it has no known permanent ill effects. They also tend to agree that the ameliorating effect is wholly "empirical," that is, without known scientific or theoretical explanation.

Summing up his lifetime experience as a world authority and advocate of ECT, Lothar Kalinowsky (McDonald, 1978), recalled a sentence in his 1946 edition with Paul Hoch: "At present we can only say that we are treating empirically disorders whose etiology is unknown, with methods whose action is also shrouded in mystery." Kalinowsky stated that he was "proud" of that sentence and declared, "Today we are in 1978—30 years later—and exactly the same is true."

It is time to take the shroud off the mystery. For 40 years a massive amount of evidence has been accumulated that proves that ECT causes brain damage and dysfunction. The purpose of this book is to amass and to analyze that evidence, to examine alternative explanations of "efficacy," and to demonstrate what I call the brain- and mind-disabling hypothesis—that ECT and the other major somatic treatments achieve their effects precisely by producing brain damage and mental dysfunction (Breggin, 1979).

Epidemiologic Data

Although advocates of ECT have noted a resurgence of the treatment (Kalinowsky, 1975a, p. 545), epidemiologic data concerning ECT usage have been very sparse until a recent series of reports. Because the profession and the public alike have had very little awareness of the large numbers of patients receiving the treatment, I will review the available facts in some detail. They will raise important issues for further analysis.

Prevalence of Usage

The most accurate data concerning the prevalence of ECT have been collected from private and public hospitals in Massachusetts. A survey conducted by the state's Department of Mental Health between May 1, 1973, and May 1, 1974, disclosed that 2,241 individuals were administered ECT (Grosser et al., 1974; Dietz, 1975). Official U.S. Census figures indicate that Massachusetts possessed 2.76 percent of the population during July 1973, from which we can roughly extrapolate a national annual rate of 81,195 ECT patients. The survey did not include patients treated as outpatients or as patients on the psychiatric units of general hospitals. In addition, it was conducted in response to severe criticism in local newspapers concerning the use of ECT in private psychiatric hospitals (Dietz, 1972; Harris, 1972), and these institutions were known to have curtailed their activities somewhat following the scrutiny that gave rise to the survey. From this we can conclude that the corresponding national number may approach or possibly exceed 100,000 patients per year.

A survey conducted by the National Institute of Mental Health for the year 1975 (Taube & Faden, 1977) generated a figure of 60,000 persons receiving ECT in the United States in all types of psychiatric inpatient facilities. The total is certainly larger, however, because of several limiting factors in the sampling technique (Faden, 1978): (1) Data collection traced patients only through the first three months of hospitalization, thus missing patients who were given ECT as a "last resort" after three months of unsuccessful treatment by other methods, and also missing chronic patients who were given ECT many months and even years after their admission. This review will suggest that both groups of patients may be substantial in number. (2) Psychiatrists administering outpatient ECT in private offices were not included in the survey of outpatient ECT. This is probably a relatively small number, however. (3) Outpatients in licensed psychiatric facilities were also excluded because the number of cases located were too small to make adequate statistical inferences. Nonetheless, according to Faden, an extrapolation would have added an additional 947 patients. (4) No attempt was made to focus on private profit-making psychiatric hospitals, which, we shall see, perform ECT at a ratio of 20:1 in comparison with public hospitals. Here large numbers of patients could have been overlooked through a small sampling error. (5) Most important, the sampling was entirely voluntary, and hospitals returned the forms or filled out various parts of the forms entirely at their own discretion. Because the disproportionate use of ECT in private profit-making hospitals was already a national controversy, and in some cases a scandal (*Psychiatric News,* 1971, 1973), it would have served the interests of these hospitals to neglect to answer or to report inaccurately in a survey requesting information concerning their rate of usage of ECT. Indeed, this conjecture on my part is confirmed by the relatively small percentage of admissions reported to be receiving ECT in private profit-making hospitals in this mail survey (7.5 percent) compared with the percentages reported (21 percent and 25 percent) from similar hospitals in two local surveys that collected data more systematically (Asnis et al., 1978; Grosser et al., 1974). Overall, then, the NIMH study provides us with a useful lower floor of *more* than 60,000 patients given ECT in the United States in 1975, but does not preclude a figure of 100,000 as the actual total.

As this book goes to press, another survey of ECT usage has been completed that suggests a lower national rate. A survey of all New York State facilities by the New York State Department of Mental Hygiene (Morrissey et al., 1979) found a total of 247,033 individual ECT treatments given during a five-year period from 1972 through 1977. The data disclosed a sharp 50 percent decline in usage from a high of 53,515 treatments in 1972 to a low of 27,201 treatments in 1977. If we assume an average number of ten treatments per patient, this means that approximately 2,700 patients were given ECT in New York State in 1977. Extrapolating this figure to the United States suggests a national rate of 32,000 patients treated in 1977.

The authors of the survey admit to several possible errors that would tend to underestimate the totals for New York. All the data were reported by staff at the hospitals "without independent validation by the study team." Also, the survey may have failed to record the administration of ECT on an outpatient basis by physicians practicing at general hospitals, while the investigators admit that "many private physicians" practice in this manner at general hospitals. The study may have also missed patients sent from state hospitals for brief stays at nearby general hospitals for the purpose of receiving ECT. Since the missing data admittedly would have come largely from the private sector, where most ECT is performed, it may have affected the totals to a significant degree. Nonetheless, I doubt if these omissions could account for the great discrepancy between this survey and the NIMH and Massachusetts studies. Of interest is the question "Is the national rate declining as the New York State rate seems to be declining?" We must wonder if some of the New York State decline is the result of a growing reluctance to report the number of ECTs being given. A decision on the part of only one or two private hospitals to report a relatively low rate to protect themselves could have substantially lowered the apparent rate. Indeed, one private profit-making hospital accounted for 22 percent of all the ECT treatments given in New York State during this period (see next section). It is also clear that the ECT rate will vary widely from state to state depending on the presence or absence of a few private facilities that perform a relatively large proportion of the total number of treatments.

Problems in evaluating the rate of ECT usage are also complicated by possibly vast differences in usage in differing localities. St. Louis, Missouri, for example, is well known for its leadership in the field of somatic psychiatric therapy. Based on an informal survey of St. Louis, Pitts (1972) estimated a rate of 10,000 treatments per day in the United States, which is surely unrealistic as a national rate since other areas of the country do not usually use as much ECT.

ECT in Private Profit-Making Hospitals

The Massachusetts survey disclosed the main reason why the prevalence of ECT frequently has been underestimated: by a ratio of 20:1, the vast majority of patients were treated in small private facilities rather than in public facilities. More than 25 percent of private admissions in the state were given the treatment (Grosser et al., 1974):

> Three public mental hospitals reported no use of ECT during the year. The ratio of patients treated with ECT to total number of inpatient admissions ranges from less than 1% to 70%. Two private psychiatric hospitals reported administering ECT to more than 50% of their inpatients, and a total of five of eleven private hospitals reported administering ECT to a third or more of their patients.

A less rigorous recent survey of New York City (Asnis et al., 1978) confirmed that the preponderance of ECT treatments are carried out in private profit-making psychiatric facilities:

> Five percent of patients in university and private nonprofit hospitals, less than 1 percent in public hospitals and 21 percent in private for-profit hospitals receive ECT. . . . Differences in incidence of use result from staff training, public antipathy, and economic factors.

Six of the surveyed psychiatric facilities did not use ECT at all, whereas in four institutions ECT was given to 40 percent of the patients. City, state, and veterans' facilities gave ECT to an average of 1 percent of inpatients, whereas private for-profit hospitals administered it to an average of 21.3 percent. Thus, in New York City as well as in Massachusetts, the rate of ECT use in private for-profit hospitals exceeds that in public facilities by 20 to 1 (or more).

Finally, the very recent study by the New York State Department of Mental Hygiene (Morrissey et al., 1979) confirms that the vast proportion of ECT is performed in private hospitals. Although treating a small proportion of the total psychiatric patients in the state, private hospitals accounted for 86 percent of the total ECT treatments. Private profit-making psychiatric hospitals performed almost 41 percent of the treatments, while private nonprofit general hospitals accounted for 33 percent. Although the latter hospitals are nonprofit institutions, the physicians treating private patients in these facilities would themselves be profit-making.

The New York State survey found considerable variation in the amount of ECT even within separate categories of facility, such as state hospitals and private profit-making hospitals. State hospitals accounted for only 11.7 percent of the treatments, even though they treat the vast majority of hospitalized patients; and among state hospitals, only 5 of 22 facilities accounted for more than half the treatments carried out in state facilities. These hospitals were described as "relatively older and larger hospitals which have a proportionately much larger chronic patient case-load." In private hospitals, a great disparity was again reported. Three of twelve responding hospitals reported no use of ECT, and four of twelve on the other end of the continuum performed 96.6 percent of the treatments administered in private hospitals. "Actually, one of these latter hospitals alone accounts for a five-year total of 54,688 treatments or 22 percent of the entire 247,033 treatments rendered by all facilities in New York State." No figure more graphically illustrates the truth that a patient's likelihood of receiving ECT depends mostly on the treating physician or the facility to which he or she is admitted.

The tremendous disparity between the use of ECT in private profit-making hospitals and academic as well as public facilities has been noted by several other observers. J. B. Robitscher (1974) has commented that "a proprietary hospital may give ECT to 60 percent, 70 percent, or even 100 percent of its patients—some hospitals use this as the only treatment modality." In Michigan, Tien (1975) reported that one state hospital did not use ECT at all and that another had reduced its usage to a "bare minimum" of less than 0.5 percent of its admissions.

It can be concluded that the private profit-making psychiatric hospitals and general hospitals use ECT far more than academic, public, and other nonprofit facilities, and that the utilization rate among hospitals varies enormously, from zero to 70 percent or more.

It is important not to accept personal impressions that ECT is used infrequently, even in relatively small institutions with which one is familiar. During my internship in a psychoanalytically oriented university hospital, most of the staff members thought that ECT was "rarely" used. To everyone's surprise, when I reviewed every discharge summary for an entire year, I discovered that 10 percent of the discharged patients had received ECT (Breggin, 1964). Similarly, when I questioned a knowledgeable state hospital director about the resurgence of ECT in his region, he responded that ECT was never used at his hospital, and rarely if ever used in the immediate vicinity. Later he checked more carefully and was surprised to find that ECT was being used extensively at a local private hospital and that staff from his own state hospital on two occasions sent outpatients for ECT.

ECT and the Individual Psychiatrist

The use of ECT varies enormously from psychiatrist to psychiatrist. Some use it frequently, as Perlson (1970), who described administering 50,000 treatments, or as one Veterans Administration physician, who personally informed me that he had given 100,000 treatments. On the other hand, many psychiatrists never use the treatment at all (Frankel, 1973).

An indication of the number of individual psychiatrists extensively involved in the use of ECT came indirectly from a recent report concerning the surcharge on malpractice insurance policies carried by doctors who perform ECT. Many members of the American Psychiatric Association are covered by a group malpractice contract (*Psychiatric News,* 1978b), and 14 percent of them carry additional expensive coverage for ECT (*Psychiatric News,* 1978a). If this percentage holds for the nation's 30,000 psychiatrists, we can reach agreement with Cammer's estimate (*Clinical Psychiatry News,* 1975) of between 3,000 and 4,000 psychiatrists significantly involved in using ECT. To account for an estimate approaching 100,000 patients treated with ECT each year in the United States, each psychiatrist in this group need only treat 25 to 35 patients a year with ECT.

The relatively uncommon use of ECT by the typical psychiatrist is also indicated in a recent survey by the American Psychiatric Association (1978), which found that only 16 percent of respondents to the survey had personally administered ECT in the previous six months, and that only 22 percent had administered it or recommended its use to psychiatric residents in the previous six months.

Numbers of ECT Administered to Individuals

Next to the overall prevalence of the use of ECT, the most important concern is the total number of treatments given any individual patient, because experimental and clinical data indicate that the damage inflicted by ECT is often proportional to the number of treatments. Very little data are available on this subject. The Massachusetts survey found that an average of 10 treatments were given to each individual, but that many patients received 35 or more during a one-year period, up to a maximum of 77 (Grosser et al., 1974). Reports that originally inspired the survey indicated that in years before the survey more than 100 ECT were given to some patients (Dietz, 1972; Harris, 1972). I personally have evaluated several patients who have received between 100 and 150 or more treatments at private psychiatric hospitals in the last decade. Cases of patients given more than 100 treatments also appear in the literature (Rabin, 1948; Perlson, 1945; Holt, 1965). Patients given intensive ECT (more than one a day) may also be given large numbers (Blachly & Gowing, 1966).

Fink and Abrams (1972) have advocated a range of 6 to 10 treatments for depression and 18 to 20 for schizophrenia, with a maximum of 40 treatments in some cases. My own examination of several hundred articles and my clinical and forensic experience confirm that this is the common range of treatment. In the United States a patient rarely receives fewer than six to eight treatments, and frequently many more.

The Type of ECT Administered

Another important variable is the type of ECT administered, a subject requiring some analysis throughout this review. In general, the vast majority of ECT given in the United States are "modified ECT"[1] accompanied by premedication, a general anesthetic, and an agent to paralyze the musculature, as well as by artificial respiration with oxygen (Asnis et al., 1978; Beresford, 1971; Grosser et al., 1974). Fewer figures are available concerning variations in the placement of the electrodes, although it is apparent that the traditional bilateral placement across the forehead is by far the most common. The New York survey (Asnis et al., 1978) found that 25 physicians used bilateral ECT exclusively, two used unilateral exclusively, and three used both. Experienced clinicians believe that bilateral ECT is more effective (Abrams & Taylor, 1976; Kalinowsky in McDonald, 1978). An American Psychiatric Association survey conducted in 1976 and published in 1978 found that 75 percent of psychiatrists reporting used bilateral ECT exclusively.

The Patient Population

The sex distribution of ECT is striking. In the Massachusetts survey, excluding the Veterans Administration hospitals, ECT was given to more women than men by a ratio of 2.35:1. The NIMH survey confirmed a ratio of at least 2:1. So do most of the reports in the literature. Accounting for this sex distribution is an important task of any theory that attempts to explain the use of ECT.

Information concerning the age of patients given ECT is difficult to find. The Massachusetts study stated that a "substantial number" of patients between 16 and 19 years of age were given ECT. The New York survey observed, "All physicians occasionally treated adolescent patients; only one reported giving ECT to children under the age of 13." The NIMH study shows that small percentages of individuals under age 18 were given ECT (4.4 percent in general hospitals, 1.1 percent in private hospitals), but these figures may be underestimated for the reasons I have already elaborated. The NIMH data do show that a substantial number of people age 65 and older are given ECT (16.1 percent in general hospitals, 11 percent in private hospitals). The use of ECT for the aged is important in the light of evidence that ECT is most dangerous when given to older people (Impastato, 1957).

---

1. On occasion throughout the text brief definitions or explanations will be provided for the nonmedical reader. For more exact information, the reader should consult an appropriate dictionary or the references.

   Modified ECT and *bilateral ECT* will be discussed and defined on pages 17 and 18.

In general the psychiatric literature most consistently advocates ECT for psychotic depressions (including involutional melancholia and manic depression, depressive phase). The data now available confirm that these are the most frequent diagnoses among patients given ECT, but that there is a very wide distribution among all functional diagnoses. In the Massachusetts survey schizophrenia of all types was the diagnosis for 26.3 percent of public hospital ECT patients, 23.8 percent of private hospital ECT patients, and 51.9 percent of veterans' hospital ECT patients. In private hospitals a large percentage of ECT treatment was accounted for by neurotic patients (25.9 percent) and by patients with personality disorders (9 percent). The New York survey did not break down the patients receiving ECT according to diagnostic categories, but did give data concerning the viewpoint of psychiatrists who give ECT. ECT was considered the treatment of choice for psychotic depression, but it also was recommended by a large percentage of psychiatrists for occasional use in childhood schizophrenia, acute schizophrenia, postpartum depression, neurotic depression, and personality disorders. In the NIMH survey in general hospitals and in private mental hospitals, a significant percentage of patients receiving ECT were diagnosed as schizophrenic (11.3 percent and 9.0 percent, respectively) and as neurotic (6.6 percent and 2.2 percent, respectively).

Statistical averages do not convey the wide variation among psychiatrists as to which individuals they treat with ECT. On the conservative end of the spectrum, many psychiatrists who use ECT recommend it for psychotic depression only, whereas some advocates of ECT are far more liberal. In a book for the layman, entitled *The Miracle of Shock Treatment*, psychiatrist Robert E. Peck (1974) advocated ECT for the pain associated with back ailments and cancer, for heroin withdrawal, for colitis and psoriasis, for the depression associated with multiple sclerosis and other diseases, and for schizophrenia. He declared, "Surely shock treatment represents one of those medical miracles that the *Reader's Digest* likes to write about."

The Legal Status of ECT Patients

No data are available concerning the most important legal and ethical issue surrounding ECT—the patients who are treated against their will. The definition of "voluntary" or "willing" in regard to ECT is itself fraught with difficulties that will require further analysis. At this point it is important to acknowledge that those who have surveyed ECT usage have not collected data pertinent to this issue, and that, among those who advocate and administer ECT, voluntary consent has not been an important or well-defined issue. Impastato (1957) advised that because many patients are afraid of ECT they should not be told when they are about to receive the treatment. He recommended informing a relative instead. Kalinowsky and Hoch (1961, p. 173) and Kalinowsky and Hippius (1969, p. 212) have written: "It is gratifying that the Pennsylvania Department of Justice . . . expressed an opinion to the effect that ECT is of recognized value and, therefore, may be applied to mental patients without the consent of the patient or his family."

The idea that a treatment can be imposed on a patient because it is considered *valuable* is foreign to medical practice, but commonplace in psychiatry. Beresford (1971) received answers to a questionnaire from 54 psychiatric units using electroshock, including 30 state hospitals and 24 hospitals or services affiliated with university medical centers. The response to his questions concerning consent for treatment illustrate the wide latitude assumed by psychiatrists in the exercise of their powers, including the enforcement of treatment without consent of the patient, relative, or legal representative:

> In the matter of obtaining consent for the use of ECT, 36 of the respondents had governing regulations requiring that they obtain before treatment a consent to ECT from each patient or his legal representative. Three units had rules which permitted them to perform ECT without the consent of patients or their legal representatives only if the patients were under involuntary commitment orders. Ten units had no rules requiring advance consent to ECT, but most of these customarily sought such consent. However, during 1968 eight units did use ECT in a few cases without the consent of patient or his legal representative.

A more recent survey of New York City hospitals by Asnis et al. (1978) indicated a similar situation. The authors found that "procedures for patients who refused to consent differed and were poorly defined. Procedures varied from consent of a close relative to authorization of the treating physician and to strict requirement of a court order." In other words, if a patient refused ECT in New York City, a psychiatrist, on his own discretion or according to hospital policy, might seek a court order, obtain the consent of a relative, or go ahead strictly on his own. Current attempts to improve the legal status of mental patients will be discussed in Chapter 13.

The ECT Controversy

From its inception in 1938 and its introduction into the United States in 1940, ECT received wide and enthusiastic support from many psychiatrists. But the voices of concern were raised almost as quickly. One of the nation's most esteemed neurologists, Roy Grinker, Sr., drew attention to the brain-damaging effects of ECT in 1942 (see Levy et al., 1942, especially the discussion); another neurologist, B. J. Alpers, also published research reports indicating brain damage in animals as early as 1942 (Alpers & Hughes, 1942a, 1942b) and warned about its threatening implications for human beings.

By the war years, concern about ECT was sufficient to curtail its use in some areas of the military. M. T. Moore (1947) complained that ECT was prohibited "by Washington," and that American soldiers had to be "bootlegged" to an English hospital for the treatment. He also observed that ECT had been given to soldiers at the front even though it was against the regulations.

By 1947 many American psychiatrists had become seriously distressed about the abuse and the hazards of ECT. The prestigious Group for the Advancement of Psychiatry (GAP), a committee of 150 establishment leaders, chastised both sides in the rising controversy. The unanimous GAP report (1947) declared:

> In view of the reported promiscuous and indiscriminate use of electro-shock therapy, your Committee on Therapy decided to devote its first meeting to an evaluation of the role of this type of therapy in psychiatry. Both the extravagant claims as to its efficacy made by its proponents and the uninformed condemnation of its use at all by its opponents indicate the emotional aura which surrounds this whole topic.

In a move still unparalleled in the history of psychiatry, GAP made serious criticism of the advocates of a major psychiatric treatment:

> The complication and hazards in its use should be reemphasized, since they appear to have been minimized by some workers. . . .
>
> Your Committee deplores certain widespread abuses of electro-shock therapy, amongst which are:
>
> a. Its use in office practice.
> b. Its indiscriminate administration to patients in any and all diagnostic categories.
> c. Its immediate use to the exclusion of adequate psychotherapeutic attempts.
> d. Its use as the sole therapeutic agent, to the neglect of a complete psychiatric program. . . .
>
> Abuses in the use of electro-shock therapy are sufficiently widespread and dangerous to justify consideration of a campaign of professional education in the limitations of this technique, and perhaps even to justify instituting certain measures of control.

In the years following the report the abuses of ECT did not abate. It continued to be used in state hospitals as an agent to suppress difficult patients, without even a pretense at "treatments." Shoor and Adams, in *The American Journal of Psychiatry* (1950), described and advocated the use of "intensive electric shock" in "chronic disturbed psychotic patients," declaring, "Our goals were not curative; they were limited to the level of improved ward behavior." Improved ward behavior meant subduing the patients: "Within two weeks from the beginning of our intensive electric shock treatment the character of the ward changed radically from that of a chronic disturbed ward to that of a quiet chronic ward." Giving some of the individuals more than 100 ECT treatments, they were "impressed" with the resemblance of some of the post-ECT patients to "the lobotomized patient."

The use of ECT to intimidate patients into submission was so commonplace (see Chapter 10), that Bennett (1949), a very staunch advocate of the treatment, declared:

> The promiscuous use of E.C.T. without adequate psychiatric therapies has become a medical scandal. Many institutions use it wholesale for all forms of mental illness without any other therapy—no proper nursing supervision, no occupational therapy, no psychotherapy—simply a pure physio-therapeutic procedure. They do not follow up patients or note relapses.

Bennett not only protested the "medical scandal," he warned that because of the abuse of ECT, "Patients' fears drive them to suicide. . . ."

Despite mounting abuses of the treatment, as well as growing evidence that it produced brain damage, within three short years of its initial report the Group for the Advancement of Psychiatry (1950) issued a revised report on ECT, softening its criticism on the basis of new "clinical" and "scientific" evidence. Concern was still voiced about "widespread abuses" and about the danger that "electroshock nullifies attempts at psychotherapy," but ECT was now seen as having almost unlimited applications to psychiatric disorders. Most importantly, there was no longer any suggestion of a need for an educational campaign or controls. The most severe criticism in the report was relegated to an addendum of dissenting opinions, which concluded, "Since the real situational factors and their attendant emotional problems are not affected by this treatment, the patients continue to live unhappy, maladjusted lives."

Why should this prestigious group soften its originally unanimous report in the space of three years—three years that witnessed increasing evidence of widespread abuses as well as brain damage? Promoters of the treatment had been caught off guard by the unexpectedly strong criticism in the initial report, and now brought influence on the GAP to revise its statements. The alleged clinical and scientific evidence was not cited. But the new report had the benefit of several well-known special "consultants," including Kalinowsky, Hoch, and other staunch advocates of the treatment.

From this time on, advocates of ECT became much more cautious about mentioning the brain-damaging effects of the treatment, and research into these effects practically came to a halt. Whereas the first definitive textbook on the shock therapies, by Jessner and Ryan (1941), had cited massive evidence that all the convulsive therapies cause brain damage, newer textbooks literally expunged these data from history and took the position that no such data ever existed. This viewpoint was maintained in the face of increasing evidence confirming the many early studies that had proved that ECT causes brain damage.

Kalinowsky has been the main voice promoting the viewpoint that ECT is utterly harmless and that no evidence exists to bolster fears about the treatment. He has done this in a series of review articles (1959, 1975a, 1975b) spanning four decades in the most widely read psychiatric textbooks, and in his own textbooks, as co-author with Paul Hoch (1946-1961) and with Hans Hippius (1969). He has been quoted in the nation's leading newspapers and magazines, and was sought by the *Journal of the American Medical Association* (1971) to answer questions on ECT.

Kalinowsky has not merely disagreed in his interpretation of the evidence. He has denied the existence of any evidence to back up fears about ECT. In defending ECT in this manner he sometimes has linked his statements directly to his concern about public and professional antagonism to the treatment (Kalinowsky & Hoch, 1961):

> No evidence has been brought forward to indicate that perma-
> nent mental sequelae are caused by the treatment. The question
> has received undue attention in the lay press and by those
> objecting to organic treatments on theoretical grounds.

Other major authorities in psychiatry have been equally adamant about the harmlessness of ECT. Perhaps the most widely read textbook of all stated, "Full return of memory finally occurs. Psychological investigations indicate that electric convulsive therapy is not followed by any intellectual impairment" (Noyes & Kolb, 1973). This book failed to mention a single one of dozens of studies indicating brain damage and associated mental impairment from ECT.

The myth of ECT's harmlessness has been fostered by the federal government. In an official pamphlet put out by the National Institute of Mental Health (1972), these comments were offered to soothe the anxieties of the public:

> The most common side-effects of ECT are confusion and temporary memory-loss (amnesia), seen most obviously immediately after a treatment. These memory changes include forgetting some recent events and a tendency to forgetfulness in day-to-day matters. Amnesia does not always occur with ECT, but when present it increases as more treatments are given. These memory changes disappear slowly over the weeks following ECT, and memory is usually fully restored by one or two months after ECT. Much research has been done over the past 35 years to investigate the possibility of permanent memory changes occurring with ECT. Research now suggests that such changes do not occur regardless of the number of treatments given.

A survey of psychiatrists by the American Psychiatric Association (1976; reprinted in American Psychiatric Association, 1978) was designed in such a way that severe brain damage did not appear as one of the possible alternatives in the 12 pages of multiple choices concerning ECT. The most negative item a psychiatrist could check was, "It is likely that ECT produces slight or subtle brain damage." The possibility of reporting brain-damage-related death following ECT was drastically reduced by the wording of the survey question: "How many deaths have occurred among your patients during, or within 24 hours, of ECT?" Brain death from ECT frequently follows days and weeks of prolonged coma (Impastato, 1957). Finally, only psychiatrists who "use" ECT were supposed to complete the lengthy Section II, which sought information about the possibility of memory loss. This precluded negative reports from psychiatrists who did not use ECT but who had seen or were seeing patients who have been damaged by the treatment. The questionnaire exemplifies how the myth of ECT harmlessness has been perpetrated within psychiatry—by failure to examine certain assumptions and by reliance within the profession on the opinions and reports of individuals who highly favor and actively promote the treatment.

The official American Psychiatric Association report (1978) that followed the survey was written with the clear intent of improving the image of ECT. It laments public criticism of the treatment and legislative attempts to enforce informed consent, and it questions the motives of those who criticize the therapy. It urges discarding the time-honored name "shock treatment" because it arouses fear, and further argues that even "convulsive therapy" is inappropriate because the muscles no longer twitch during the treatment (p. xi). The composition of the Task Force was dominated by some of the best-known advocates of the treatment, including Max Fink, T. George Bidder, Iver F. Small, and Fred Frankel, as well as psychologist Larry Squire (1977), who claims that frequent complaints of memory loss reflect an "illusion" on the part of patients. The Task Force noted with pride that it also extended invitations to address the Task Force to two *neurologists* known to oppose the treatment (p. ix). It does not mention that it also invited one of these neurologists to participate in the Task Force's all-important "open forum" at the Annual Meeting of the American Psychiatric Association, but would not permit any *psychiatrist* to speak in opposition to the treatment at the "open forum," even when the neurologist offered to step down in exchange. Thus, the papers published from the Task Force's "open forum" were heavily stacked with several advocates of ECT aligned in opposition to one neurologist (see Fink 1977; Frankel, 1977; Greenblatt, 1977; and Salzman, 1977 versus Friedberg, 1977b).

During this period in which advocates of ECT began actively promoting their new viewpoint, some medical authorities continued to cite contrary evidence. In his textbook of neurology Roy Grinker, Sr. (Grinker & Sahs, 1966), described the brain pathology associated with ECT, and in his textbook of psychiatry Ian Gregory (1968) showed dismay that advocates of ECT could overlook these proved findings of brain damage. Slater and Roth warned in *Clinical Psychiatry* (1969) against serious memory defects following ECT. An internationally known Russian textbook of psychiatry called for limiting the use of ECT on the grounds that it causes brain hemorrhages and amnesia (Portnov & Fedetov, 1969).

Supporters of ECT remained well aware that a controversy continued to boil beneath the surface, and occasionally they made references to it in print. In a 1964 review article, Smith and Biddy lamented a "strong desire" in the profession for "the elimination of ECT entirely." Max Fink, a well-known proponent of the treatment, underscored the unabating controversial nature of the treatment in 1972 when he stated, "ECT is used sparingly and, in many academic institutions, is considered inelegant, bizarre, dangerous and antithetical to the prevailing philosophy, and even expensive."

In the 1970s more aggressive criticism of ECT began to be made by psychiatrists and neurologists, including Friedberg (1975, 1976, 1977a, 1977b), Grimm (1976, 1978), Coleman (1978), Giamartino (1974), Szasz (1971), and Breggin (1977a). For the first time it could not be contained within the confines of the medical profession. In Boston reporter Jean Dietz broke a story about the abuses of ECT in private hospitals, leading to the closing of one hospital and to a series of related newspaper exposés, legislative hearings, and the promulgation of rules governing ECT within the Department of Mental Hygiene (Dietz, 1972, 1975; Harris, 1972; Cowen, 1972). In San Francisco neurologist John Friedberg took his medical opposition to ECT to the public in a series of publications and received national attention (Clark & Lubenow, 1975). Simultaneously, a group of former psychiatric patients, including Leonard Frank (Friedberg, 1976; Frank, 1978), organized systematic opposition to ECT in the press and in the California legislature (*Psychiatric News*, 1973, 1975a; *Clinical Psychiatry News*, 1975).

Advocates of ECT responded vigorously with the formation of a new organization to educate the profession and the public concerning the safety and value of the treatment (*Psychiatric News*, 1975b; *Clinical Psychiatry News*, 1975). Many articles defending ECT appeared in the psychiatric literature (Arnot, 1975; Frankel, 1977; Greenblatt, 1977; Allen, 1978). Without citing evidence, M. L. Cunningham (1975) wrote:

> Despite a very large volume of writing in this area, there has been no incontrovertible evidence produced that either intellect or behavior are [sic] significantly affected in any way to the patient's detriment.

In a panel presentation at the annual meeting of the American Psychiatric Association, defenders of ECT unanimously agreed on the harmlessness of the treatment. Max Fink (1977) declared:

> It is difficult to negate the global judgment that ECT causes permanent brain damage. Except for persistent subject complaints of memory defect, however, the evidence for such injury or its persistence is lacking, despite extensive study.

Fink and other members of the panel (Frankel, 1977, Salzman, 1977) made clear that their efforts to improve the image of electroshock were made in direct response to criticism being generated by Friedberg and by groups representing former psychiatric patients. Not surprisingly, the American Psychiatric Association report (1978) by a Task Force including Fink and Frankel took the same promotional view toward ECT.

Basic Issue: Is There Complete Recovery from the Acute Organic Brain Syndrome?

Reviews by Sanford (1966) and by Goldman (1961), as well as almost any biologically oriented textbook of psychiatry, can provide a history of ECT and a description of modifications that became popular in the

1960s. For the purposes of this study it is most important to recognize the distinction between unmodified and modified ECT. In unmodified bilateral ECT an electrical current is applied to both sides of the forehead of an awake patient, simultaneously rendering him unconscious and eliciting a grand mal or generalized convulsion with tonic-clonic muscle spasms.[2] In appearance the physical response of the body and the brain wave reaction do not differ significantly from those in a severe spontaneous convulsion.

The amount of the current varies widely from machine to machine and from clinician to clinician (Davies et al. 1971). Kalinowsky (1975b) described a range of 70 to 130 volts (v) for 0.1 to 0.5 sec, with the delivered current varying from 200 to 1,600 milliamperes (ma). As this review proceeds, it will become apparent that the range is vaster than this, especially in the duration of application. Different currents have been tested over the years, but the great majority of machines, and most practioners of ECT, employ the same type of electric current (60 Hz. bipolar sinewave) used in the first ECT treatments in 1938, and the actual strength of the current has been increased in most cases (see Chapter 8 for details). For comparison's sake, only 100 ma delivered across the brain stem can be fatal (W.A.D. Anderson, 1971).

Experiments in varying the amount of electrical energy delivered to the brain have not led to any regularly adopted changes, but modifications through the introduction of anesthesia have become almost universal. The term "modified ECT" now customarily refers to treatment in which the patient is given a general anesthetic (an intravenous sedative) and a "muscle relaxant" immediately before ECT, and then artifically breathed with oxygen during the period of anesthesia and the subsequent apnea.[3] The term muscle relaxant is a euphemism because the patient is paralyzed by means of a neuromuscular blocking agent that renders him unable to blink or breathe. The purpose is to prevent severe muscle spasms and thereby to avoid fractures.

Other modifications aimed at reducing intellectual impairments involve unilateral application of both electrodes to the nondominant side of the head. Dominance designates the cerebral hemisphere that controls the physical or motor activities of speech, and to some degree their related mental/verbal activities. It is usually the left side of the brain in right-handed individuals. By applying both electrodes to the nondomi-

---

2. *Tonic-clonic spasms* are typical of generalized convulsions of any origin and consist of tonic spasms during which the muscles remain tense, followed by clonic spasms during which the muscles intermittently tense and relax. The patient appears rigid during the tonic phase, and thrashes about with enormous vigor during the clonic phase.

3. *Apnea* is the abnormal cessation or suspension of breathing. It is produced both by the convulsion and by the pharmacologic agents that paralyze the patient. It can also be intensified by the addition of the general anesthetic that renders the patient unconscious.

nant side of the brain, it was hoped to reduce memory loss. However, as this review will indicate, the application of electrodes to the nondominant side of the head *increases* visual memory loss while reducing verbal memory loss. The higher concentration of electrical energy in one area may also produce more intensive localized brain damage.

After ECT, the initial period of unconsciousness is accompanied by apnea, usually of no more than one to two minutes' duration, and cyanosis.[4] The patient then resumes spontaneous breathing and gradually awakens over a period of many minutes to half an hour or more. On awakening, depending on the number and severity of his treatments, the patient suffers from an acute organic brain syndrome, which will be documented in detail in subsequent sections. It is characterized by (1) confusion and disorientation to time, place, and person; (2) impaired memory, especially for prior events; (3) global disruption of all intellectual functions, such as comprehension, learning, and abstract reasoning; (4) impaired judgment and insight; and (5) shallowness or inappropriateness of emotional reactions, varying from euphoria to apathy. The patient frequently experiences a severe headache, nausea, and physical exhaustion or malaise. Typically the patient also feels "out of touch" with reality and very helpless and frightened. This acute organic brain syndrome is nonspecific, and follows a variety of other general traumas to the brain, including epileptic convulsions, electrical trauma, intoxication, anoxia[5] of any origin (strangulation, suffocation, breathing nitrogen), blows to the head, or lobotomy, as well as electroconvulsive therapy (Brosin, 1959; Weinstein & Kahn, 1959). However, the syndrome following ECT displays an unusually severe memory loss, a phenomenon that will be documented and accounted for in the following chapters.

Kalinowsky (1959) described the acute organic brain syndrome following one ECT in the following words:

> All patients show confusion immediately after a convulsion, and a retrograde amnesia which usually clears up in 1 to 2 hours. The memory impairment becomes longer in duration after several treatments. The intellectual impairment is always accompanied by some emotional disturbances, and the patient is sometimes dull or sometimes silly. Fear develops almost invariably after a certain number of treatments, and no satisfactory explanation has been found for this fear which the patient also is unable to explain. Some people are frightened by the

---

4. *Cyanosis* is the bluish purple discoloration of the skin due to deficient oxgenation of the blood. The condition can be brought about by apnea or by other disruptions in the respiratory process.

5. *Anoxia* is the absence of oxygen.

awakening and the ensuing difficulty in orienting themselves, and by a very characteristic feeling that everything looks either strange and unfamiliar, or, to the contrary, that all strangers look familiar.

Kalinowsky (1945), Kalinowski and Hippius (1969), Elmore and Sugerman (1975), and others have described a still more severe "organic-psychotic reaction" that sometimes occurs in the course of routine ECT. It can appear in patients who have not previously been psychotic, and includes extreme confusion, bewilderment, severe emotional lability, delusions, and vivid hallucinations. The patients also may become incontinent and utterly unable to take care of their daily needs.

If ECT is given more intensively, at the rate of two or more per day, nearly total neurologic collapse *routinely* occurs. Using unmodified ECT, Rothchild et al., 1951, describe the response of patients to 28 ECT at the rate of four per day for seven days:

By the end of this intensive course of treatment practically all patients showed profound disturbances. They were dazed, out of contact and for the most part helpless. All showed incontinence of urine, and incontinence of feces was not uncommon. Most of them were underactive and did not talk spontaneously. Many failed to respond to questions but a few patients would obey simple requests. They appeared prostrated and apathetic. At the same time most of them whined, whimpered and cried readily, and some were resistive and petulant in a childish way. They could usually be made to walk if led and supported, but their movements were slow, uncertain and clumsy. Most of them liked to be coddled. Masturbation was not uncommon. They seemed to have lost all desire to eat or drink and showed no discrimination as to what they were eating. They had to be spoonfed, and most of them lost from 3 to 12 pounds in weight during the course of treatment. They could not dress themselves and none of those tested during this period could complete the task of extracting a match from a matchbox and lighting the match.

The foregoing symptoms usually began to appear during the course of treatment, but became fully developed at the end of the course and lasted for approximately one or two weeks thereafter. Recovery was gradual, with the ability to walk, to feed oneself and to talk ordinarily being re-established within a week after termination of treatment. Incontinence usually ceased at about this time. Interest in their own appearance and in persons or objects was shown as a rule for the first time during the second post-shock week.

This form of ECT has been enjoying something of a resurgence in the last five to 10 years. Using modified ECT, Exner and Murillo (1973) described achieving essentially the same regression with a schedule of ECT twice daily seven days a week, until "the signs of regression occur." This may be achieved with as few as six ECT treatments, but requires an average of 26.3. The reaction "is characterized by complete helplessness, confusion, mutism, etc., and by neurologic signs of altered cerebral activity such as a positive Babinski, ataxia."[6]

As the literature unfolds it will become apparent that there is no debate about whether modified ECT produces an acute organic brain syndrome. Given that routine ECT does cause a severe acute organic brain syndrome and occasional neurological dilapidation, and that intensive ECT regularly produces nearly complete neurological collapse, the questions concerning the damage produced by ECT become narrowed. Specifically, the questions become: Does the acute organic brain syndrome or the immediate destructive effect of ECT leave any lasting effects? Does it become a chronic or permanent organic brain syndrome, or does it leave other more limited sequelae, such as permanent memory loss for important past experiences? Are the aftereffects substantially reduced by the various modifications?

Most of the literature pertaining to brain damage after ECT involves unmodified ECT; based on this literature, pro-ECT reviews claim that the treatment causes no harmful effects. It is therefore imperative to review the older literature, first because it is the main body of evidence cited in support of ECT even in recent reviews, and second because much less research is available concerning modified ECT. Furthermore, if it can be shown that the literature on unmodified ECT demonstrates brain damage, then there is a presumption that modified ECT also causes damage. This presumption is bolstered by data in this review indicating that the most frequently used newer modifications often have increased the amount of electrical energy delivered to the brain and the strong evidence that the electrical current as well as the convulsion causes severe and permanent damage. Each section, when possible, will be divided into two portions, the first dealing with unmodified ECT and the second dealing with modified ECT.

I will begin with six clinical cases of my own that demonstrate permanent, serious mental impairment resulting from *modified* ECT.

---

6. The *Babinski* is a neurological reflex that can be elicited normally in small infants and abnormally in adults. *Ataxia* is an uncoordinated or clumsy walk. In this context both indicate significant malfunction in the central nervous system.

2

Six Cases of Mental Dysfunction following Modified ECT

Over the last 20 years I have met, interviewed, and studied the life histories of many individuals suffering from severe mental dysfunction following ECT. The most frequent disability is *retrograde amnesia*, or the inability to recall experiences known to the individual before ECT. It refers to the loss of some portion of the memory bank. Whether the memory has been erased or whether the retrieval mechanism has been disrupted, it is no longer available. The next most frequent disability is a more general *anterograde mental dysfunction* or the inability to learn, memorize, or recall new material or current or immediate experiences after ECT. Using a computer model, the difference would be between a computer that has lost contact with some of its *past* input and a computer that can no longer effectively handle some of its *new* input. Anterograde dysfunction is far more crippling to the individual. It reflects an ongoing, continuing, or current brain disability.

Within the last few years in my private practice and as executive director of the Center for the Study of Psychiatry, I have worked closely with many individuals who suffer severe, permanent mental disabilities of both kinds following ECT, and many others have written or spoken to me.

Background of the Losses

The six cases I have chosen to summarize reflect my overall experience that ECT usually or typically causes some degree of significant permanent mental dysfunction, and often causes severe, lasting disability. I have selected these particular individuals to summarize based on the following criteria: (1) At least a four-year follow-up was possible since the last ECT; (2) many sources of information were available concerning their pre- and post-ECT mental functioning; (3) their psychological problems did not confound my evaluations of their mental function; and (4) other physical trauma or illness could not account for their disability.

Many people are very concerned about confidentiality, especially in regard to their disabilities following ECT, and I have therefore taken every precaution to make it impossible for them to be identified, even by the number of ECT they received. For this purpose I have divided the six individuals into two groups, three who received a typical short course (less than 10 ECT), and three who received very long courses (more than 45 ECT); I will refer to them by these categories. Because their reactions are rather uniform, this will not be a significant difficulty.

All of the patients received modified ECT between the mid-1960s and early 1970s, and none received regressive ECT. Four were treated in private psychiatric hospitals and two in general hospital psychiatric units. The hospital and physician differed in each case. Three individuals are male and three female. They varied in age from 18 to 50 at the time of the first ECT. The time elapsed since the last ECT varied from four years to more than 10 years, with an average of about six, so that all changes had been stable long enough to be permanent.

In five of six cases I had access to hospital records to confirm the treatment course and the pretreatment evaluations of the patients. In all but one instance I had seen the person myself before and after ECT, or I had confirmatory evidence from others who had known the person before and after ECT. In most instances I was able to study before and after reports, and letters and projects written by the individual. In every case I had multiple sources of information to give a complete and continuous picture of the individual's course. Each person was interviewed by me personally for at least six hours, and all were interviewed on several occasions over several months or more.

The three people in the short-course group were given ECT on their first and only psychiatric hospitalization. One person in the long-course group was given ECT in the first of several hospitalizations, and the other two as part of a series of hospitalizations in rapid succession. None of the individuals was given any intensive psychiatric treatment before being hospitalized. For four of the six, ECT was instituted as the first major psychiatric intervention, shortly after the beginning of their first hospitalization, and the others received medication in the hospital before ECT. None had been involved in intensive or analytic psychotherapy, group therapy, or family counseling at any time before ECT. In four cases the prescribing physicians justified ECT on the basis of depression. In two cases in the long-course group, clinical justifications were lacking despite detailed records. These patients had resisted lengthy hospitalizations, and appear to have been given ECT to overcome this resistance. Both were diagnosed as "paranoid" largely on the basis of their resentment toward involuntary treatment.

Three of the six patients sought my help with their personal problems (two with additional concerns about post-ECT mental deficits), and three sought my help as an expert witness in malpractice actions that they had already initiated. None of the patients felt that they had been helped by the treatment; all felt they had been harmed.

There are some common features among the individuals. Each was above average in intelligence and most had prided themselves on their intellect and their memory. Their educations ranged from high school to postgraduate work; all had performed well before ECT, either in school or subsequently at work. Four of six were very active professionally within the year before ECT. None had been chronically or totally disabled by their personal problems during the several months before hospitalization. None was suicidal at the time of treatment, although one had been years earlier.

The initial diagnoses of the individuals varied from reactive depressions to paranoid schizophrenia, but I could find no relationship between diagnosis and degree of post-ECT impairment. Even among those with more serious diagnoses, none had hallucinations, delusions, or thought disorders before ECT, and other psychiatrists, including myself, have seriously questioned their diagnoses by ordinary professional standards. In no instance did I feel that the complaints of amnesia or mental dysfunction were in any way a product of personal problems, and indeed, as the persons overcame their personal problems, their awareness of and concern about mental dysfunction seemed greater.

The patients varied a great deal in their initial attitudes toward ECT, from actively seeking it (one patient) to having it forced upon them (three patients). Each patient had complained about the treatment's effect on the mind once it had begun, but in only one case did this possibly influence the psychiatrist to shorten the therapy; in no case did it influence the psychiatrist to terminate the therapy immediately at the patient's request.

Permanent Retrograde Amnesia

From various sources I was able to document and to trace each person's progression from a severe acute organic brain syndrome following ECT into a more lasting mental deficit with a marked amnesia for events before ECT. Four of the five hospital charts are very detailed and show marked confusion, disorientation, mood instability, and memory loss during and after the course of the treatment. The fifth chart is very skimpy and lacks nursing notes, but the doctor's abbreviated observations include confusion and memory loss during a short course.

The doctors' progress notes in the charts usually stress memory loss and confusion, and often fail to give a full picture of the patients' disability. The nurses' notes, occupational therapy reports, and other services describe the patients' progressive disorientation, mood instability, helplessness, and dependence. Occupational therapy notes show the patients willing but unable to carry on any kind of activity as ECT effects accumulate.

There is little difference between the quality of the acute brain syndrome in the short and long courses, for the overall symptoms began to appear after two to four treatments, and none of the patients became neurologically dilapidated with complete helplessness, incontinence, or the inability to perform routine self-care. The hospital charts do not provide a suitable comparison for the intensity of each person's acute organic brain syndrome, as the depth or richness of the reporting is too variable. However, a general worsening with increasing ECT can be observed in each chart when the notes are sufficient.

Following termination of the ECT, the charts and associated materials and interviews clearly document the gradual reduction of most of the signs of the acute brain syndrome, leaving residual amnesia for events before ECT in all six cases, plus other lasting symptoms in at least four cases. It appears that memory losses maintained after several weeks are stable and permanent.

The *least* severe permanent aftereffects of the six occurred in a patient in the short course and involved a nearly complete amnesia for all experiences over a three- to four-month period before ECT, plus a sense of unfamiliarity or alienation with events earlier than that, spanning a period of several more months. Each of the other five individuals had a much more severe permanent loss, blotting out most experiences for at least one year before ECT. In four cases, two in the short-course group and two in the long, the individuals had difficulty remembering most of what had happened over two or three years before ECT, with lesser but significant losses reaching back five to 10 years—including major events such as important vacations, a wedding day, family get-togethers, and educational and professional experiences. One of the two with a very long course lost much of the previous five- to 10-year period, although the other person, who had the longest course, lost only about a year. In these four cases, too, previously familiar memories for childhood seemed less clear, with occasional definite losses of important recollections, such as houses lived in before age 10 or elementary schools attended as a child. Relatives of these individuals would tell them anecdotes or describe places or persons from childhood, which they once could recall but now had lost. In three cases, one from the short course, childhood generally seemed more vague, but in no case was most of childhood lost.

I was surprised by the similarity of the subjective quality of the retrograde amnesia from person to person. Memories would be impaired along a continuum from obliteration on one end to a sense of "vagueness" or "unreality" on the other. On the obliteration end, which dominated nearer to the time of the ECT, the individual would have no idea that the lost memory ever existed, and would be surprised when reminded of it by a therapist, friend, or relative. Obliteration was prominent for a one- to three-year period before ECT for four of six individuals. On the other end of the continuum, individuals would have a vague recollection for an important event, but would feel as if they had not really been present at the event. They might have a sense of recalling through a screen or filter, almost as if they remembered a movie or a second-hand description, rather than the experience itself. When memories were recovered after work in therapy, or with friends, or after reading earlier letters or looking in photograph albums, the events recalled would usually have this unreal quality. Rarely after the first few weeks following ECT was a lost memory recovered in any richness or with any sense of personal participation.

There were exceptions to the general tendency for the blanks to be greatest closer to ECT. At least two patients remembered details of the ECT treatment itself, including severe panic as they awaited ECT in the morning, fragmentary recollections of being given the anesthetic, and frightening, confused memories of events soon after ECT, such as the gasping, coughing, and moaning of people in the recovery room. Several also recalled enduring the worst headaches of their lives on awakening from each ECT.

Because some clinicians maintain that it is impossible for patients to recall such details of the treatment (Kalinowsky, 1975a, 1975b), I want to emphasize that I have found fragmented recall of the ECT experience in many other patients as well, including some to whom I gave ECT as a psychiatric resident. These fragmentary memories add to the nightmarish sense of fear associated with the treatment for many patients, and often become a part of actual nightmares that last years after the treat-

ment. Nightmares of this kind persisted for several years in three cases
in this clinical sample. Two of these also recalled fragments of the actual
treatment.

On the other hand, at least two of these six patients had no recall
whatsoever for short courses of ECT and only knew of their ECT from
the reports of others.

Similarly, some people lost all or most of their recollections of the
events taking place or the individuals met in the hospital during their
stay, whereas others had partial recall for these experiences. None of the
six had a very clear memory for any of the treatment period, however,
and those with long courses lasting many weeks or months lost the vast
body of those weeks or months. The few who later read their hospital
records were introduced to an era of their existence that was entirely or
almost entirely new to them. They read about their daily activities with
little if any recognition, and no matter how much they could reconstruct
from others or from records, they regained no sense of personal participation and no flood of returning reactivated memories. One person from
the short-course group drew a total blank about the hospital experience,
despite many interviews touching on the subject and reminders from the
hospital chart. As far as personal memories went, the experience had
never happened. Another person from the short-course group had only a
very vague recollection of the hospital. In the long-course group the
general familiarity with the hospitalizations in two cases seemed to stem
largely from the fact that they had been in the hospital for some time
after their treatment ended. The degree of amnesia for these periods is
not surprising, considering that all six had acute organic brain syndromes at the time.

There is also irregularity in the loss of events remote from the treatment. One person who had had a variety of complex skills was unable to
recall how to operate an apparatus that had been a routine part of office
work for 15 years, although other long-practiced skills were relatively
unimpaired. Another person lost several well-practiced household skills,
including sewing and cooking. These losses reached much further into
the past than the more global amnesia for periods nearer to ECT. Another person was completely blanked out on a previously well-remembered long trip abroad 11 years earlier, but retained memory for other
important events of that time. Still another lost a period of a year or two
in childhood, with clearer memories before and after that time.

Some of the irregularity in memory loss seemed attributable to the
general irregularity of memory recollections, with stronger memories
tending to remain while weaker ones tended to be lost. But this does not
explain the phenomenon fully, especially the loss of well-learned skills
and previously well-remembered experiences. Some very important,

powerful, or traumatic recollections were also lost, while some "trivia" were retained. This inexplicable irregularity often made the patients fear that others would doubt the validity of their recollections. Despite the irregularity, however, each person had a largely global loss for the period of severe amnesia, including one to three years or more in five cases.

The Assessment of Global Memory Loss

Despite the considerable irregularity in materials lost or maintained during the period of amnesia, the amnesia nonetheless tended to span all categories of life experience. To assess global, overall, loss, I have used the following categories.

1. Educational and professional experiences, including projects at work, important reports or memos, conferences, special briefings or courses, major assignments, noteworthy successes or failures, highly technical information, coworkers, physical environment, and routine activities such as lunchbreaks.
2. Movies, books, plays, and other forms of entertainment.
3. Important social events, such as vacations, parties, dinners, birthdays, anniversaries, family get-togethers, unexpected visitors; particularly enjoyable, funny, or unpleasant incidents.
4. People, such as friends, family, and business acquaintances (names, faces, time of meeting, identity).
5. Household activities, such as clothes or furniture purchased; the layout of various rooms; the organization of possessions; old bills and tax forms; important chores, cooking recipes, dressmaking, or other home-related activities.
6. Once-familiar places and locations involved in daily living, such as the location of stores or theaters, the layout of the city or town, and the aisles of the supermarket.
7. Medical and psychiatric experiences during and before treatment.
8. Thoughts, feelings, and other subjective, inner experiences, including personal conflicts.
9. Public events, such as elections, international crises, and economic or sporting news.

Each of the individuals had losses in *all* areas, with four important emphases.

1. The three women had greater awareness of the loss of household experiences. In two of three cases, their homes felt wholly strange to them.
2. All five who had vocational experiences had special awareness of the loss of their professional knowledge, three feeling that the amnesia was sufficient to render them permanently unable to perform at their peak. Four lost significant portions of professional knowledge, spanning several years.
3. Five of six experienced enormous losses in regard to persons known before ECT, with many people met one to three years before ECT often obliterated wholly from their memories.
4. Each lost almost all sense of inner self—thoughts, feelings, inner conflicts—for the period of most severe amnesia, resulting in a sense of alienation from self, or emptiness.

The special attention given these four areas of loss seem easily explainable. Women are more likely to have an awareness or concern about lost household experiences, and professionals of both sexes are likely to focus on occupational losses. The loss of persons known before therapy is highly embarrassing, and was repeatedly brought to each person's attention. The loss of inner, subjective experiences may relate to the general lack of strength of these memories in most people. Furthermore, no one else is in a position to help remind the individual of his or her past subjective feeling. Because every one of these individuals went through extensive attempts to regain memories by reading books once familiar to them, looking at photos, talking with friends and family, reading old letters, and so on, much of what they recollect has actually been relearned from other sources. They cannot relearn their inner experiences through outside sources.

It is important to note that descriptions of the patient's losses as found in charts or reported to me by other interviewers often missed the global nature of the amnesia. Comments in hospital charts typically noted that the person could no longer identify "what was upsetting him so much before he had his treatment," as if it were assumed (but not checked out) that he could recall other things from the same period of time. Or it might be reported by an observer that a housewife had forgotten data pertaining to housework, whereas a professional person had forgotten subjects related to professional work. Occasionally there would be an air of mystery or doubt surrounding the report as the observer questioned the reality of such a selective loss. But on careful questioning, I have always found that the losses were global, especially for the period of most severe amnesia. The reported "spottiness" of the amnesia often reflected the observer's own "spottiness" in failing to take a very careful inventory of losses. I myself fell into these errors until I began taking careful inventories. Sometimes the patients themselves were selective because of their own concerns over these specific losses, or because of shame and anxiety over the extent of other losses.

The memory losses thus far examined fall into the general category of *retrograde amnesia*—loss of memories that had been available to the person before ECT. This is by far the most common complaint made by patients who have otherwise recovered from their ECT.

Permanent Anterograde Mental Dysfunction

Many post-ECT patients complain about the inability to retain new material confronted since their treatment. This is called *anterograde amnesia*. Anterograde amnesia is a much more complex function than retrograde amnesia. Recalling old material involves the storage and retrieval of previously learned information, but anterograde amnesia involves learning as well as memory. Learning itself can be broken down into many components, such as perception and abstract reasoning. Anterograde amnesia, as it is commonly called in the literature, actually encompasses most or all mental functions, and a patient who complains about inability to remember new material may in fact be suffering from what Stone (1947) originally described as the "general impairment of cognitive functions resulting from electro-convulsive shocks." For the purposes of this study we need only acknowledge the complexities of these distinctions without analyzing them. In determining whether a patient suffers residual symptoms of an organic brain syndrome, we need only determine whether a generally identifiable mental function has been impaired. For this purpose a very loose reliance on the terms retrograde amnesia and anterograde amnesia (or anterograde mental dysfunction) is sufficient.

In regard to anterograde mental function, each of the persons experienced considerable intellectual malfunction during the period of recovery from electroshock. This merely confirms the presence of the documented acute organic brain syndrome. But in every instance the subjective sense of impaired function considerably outlasted the most severe symptoms of the organic brain syndrome. Each individual felt that several weeks or months were required to begin functioning on a relatively high level again, and some believed they never achieved this. Recovery was often accompanied by headaches and nightmares as well as apathy, lethargy, and fatigue. Most felt as if they were recovering from a traumatic physical illness.

There was great variation in the permanence and the strength of anterograde mental impairment, as well as in the accuracy of the individuals' perception of that loss. Two individuals—one from the long course and one from the short—felt fully recovered in regard to current mental capacities. One worked at an intellectually demanding job, the other at a blue-collar job. In interviews and other situations these individuals appeared alert, sharp, and clever, confirming their sense of recovery. They also had the least severe retrograde amnesias. There is no way to prove that their capacities had returned to normal, but there is no way to prove otherwise.

Two other persons—again one from the long course and one from the short—believed that their mental functioning was now as good as before, or even better, despite severe retrograde amnesias, but other evidence proved the contrary. The person in the short-course group who felt mentally recovered did display a remarkable degree of continuing intelligence, but this had to be weighed against a past history of mental brilliance. Five years before ECT the patient had received a negative neurological evaluation, including skull films and an EEG, and immediately before ECT a history and physical examination were entirely normal. During and immediately after ECT the patient developed a severe acute organic brain syndrome, mild euphoria, and lasting retrograde amnesia. When evaluated two to three years after ECT, because of persisting complaints of retrograde amnesia, objective signs of brain damage were found: on neurologic examination, a snout reflex and Hoffman reflex, and astereognosis and clumsiness of the left hand; on computerized tomography (CT scan), right temporal lobe atrophy and ventricular enlargement (two and one-half times normal); and on EEG, temporal lobe abnormalities consistent with those typically reported following ECT.[1] Psychological testing revealed a loss in abstract reasoning and right hemispheric deficits in the area of nonverbal memory and concepts. The highly experienced professor of psychology who conducted the tests concluded that these defects represented "a devastating loss on the phen-

---

1. An elucidation of these various neurologic findings is beyond the scope of a footnote. Of importance to the nonmedical reader is the consistent picture of brain damage that they present. The temporal lobes extend like the thumb of a mitten on both sides of the brain, and lie in part beneath the region of the skull to which the electrodes are applied. These lobes are crucial in memory function, and damage to them frequently results in memory deficits. *Atrophy* indicates a decrease in the size of an organ, in this case presumably due to cell death and shrinkage.

omenological level" despite a persisting high IQ. He reported that this person's subjective experience of losses in the "richness" of mental life was a "common complaint in exceptionally bright people who suffer even a 'slight' organic impairment of intellectual functioning." The patient's history and physical findings could suggest no cause other than ECT for these organic changes and mental losses.

The person in the long course who felt better than ever in regard to mental function was judged impaired in this regard in before-and-after observations by others, and showed clinical signs of a chronic organic brain syndrome several years following ECT, including confabulation[2] when confronted with the severity of the retrograde amnesia, difficulty in focusing and maintaining attention, inappropriate levity, and poor judgment. This person did not receive an EEG or other neurologic tests.

The other two individuals experienced continuing impairments, one a relatively mild but frustrating difficulty memorizing new material, the other a more significant sense of difficulty in concentrating, thinking, learning, and memorizing.

The retrograde amnesias were extremely upsetting to most of the individuals in this group, but the anterograde mental problems were far more disturbing. They had a sense of being "defective" and were conscious of the realistic cost in terms of a full, rich life in the future. Therefore it was difficult to evaluate these losses without dealing with a great deal of understandable mental anguish. Much more than their retrograde amnesia, individuals tried to ignore or overlook their current mental disabilities, and when confronted with them through new failures at learning or memorizing, they felt angry, frightened, and humiliated. As noted, two of them denied staggering losses in current mental function.

The Reliability of Clinical Observations and Subjective Reports

Questions may be raised about the reliability of clinical reports based on the subjective productions of the patients themselves. Surely there are some real problems in this method, but just as surely clinical observations and self-reports are the most sensitive indicators of metal dysfunction. We are therefore compelled to give them serious consideration (see Chapter 7).

A number of factors have been taken into account in both the selec-

---

2. *Confabulation* is the fabrication of ready answers and false stories in compensation for and to hide actual memory gaps. It is seen following amnesia due to organic brain damage or dysfunction. Chapter 7 examines confabulation in post-ECT patients.

tion of these patients and in the methods of interviewing and evaluating them to guard against lying or exaggerating. I have already noted that each of these patients was selected because of a plethora of information concerning their clinical course before, during, and after ECT. All sources confirmed the changes that the patients reported. In addition, I took great care in checking and rechecking their reports against themselves during various interviews, and in using test questions to see if anyone were overeager to find or to report new losses. I never discovered any tendency to exaggerate in any case I included in the study. To the contrary, I frequently found a tendency to deny impairment. At least eight points can be made in this regard.

1. No one had a past history of complaining about mental dysfunction.

2. The descriptions of retrograde amnesia were uniform in quality among the six cases.

3. Their attitudes toward anterograde losses were consistent with clinical observations concerning brain damage. The two patients who were apparently undamaged in this regard showed the least upset about their losses, whereas the two people with the most loss actually denied them entirely. The two people with the more moderate losses had very similar complaints of difficulty recalling new material and a lack of mental agility.

4. Because several of the individuals were self-supporting at the time they were evaluated, they had little to gain from exaggerating their disabilities so as to escape responsibility for work. Before consulting with me, three had brought malpractice suits against psychiatrists, wholly or in part relating to ECT; but all three continued to deny any anterograde mental problems despite the advantage such claims would have afforded them.

5. None of the individuals involved originally anticipated any permanent memory loss from ECT, and most were reassured by their psychiatrists that none would occur. Yet all experienced these losses in a very similar manner. None of them knew each other, and none of them had read anything about ECT memory loss until the patterns of their losses were well-established; even then, only two studied the subject. Yet their losses, as we shall see, closely mimic those described in many other

reports in the literature on both unmodified and modified ECT.

6. In every case there is a continuity that can be traced from the original acute organic brain syndrome to the residual amnesias and anterograde difficulties.

7. None of the individuals had a history of lying, deceit, or malingering.

8. Two did have persistent medical difficulties unrelated to the central nervous system, but as a group they appeared to be at least as free of chronic physical complaints as the general population, and several had remarkably negative histories in this regard.

9. Unlike most people who try to fake organic illness, these people were very ashamed of their disabilities, and tried hard to improve on their recollections and their capacities through study and practice.

Let me place this group of patients in the overall perspective of my clinical and forensic experience. I have worked closely with one patient who may have suffered a lesser degree of loss than any of these patients following a short course of ECT and I have seen several after lengthy treatments who have suffered as much or greater loss than the most extreme examples in this series. I have not included these other cases in this study because of the individuals' unwillingness or inability to talk about their experiences, because of inadequate corroborating records, or because other extreme treatments or long-term personal difficulties clouded an evaluation. In general this group of six cases reflects my experience concerning the typical range of effects of ECT, but obviously it is not a controlled sample. Its purpose is to illustrate and describe frequent types of post-ECT disability, without claiming to establish actual frequency.

In summary the least severe retrograde amnesia following ECT among the six cases involved a nearly total loss of three to four months before ECT, plus some general unfamiliarity with life events several months earlier; the most severe reaction involved the obliteration of most experiences for three years or more before ECT, with some losses extending back to childhood. In general, losses declined on a gradient from the time of ECT into the past, but there were exceptions and the gradient seemed irregular. Two individuals described no anterograde or current problems in regard to their mental functioning, and clinically showed no unequivocal symptoms. Two others described significant permanent losses in their ability to learn and retain information, and one of them also had more severe difficulties focusing and concentrating. The two patients with the most obvious anterograde difficulties denied experiencing any loss whatsoever in their ongoing mental function, but one had documented organic brain damage and the other displayed signs of a chronic organic brain syndrome. Most felt enormous shame and anguish over their mental losses, a subject requiring special attention.

The Subjective Experience of Anguish and Shame

The abstract presentation of the case material cannot communicate the anguish experienced by many electroshock patients for years after the termination of the treatment. I have seen people who have been reclusive for years after electroshock for fear of entering a social world in which they would not recognize old friends and relatives and in which they would be unable to find their way to places they had frequented in the past, such as grocery stores and the homes of friends.

I have selected statements from two individuals among the six who were especially verbal in expressing their feelings of shame and helplessness. It may be argued that some of their anguish pertained to long-standing personal problems, and it is difficult to disentangle the pained response to memory loss and brain dysfunction from other emotional reactions that reach back to periods long before the shock treatment. Nonetheless these responses have been so uniform in quality and so frequent in my clinical experience and in the clinical literature that they must be taken seriously. With the notable exception of one patient, shame over disabilities had played no significant role in the lives of these individuals before their treatment with ECT.

Before ECT Mrs. Jackson had been seriously depressed over a number of losses and crises in her life. Nonetheless she had functioned as an administrator in a large corporation up to the day in the early 1970s that she admitted herself to a nationally known private hospital. It was her first psychiatric hospitalization, but she was started immediately on a long course of ECT.

Mrs. Jackson's recall for the period of shock is spotty and fragmented, but certain experiences have remained emblazoned on her mind:

> When the nurse came by and said "No breakfast" you knew
> you were scheduled for shock treatment. Grown men would be
> shivering, and I saw grown women crying and saying, "No,
> no, not again today," and carrying on all the way to the shock
> room. I remember my girl friend who moved her bowels in her
> bed when she heard she was getting shock again. It was terri-
> fying and it was humiliating. Pure fear. I used to say my

prayers. I'd pray that I would live through it, and that I'd never have it again. But when I first complained, I was put in solitary, and taken to shock from there. After that happened a few times, I realized that my only hope of getting out was to conform and not to say anything. I'd wait until my husband came and then plead with him to take me out.

Mrs. Jackson vividly recalls her upset over witnessing other people being treated ahead of her.

I'd have to wait there lying on one of the cots with rows of other cots around me as each person got the treatment. If you were the first one to get the needle you were all right, but if you weren't it was horrible. I couldn't bear to look from my cot to the others to see the way everyone looked as they were waiting. And then those who got the shock ahead of me, I'd hear them on their cots choking and gurgling like water going through their nose and mouth, and gasping and other horrible sounds.

Waking up afterward in a confused stupor, she would experience an immense desire to disappear into sleep. But sleep was made difficult by agnoizing headaches that lasted for hours after treatment. After discharge, she also developed fearful nightmares containing fragments of the ECT experience.

Mrs. Jackson felt mentally disabled after her release.

When I got out, I spent most of my time in bed, unable to read because of the headaches, unable to function on a daily basis, like the cooking. In general, doing nothing.

I couldn't remember my own home. I couldn't remember the day I was married. I couldn't remember my children's hobbies. I couldn't remember faces. I'd be shopping in grocery stores and have people call me by name and ask "How are you?" and I'd look at them, unable to remember who they were or what they were to my life. I was shopping one day and ran into a woman I had known for years, but to me she was a complete stranger. This was nine months after the electroshocks! I was dreadfully ashamed, and I would cry. And then after the frustration of the tears I would get angry.

The personal and family problems that existed before I went for treatment remained, only now I had the added problem of having my memory erased.

Three years after treatments, Mrs. Jackson still met previously well-known individuals whom she could not identify, and she had lost important parts of her past.

I don't remember things I never wanted to forget—important things—like my wedding day and who was there. A friend took me back to the church where I had my wedding, and it had no meaning to me. All I could do is cry in frustration. That just about sums it up. Just recently another friend reminded me of the time that she and I ran a beach party for the office two years before the treatment, and when she told me all I could do was cry because these experiences aren't a part of my life anymore.

There are a lot of blanks that have pieced together for me. Sometimes when I get very frustrated and angry, I ask my husband or father to tell me different things that I've known since childhood, like my relatives and uncles, and what their children's names were, and where they were and what they did. I always had a very good knowledge of this because I had been the one in the family who kept in communication and kept the family aware of each other's doing. Just recently an uncle of mine told me about things we used to do together when I was little—things we used to joke about together when I was an adult, and now it is lost.

Three years of piecing together the facts. But I cannot go back and feel the feelings I had then. I told my sister one day that I don't remember the things shown in the pictures from my honeymoon, but I can see a happy female in the photographs. The experience is lost. I have the data that somebody gave me, I have the pictures, and therefore I know it did occur. And people tell me I used to remember it well. But the actual physical feeling of being there—no, it's gone.

Mrs. Sheffield's subjective viewpoint of the post-ECT experience shares many qualities with Mrs. Jackson's. Mrs. Sheffield had seen a psychiatrist for a few sessions when he encouraged her to enter a hospital for a short course of ECT. More typical of most postshock patients, she cannot recall anything about her decision to accept the treatment or about her relatively short course of therapy. Indeed, she has no recollection whatsoever of the hospitalization. She also experiences more anterograde dysfunction. The emotional pain, however, is very similar.

Returning to a home and family following shock was a truly bewildering experience. I had entirely forgotten how to accomplish even the simplest tasks. To this time, years later, many of the memories needed daily to accomplish my duties as a human being and also wife and mother of other human beings remains shrouded. It was like moving into the home of a complete stranger—myself. Many times I have felt like a second wife; I often find traces and marks of the other wife and feel she was then a much better person than I am today.

Any relatively new skills or knowledge acquired prior to shock were forgotten. A few remnants remain in corners of my mind, but realistically speaking they are gone. So far I have not been able to relearn them, although I have tried.

Trying to find my way around town was very frightening. I could not remember the way, none of the way looked familiar to me, and when I arrived at a supposed destination, if it did not have a sign I would not be sure that was where I wanted to be.

Any efforts at travel were accompanied by a peculiar and almost overwhelming feeling of anxiety, loss, and terror. Only repeated efforts over the same way diminish this, but it is still there.

Mrs. Sheffield was especially articulate in describing the loss of independence, personal strength, and energy following ECT.

After shock the simplest decision felt more like trying to walk through a marsh. Suggestibility was so strong and my own reactions were so shattered that I could not be sure if I really didn't want to do a certain thing, if it was a good or a bad thing for me, or even if it truly interested me or not.

She felt that she was able to gain considerably greater autonomy as the months wore on, but that the recovery was far from complete. Four years after her electroshock, she was still angry and ashamed. She felt her mind had been partially destroyed, and that she would never be able to recapture her former skills or intelligence. She felt isolated and estranged in an unfamiliar environment. Her memory and her ability to learn, she believed, were permanently impaired.

All six of the patients in this series showed, directly or indirectly, a great deal of shame and anguish at the loss of mental faculties. This shame, combined with the actual memory loss and mental disability, may account for why ECT patients did not often speak out in public against the treatment until the development of moral support groups among ex-mental patients in recent years.

3

ECT Brain Damage in Animal Experiments

Gross and Microscopic Pathology Produced by Unmodified ECT

There are many animal experiments indicating that unmodified ECT can produce severe and often permanent brain damage, and many human autopsies yielding a similar pattern of destruction. The most common findings are diffuse damage to small blood vessels with vessel wall deterioration, petechial hemorrhages, gliosis, neuron degeneration, and neuron death. These changes often are scattered throughout the brain in small clusters, but the most severe and frequent ones develop in the frontal and the frontotemporal cortex. In addition, larger hemorrhages are frequently reported in individual cases, as are areas of greater devastation. Edema of the brain is also a frequent finding.[1]

---

1. *Petechial hemorrhages* or *petechiae* are minute, rounded spots of bleeding. They may be visible to the unaided eye as small dots. *Gliosis* is the proliferation of specialized cells in the central nervous system in the wake of damage or inflammation. When permanent or chronic, gliosis may be roughly compared to the scarring process in other tissues of the body. Gliosis indicates brain damage and may in itself compromise brain function. *Neurons* are the brain cells that conduct nerve impulses. They cannot regenerate, and their loss is permanent. The *frontal* and the *frontotemporal cortex* designates the gray matter or surface of the anterior of the brain, including those parts most crucial to the highest human functions, such as abstract reasoning, judgment, insight, self-control, and, in the case of the temporal region, memory. *Edema* is the swelling of tissues, and is in itself potentially damaging to the brain. Because the brain is encased in a rigid skull, swelling increases the pressure on brain tissue, and may eventually cause serious dysfunction or damage.

The definitive study on the brain-damaging effects of electroshock was carried out by Hans Hartelius and published in 1952. It is a treatise that piles detail upon detail in explanation of the theory and the method of the experiment. Unlike any previous study, it critically reviewed most earlier studies and provided objectivity unique in the electroshock literature.

Forty-one cats were subjected to ECT, and 16 others were used as controls. The largest group of 23 animals received four ECT in one day at two-hour intervals. Another group received 11 to 16 treatments at the same rate of four per day. A third group received up to 12 ECT, mostly at three per week. The animals were fed and housed under good conditions and their health carefully evaluated.

The minimal amount of shock necessary to produce a convulsion was used; in some instances small electrodes proportional to the size of the cat's head were employed. The heads were protected during the seizure, and both monophasic and diphasic currents were employed. The experimental and control animals were sacrificed in the same manner, by the removal of their brains under anesthesia.

In one phase of the evaluation of the pathology slides, the pathologist rated the slides from the animals without knowing their origin. In another phase, fresh slides were made from eight ECT animals and eight control animals, and in a double-blind experiment, the pathologist was asked to evaluate whether or not the animals had been shocked. The entire process was subjected to careful statistical analysis. Judgments concerning the presence or absence of pathological findings were carefully described and appear to be conservative.

In the double-blind portion of the experiment, the pathologist was able to discriminate between the eight shocked animals and the eight nonshocked animals with remarkable accuracy:

> This resulted in 7 out of 8 control animals being diagnosed as controls (although one of them with some doubts). Of the 8 treated animals, 7 were diagnosed as treated (3 of them with some doubts). On the basis of the findings, 1 of the 2 remaining animals was denoted as presumably shocked and the other as presumably a control: this proved to be correct. Thus, no definitely incorrect diagnosis was made in the case of any of the animals. On the hypothesis that this distribution was purely random, the probability of classifying the animals correctly is less than 0.0001.

The experimental animals showed vessel wall changes, gliosis, and nerve cell changes:

The *vessel wall changes* found more frequently and more distinctly in the animals subjected to ECT consist of characteristic, sac-like dilatations of the perivascular spaces, which in some cases contain histiocytic elements. The *glial reaction*, of the progressive type, consists of an increase in the number of the smaller glial elements in the parenchyma and of satellitosis beside the nerve cells. The *nerve cell changes* observed are in the form of various stages of chromophobia, frequently with coincident nuclear hyperchromatism. The arrangement of such cells is mainly focal.

The difference between the shocked and control groups was statistically significant when the evaluations were done without knowledge of which animal the slides were derived from (p<0.01). Confirming their basis in reality, the abnormalities were found most heavily in the animals subjected to the greater number of ECT, were most dense in the frontal region, and were correlated with the increasing age and presumed vulnerability of the animal.

Hartelius used very conservative criteria for determining if changes were irreversible. He assumed that findings such as hemorrhages, vascular wall changes, gliosis, and cellular degeneration *might* be reversible, although in some cases they might be permanent. For his criteria of irreversibility he used the appearance of shadow cells and neuronophagia.[2] No signs of unequivocal permanent brain damage were found in animals subjected to 4 ECT or in control animals, but some were found in the 11 to 16 ECT group:

> The question of whether or not irreversible damage to the nerve cells may occur in association with ECT must therefore be answered in the affirmative. This is the first conclusion to be drawn from the observations reported. The changes found were not, however, extensive; they affected only a small minority of the nerve cells and occurred principally in those animals given the largest series of ECT's. On the other hand, only a very small proportion of the cells in the cerebral cortex were examined in the individual animal. In absolute figures, the number of damaged nerve cells in the whole cortex should be considerably greater.

It should be reemphasized that Hartelius' animals were subjected to minimal electric currents in a carefully controlled manner, and that very conservative criteria for irreversible changes were used.

---

2. *Shadow cells* are characterized by the disappearance of the material in the nucleus of the cell and represent a last stage before neuronophagia. *Neuronophagia* is the engulfing of brain cells by specialized cleanup cells.

Hartelius also found that the changes were most apparent in animals sacrificed between 48 and 96 hours after the last ECT, suggesting that some earlier studies that found no pathology sacrificed their animals too early. Animals sacrificed after 96 hours also showed less apparent changes. Hartelius also took great care to rule out agonal changes[3] in the manner of sacrificing the animals, in the use of controls, and in his method of pathological analysis. It is of some interest, however, that he found an increase in agonal changes in the shocked animals, suggesting that the prior trauma of ECT might have made them more susceptible. Thus even the finding of agonal changes in ECT patients may in part be the product of their treatment. Hartelius also found some gross changes in the shocked animals in the form of hemorrhages and edema, but was unable to demonstrate with statistical certainty their relationship to the treatment.

The myth that no evidence exists for brain damage following ECT is maintained in part by the failure of advocates of ECT to mention Hartelius' book-length, English-language study in their review articles and books. It is left out of both the lengthy bibliography and the text in Kalinowsky's detailed, influential review in the *American Handbook of Psychiatry* in 1959. It is listed among several hundred articles in Kalinowsky and Hippius' 1969 textbook on the physical therapies, but is unmentioned in the text itself. This tradition of ignoring Hartelius has continued (Frankel, 1977; Allen, 1978).

With the results of the best study in the animal research literature in mind, I want to review the main body of the literature in chronological order. Most of it substantiates the Hartelius study.

Evidence for permanent brain damage following ECT is found at the very origins of electroshock, in the first English-language translation of an article by Bini (1938), the coinventor of ECT with Cerletti. When they first applied convulsive shocks to the brains of their dogs, Bini and Cerletti found so much brain damage that they could not carry out satisfactory studies (Cerletti, 1950). They chose to pass the current between the rectum and the mouth of the animal in order to produce less severe brain changes. Nonetheless Bini (1938) observed, "The alterations found by us in the nervous systems of these dogs were widespread and severe." This damage included "irreversible" changes in the brain and "chronic cell disease."

Irreversible brain damage following ECT was confirmed in one of the first joint reports by Cerletti and Bini (1940) concerning ECT administered in the clinically approved manner. This publication describes the

---

3. *Agonal changes* are those due to the death process rather than to the trauma or illness that caused the death. Advocates of electroshock have taken the view that many reports of brain damage reflect agonal changes rather than the effects of ECT.

changes as "severe," including "acellular areas." Hartelius observed that their alleged control animals had been electrocuted, thus casting doubt on their claim that some damage was artifactual.[4]

Writing without Bini in later years, Cerletti (1950) presented a different version of his earlier experiments. He failed to mention the original studies and attempted to prove the harmlessness of the treatment by observing that electroshocked dogs were able to stand up and run away from the shock table following their recovery from the postshock coma. Descriptions of his pathology sections, when provided by Cerletti (1954), did acknowledge the presence of "diffuse" changes in the blood vessels and cells of the brain, as well as gliosis; but, without explanation or justification, he claimed that none of these changes were permanent.

Kalinowsky played a key role in the early years in claiming that Cerletti's studies showed no serious pathology (Jessner & Ryan, 1941, p. 108). Advocates of electroshock such as Kalinowsky and Hippius (1969), or Harms (1955), have repeated Cerletti's later assertions that ECT is harmless without mentioning the initial studies by Bini and Cerletti.

By 1941 there was so much animal experimentation evidence accumulating for cell damage following ECT that the definitive text, *Shock Treatment in Psychiatry* by Jessner and Ryan (1941), had already observed that "a great deal of evidence has been accumulated which indicates that brain damage is possible with this form of shock therapy" (p. 109; see also p. XV).

In 1941 Heilbrunn and Liebert biopsied the brains of rabbits between 2 and 60 minutes following a variety of convulsive agents, including electricity, metrazol, camphor, nitrogen, and insulin. Consistent with the earlier literature, changes were found following convulsions regardless of their origin, but the most severe ones were found following ECT. The minimum dose of electricity required to produce a convulsion was used in some animals, and damage was found proportional to increasing dosages. Agonal changes were ruled out by serial biopsies taken immediately after the inducement of the convulsions; furthermore, serious cellular deterioration was found after only one convulsion, including the loss of cellular outline, deterioration, and swelling. In the panel discussion which followed the report, Heilbrunn stressed that "specimens taken for biopsy showed no reversibility of alterations during the observation period of fifty to sixty minutes." Concern was shown

---

4. An *artifactual change* is one that is accidental, and therefore extraneous or irrelevant. Advocates of electroshock have argued that abnormalities found on microscopic examination of animals' brains after electroshock have been due to errors in staining the tissue samples. In their own studies, as this review will indicate, they have found similar changes in control animals that have not been electroshocked, suggesting that these changes are "artifactual."

by one discussant about the high voltage for the small size of the animals (80 to 90 v), but another reported that testing of similar equipment showed that no more than 100 ma were delivered to animals. Another discussant emphasized "Certainly, the available literature on careful studies of pathological changes in the brain following electric shock therapy indicates the possibility of irreparable damage to the brain."

In a less elegant study the following year Heilbrunn and Weil (1942) shocked rabbits with 60 to 150 v, 65 to 300 ma, and caused paralysis as well as brain hemorrhage. In still another study in 1943 Heilbrunn shocked rats into convulsions with 10 to 20 v, 30 to 50 ma, and found petechial and occasionally larger hemorrhages in the meninges[5] and throughout the brain, developing usually after one to three ECT. He compared these findings to those by Alpers and Hughes (1942a). Excellent pathology plates were provided.

Alpers and Hughes (1942a) subjected cats to a variety of ECT schedules varying from 10 ECT at three per week to 23 ECT on a one-a-day basis. They found a wide variety of brain changes from "punctate hemorrhages" to larger subarachnoid hemorrhages.[6] The authors note that "hemorrhage occurs with alarming frequency in experimental animals subjected to electric shock," and further, "It is probably fair to assume that there is some damage to the human brain, the difference being one of degree rather than kind." They made efforts to match clinical conditions, including proportionally small electrodes, and stated "The experimental conditions in many of these animals paralleled those used in electric shock therapy." Although Frankel in his 1977 review declares they "made no mention of the voltage used," the authors in fact specifically stated that they used a 110 v, 60-cycle current with a very small current dose of 150 to 200 ma. As in many of the studies in this section, excellent pathology plates were provided.

Neuberger et al. (1942) conducted a similar experiment with dogs. Using the same equipment as the department of psychiatry in its treatment of patients, they administered very small doses (80 v, 200 ma) at three- to five-day intervals for a total of 2 to 25 ECT. They found widespread damage in the dogs. For example, Dog 8, after five ECT, showed the following: "Changes in numerous nerve cells in all areas: swelling, vacuolation, indistinct cell borders, granular cytoplasm, occasional intranuclear granules. Occasional severe changes and ghost cells." In summarizing the findings on all dogs they described a wide variety of pathology, including some they labeled "severe," and including replica-

---

5. The *meninges* are three membranes that surround the brain and spinal cord.

6. *Punctate hemorrhages* are small clusters of dot-like hemorrhages. *Subarachnoid hemorrhages* are of varying size and occur between the membranes or meninges that surround the brain.

tion of Hartelius' finding: "small circumscribed areas" in which "only pale, ischemic, ghostlike cells remained." In addition, "satellitosis and neuronophagia were found occasionally."[7] The pathology was widespread and comparable, they believed, to that found by Morrison et al. (1930) in electrocuted animals. The changes were "most noticeable in the vicinity of the pathway of the electrical current (temporoparietal cortex)." The article provided many photographic plates to demonstrate the pathologic findings.

In 1946 Ferraro, Roizen, and Helford conducted very sophisticated research on monkeys at an institute well known for its strong promotion of ECT, and they concluded that "possibly some permanent slight structural damage" might be the basis for the ECT effect in humans. But they were pulling their punches in this conclusion. As in most other animal studies, they found scattered areas of petechial hemorrhage, especially in the frontal lobes, and they admitted, "such damage no matter how slight may ultimately become permanent. The addition of other small hemorrhages may finally influence even in a slight manner some of the mental process." Turning to their actual data—reproductions of their pathology slides and the accompanying descriptions—the picture becomes more grim. Cell *death* is seen in animal A after 12 ECT at the small dose of 120 ma; "However, here and there small areas of rarification as well as satellitosis and neuronophagia were encountered." Animal B shows a similar picture after 12 ECT, and so does animal C, which displays "slight rarification of nerve cells and a few acellular areas in the frontal and temporal lobes." Another animal has similar areas of cell death after only four ECT. From the actual data, most if not all the animals suffered some amount of cell death, as well as scattered petechial hemorrhages. The authors concluded that these findings were more extensive in the experimental animals than in the controls, especially in the frontal lobes, and therefore attributable to ECT. The overall findings are extremely close to those reported several years later by Hartelius, including the type and distribution of damage and its relative increase with greater numbers of ECT.

This two-year study was important both for the expertise of its investigators and for its design. Not only were controls used, but efforts were made to mimic clinical conditions and to answer criticisms made of some earlier studies by ECT advocates. These efforts included the use of

---

7. The variety of changes described here are beyond the scope of a footnote. They cover the spectrum of classic findings in central nervous system pathology, indicating widespread damage along a continuum from mild cellular deterioration to cell death. "Satellitosis" occurs when specialized cells gather around the brain cell prior to engulfing it in the process of neuronophagia. Hartelius also found both satellitosis and neuronophagia in some animals subjected to ECT.

a regular ECT machine, smaller electrodes to fit the monkey heads, routine numbers of ECT (4 to 18 per animal), and the minimal necessary dose of ECT (70 to 90 v, 102 to 400 ma, with an average of 129 or less). In addition the head was protected to avoid damage from trauma during the convulsion. All in all, the animals were subjected to far less trauma than in the routine use of ECT in humans.

Three years later Ferraro and Roizen (1949) published a second study of the effects of ECT on monkeys, this time with larger numbers of treatments—32 to 74—still well within the limits often used in modern practice. With the fewest shocks—32—they found "moderate nerve cell rarification" and "acellular areas." Again damage and cell death was proportional to the intensity of the current and the number of shocks, and was amply displayed on slides published in the article.

These studies by Ferraro and Roizen could not have gone unnoticed, because both men were authorities in brain pathology at the same institutes in which the advocates of ECT were at work. Armando Ferraro was clinical professor of psychiatry at the Columbia College of Physicians and Surgeons and principal research scientist in neuropathology at the New York State Psychiatric Institute. Leon Roizen was chief of psychiatric research in neuropathology at the New York State Psychiatric Institute and associate professor of neuropathology at the Columbia College of Physicians and Surgeons. Both men were acknowledged research experts, and both had individual chapters in the same *American Handbook of Psychiatry* (Arieti, 1959) in which Kalinowsky appeared as the expert on ECT. In Kalinowsky's review of electroshock in this book, with 119 citations, he omitted the research of his New York City colleagues, Ferraro and Roizen, from his text and noted only the earlier, less damaging article in the bibliography.

Kalinowsky also wrote a textbook (1961) with Paul Hoch, Professor and Director of the institute at which Ferraro and Roizen did their research. Here the earlier of the two reports on brain damage was mentioned in the text: Kalinowsky and Hoch observed that Ferraro and Roizen found "neuronal changes of the reversible type," and that's *all* they said. They did not say that Ferraro and Roizen also found changes of the *irreversible* type, including "nerve cell rarification" and "acellular areas" indicating nerve cell death.

The studies by Ferraro and his colleagues and by Hartelius met all the objections of ECT advocates to such research. Systematically criticizing the raft of animal studies indicating permanent brain damage following ECT, Frankel in 1977 and Allen in 1978 ignored these three studies, neither mentioning them in the text nor citing them in the bibliography. In reality this research was so definitive and unequivocal in its findings that it brought to an end the era of animal research on ECT in English language journals, although occasional corroborating research has appeared in other sources. Kalinowsky and Hippius (1969) cite Quandt and Sommer (1966) as finding extensive necrosis and gliosis in the anterior of the brain, attributed to the passage of the electric current during ECT animal experiments. In 1971 Aleksandrovskaya and Kruglikov also found brain damage in rats subjected to ECT.

Psychiatric textbooks and reviews frequently omit or misrepresent the important animal studies, or cite some that allegedly prove the harmlessness of ECT, when a careful examination of the material almost always proves that ECT does cause serious and permanent brain damage. Others of the studies cited are so faulty as to invalidate themselves by the authors' own suggestion that their slides demonstrate gross errors in staining technique. Because these studies are frequently mentioned favorably in the standard reviews and texts it is necessary to give them serious attention.

Globus et al., in 1943, produced the single most important study among the several frequently cited as proof that ECT is harmless. Kalinowsky and Hippius, for example, state "Globus et al. have observed no important pathology in studies on electronarcosis[8] which they rightly consider a prolongation of electric shock." However, the pathological slides from the ECT animals in Globus et al. showed classic pathological findings of diffuse brain damage. The faulty reasoning by which Globus et al. turned this study into a proof of the harmlessness of ECT is most astonishing but most important, for this reasoning has been used in several other research projects to dismiss pathological findings (Barrera et al., 1942; Winkelman & Moore, 1944) and even to invalidate independent autopsy findings (discussion in Riese, 1948).

Globus et al. found extreme, permanent pathological changes in every single one of their animals, including "ghost cells" and other signs of dead and dying cells throughout the brain. They openly admitted, "Were such to be found only in the experimental animals, they would have been regarded as evidence of an acquired pathologic condition." That is, on the face of it, these changes would have been evidence of brain damage from ECT. But while such findings were obvious in the half-dozen shocked animals, they were also found in the *one* control animal. Therefore Globus et al. concluded that the findings in the six shocked animals must have been artifacts created by errors in the laboratory preparation of the slides.

This is an incomprehensible rationalization. If their technique were so poor that all the slides, experimental and control, looked devastated, they could draw *no* conclusions; they certainly could not conclude that

---

8. In *electronarcosis* the electric current is applied for a prolonged period of time beyond the initiation of the convulsion.

none of the slides came from brain-damaged animals. For comparison let us assume a reconnaissance plane takes a picture of six cities to determine if they have been bombed. The photographs show that many areas in each city have been widely devastated in a manner typical of aerial bombing. It is then discovered that photographs of one control city—a city thought not to be devastated—show the same classic picture of devastation. Of the many conclusions one may draw from this, one can *not* conclude that the pictures prove that no devastation has occurred in any of the bombed cities. Even if it turns out that all the photographs are indeed the product of a drastic error in the darkroom, this invalidates *all* the photographs, making it impossible to draw any conclusions from them. Instead of being used as evidence to prove that no devastation has taken place, all the photographs should be declared worthless.

However, some strong alternative hypotheses suggest themselves concerning the apparently devastated control city. First, the control photographs of one city may be faulty, while the photographs of the six bombed cities may be accurate. Second, the alleged control city may not be free of damage. Perhaps it has been bombed by error, or perhaps some other form of devastation has been visited upon it. Both these alternatives are strong possibilities. In a study by Alexander and Lowenbach (1944) one of the control animals did indeed turn out to have brain disease. Perhaps this was true in Globus et al.; there would be no way to rule out such a possibility when only one animal was used as a control. Even more startling, a careful examination of the Globus study suggests that the alleged control animal may have been electrocuted—utterly ruling it out as a control animal. I believe the matter is ambiguous. The plates published with the text include shocked animals and an electrocuted animal, but no other "control." The control is mentioned, but its method of sacrifice is not made clear. At best we must guess about the nature of the all-important control. Probably because no mention of any animal is made other than the shock animals and the electrocuted animals, Hartelius (1952), on the basis on his own reading, concludes that the control animal is indeed the same one who had been electrocuted, thus invalidating it as a control.

But there is a still more obvious problem with this study. Globus and his colleagues *did* electrocute one of the animals.

Dog C. This animal was never given electronarcosis. It was killed on 2/2/42 by applying a current of about 550 ma to the head for five minutes with the electrodes in the same place as used for the other electronarcoses. The animal did not breathe during this time; the heart stopped after about three minutes and did not return.

In killing this animal the electrodes were placed on the head. This means that nearly all the electricity was confined to the skull and the brain, so that the animal was killed by the devastating effects of a prolonged current to the brain, as well as the anoxia that followed suppression of his breathing for five minutes. What did Globus et al. find when they examined the brain of this animal? The slides of this animal's brain showed all the same defects that were found in the animals treated with ECT; it was "essentially the same," meaning there were signs of cell death: "It is significant that the histologic structure of the brain in the animal killed by electrocution did not differ from that in the other experimental and control animals." These findings too were dismissed as meaningless, and it was assumed that this dog—killed by electricity— showed no changes in his brain because the same findings were found in one unspecified control.

In other words, Globus et al. found evidence of damage in the electrocuted brain, much as they found it in dogs given electroshock, but they decided that it all added up to nothing because *one* control dog *thought* to be normal had similar findings. Instead of citing this study as proof that no brain damage follows electroconvulsive therapy, advocates of electroshock should use it to cite a miracle—that no brain damage follows cranial electrocution and prolonged coma. That such a position is absurd was already well known from studies of electrocution. Langworthy (1930), for example, found this pathology after electrocuting animals:

> . . . marked shrinkage of the nucleus, which stains a uniform
> dark color, so that the nucleolus and chromatin granules may
> no longer be discerned. It is thought that cells with such
> marked changes in the nucleus no longer have the potentialities
> of recovery.

Langworthy also performed autopsies on human beings, one killed by accidental electrocution, the other in the electric chair, and he found similar changes.

Hassin (1933), again before the use of ECT on patients, found utter devastation of the brain in five victims of the electric chair, including vast cracks and fissures in the brain, as if it were "torn by some diffusely explosive or disruptive force," "almost as if the cell had been blown to bits by dynamite."

The same errors in reasoning are found in Barrera et al. (1942), another widely cited study. Much as Globus and his team, Barrera and his colleagues reported diffuse pathology in slides taken from the brains of their shocked animals.

The nerve changes were spotty in distribution and not localized to any particular portion of the brain. In the areas involved some of the nerve cells appeared shrunken with pyknosis of the nucleus, paling of the cytoplasm, and disappearance of the Nissl substance. Some of the cells were only shadow cells.[9]

These are the diffuse and spotty changes consistent with autopsy and animal studies, and accounted for by the diffuse passage of the electricity through various parts of the skull. But, as in Globus et al., this classic picture of brain damage was dismissed because an *unspecified number of undescribed control animals* had the same findings. Wholly without rational basis, the authors concluded that ECT causes no damage.

Another well-known study allegedly demonstrating no brain damage following ECT was published by Winkelman and Moore (1944). Only four cats were used, and the doses were smaller than those used on humans; but even in this study one of the four animals showed "a marked venous and venular congestion with prominence of both venous and arterial capillaries" after only *two* treatments. This finding in one of four animals is left out in all ECT texts that tout the study as another proof that ECT is harmless. Again in this study there was possible pathology seen in the brain of the other shocked animals, but these were dismissed because they were said to be similar to those in an unnamed, undescribed "control animal."

A three-dog study by Lidbeck in 1944 is also mentioned frequently as proof that no damage is produced by electroshock. The author concluded that shock is harmless. But in the fine print used to summarize their findings, a textbook picture of brain damage was reported:

In all of the sections stained by the Nissl method the nerve cells were shrunken and there was a decrease in the number of stainable granules. In addition, sections from the frontal lobe of dogs # 2 and # 3 revealed an occasional isolated area in which the nerve cells showed a greater degree of shrinkage with deeply stained nuclei and prominent, tortuous processes. A few ghost cells were noted . . .

More astonishing, a careful reading of the commentary indicates that a recent small brain hemorrhage as well as some small blood clots were found in the other dog (# 1). Still in fine print, the author concluded that: "These findings, although milder in character, are in essential

---

9. These are classic pathologic findings indicating cellular deterioration along a continuum that terminates with the shadow cell immediately prior to disintegration and neuronophagia.

agreement with those of Neuberger and his co-workers." Neuberger considered these findings indicative of brain damage.

To sum up, this "proof" of no brain damage shows that one of three dogs had bleeding and clots in his brain, and that all three displayed damage in *every* section of the brain examined, plus some *irreversible* cell damage including "a few ghost cells." ECT advocates have published the conclusions of Lidbeck without mentioning his fine print—permanent brain damage. Kalinowsky and Hippius (1969) for example, cite this study as showing only "negligible changes."

One of the most frequently mentioned studies in support of the harmlessness of ECT was published by two strong advocates of ECT, Alexander and Lowenbach (1944). Most of the animals in this study were subjected to only one ECT before they were killed for autopsy. Human beings undergoing ECT are always subjected to more than one ECT. But even the animals subjected to one dose showed some abnormal reactions of great potential importance, including "blanching," a bleaching of the brain tissue caused by temporary constriction of blood vessels in the brain. In several instances dye injected into shocked animals leaked profusely from these vessels into the brain tissue, indicating damage to the vessel walls after only *one* electroshock. Furthermore, the authors make clear that these changes took place "within the range of amperage employed in the treatment of man." The lack of diffuse cellular changes may be accounted for by the fact that many, if not all, of the animals were sacrificed one-half hour or less after ECT, too soon for the development of pathological changes (Hartelius, 1952).

Several animals that were subjected to multiple electroshocks by Alexander and Lowenbach did show more severe changes, one with heavy bleeding into the brain. This is never mentioned when the article is cited, but confirms that we are dealing with a continuum of damage, from relatively small but consistent reactions after only one ECT to greater pathology after more ECT.

Alexander and Lowenbach repeatedly stated that the main changes they found were limited to the area between the electrodes; they believed most of the electricity traveled through this area in a straight line from one electrode to another. But they were wrong about this electrical path. The resistance of the skull to the passage of electricity is so great that the outside of the entire skull collects electrical charge, which then pours through the skull in whatever areas the skull is thinnest and least resistant to the current (Hayes, 1950). Thus, when tested with implanted electrodes, "The current flow through the brain is very diffuse." As Hartelius has reminded us, those who read slides can easily see what they hope to see. Alexander and Lowenbach saw changes limited to a *hypothesized* flow of current.

In 1950 Siekert et al. published one of the few studies that does support the hypothesis that ECT is harmless to the brain. The sample is small—five monkeys—and the current is within the very low range of clinical use in humans (189 to 130 ma). Furthermore the animals were sacrificed at 24 hours, too early for the more significant brain-damage manifestations to mature (Hartelius, 1952). Considering these factors, as well as the fact that far more sophisticated studies indicating damage have been published, it seems surprising that some ostensibly detailed, up-to-date reviews cite the Siekert et al. study as the only one of significance (Allen, 1978).

Considering how much effort has gone into attempts by ECT advocates to prove that animals do not suffer permanent brain damage following ECT, it is remarkable that there is almost no research evidence upholding their position. Even when treatments in medicine eventually are discarded because of their great danger, there usually is a plethora of studies by advocates of any of these treatments "proving" that it is harmless. It is easy to *fail* to document damage. ECT, by contrast, is so damaging to the brain that few negative studies exist, and even research conducted by the advocates usually tends to confirm its destructiveness.

B.J. Alpers, professor of neurology at Jefferson Medical College and neuropathologist at the Institute of Pennsylvania Hospital, was one of the first medical professionals to caution psychiatry about brain-damaging its patients. Reviewing his own laboratory studies as well as others accumulated over the years, Alpers (1946) came to the realization that "brain changes have been found even in those cases in which the experiments have been regarded as negative." He warned against the danger of adding "injury to insult" in the life of the mental patient by electroshocking him.

Alpers also attacked the myth that ECT advocates can easily determine which brain changes are "reversible." Brain hemorrhage, in every proshock study, is listed as a temporary change. But no one can say for sure how much damage will remain after a hemorrhage has healed. This is why recovery from strokes in human beings is always difficult to predict. Many hemorrhages leave permanent damage.

Kalinowsky (1959), in perpetrating the myth of ECT harmlessness, has said,

> The question of brain damage has been thoroughly investigated since early papers mentioned petechial hemorrhages and other bleedings in the brain. Later, studies in animals and in humans after fatalities did not confirm such hemorrhages, nor did they reveal any cell changes in the brain.

To the contrary, nearly all animal studies confirm that ECT in clinical doses under carefully controlled conditions produces some degree of brain damage in nearly every animal subjected to the treatment, and that definitively permanent damage is frequently found within the range of clinical usage. The damage is diffuse and often spotty. It is heaviest across the anterior brain, and consists of vascular changes, petechial hemorrhages, gliosis, cellular deterioration, and cell death. In addition, larger hemorrhages are occasionally found.

Behavioral Dysfunction and Amnesia Produced by ECT

From early in the history of electroshock, gross behavioral inhibition and disruption were demonstrated following ECT in animals. As early as 1940, Page wrote: "After 5–10 convulsions, the rats become extremely passive, inactive and submissive. Many exhibit wax-like flexibility." These manifestations of acute brain dysfunction mimic those of more severe ECT reactions we shall find in human beings, and were demonstrated repeatedly in the literature. By 1947, Russell's review listed many studies demonstrating losses in motivation as well as in memory and learning. More recent and sophisticated studies by Routtenberg and Kay (1965) demonstrate that one ECT depresses exploratory and motor activity in rats for up to a week.

One of the most interesting early animal experiments was performed by Masserman and Jacques (1947), who subjected rats to stresses to teach them "neurotic behavior" such as fear, which would disrupt their ordinary activities. They subjected these animals, as well as "nonneurotic" controls, to 10 ECT at two- to three-day intervals. They found that the neurotic behavior did indeed disappear, consistent with the capacity of ECT to wipe out recent learning and recent memories. They also found the equivalent of an organic brain syndrome in both the neurotic and the nonneurotic animals.

Concerning amnesia itself, there is general agreement that retrograde amnesia in animals is a definite finding and that it can be permanent. Although a variety of studies indicate retrograde amnesia, few involve modified ECT. Those modifications that have been attempted rarely mimic clinical conditions. Chevalier (1965) gave artificial respiration to rats during ECT, but did not use muscle relaxants or anesthetics. With this limited modification, he was able to demonstrate retrograde amnesia. Essman (1968) used pharmacological agents to inhibit the entire convulsion in mice, and reported that "current flow through the brain, rather than an overt convulsion, accounts for the amnesic effect of electroshock." McGaugh and Alpern (1966), in a similar experiment, concluded, "These results indicate quite clearly that the retrograde amnesia produced by electroshock is due to the current and does not depend upon the elicitation of a behavioral convulsion."

McGaugh felt able in 1974 to declare that the preponderance of evidence indicates that ECT produces permanent retrograde amnesia (RA) in animals:

> Although some investigators have reported finding that memory impairment produced by ECT is only temporary, most studies investigating this problem have found that the RA is permanent, at least over intervals of time ranging from 12 hours to one month. Overall there is little evidence to support the view that ECT produces only temporary RA.

In another review of the subject, Zornetzer (1974) agreed that organic deterioration is the cause of memory loss, and he declared, "More than two decades of animal research using electroconvulsive therapy (ECT) supported the idea that recently acquired information is subject to disruption and often permanent loss." Greenough et al. (1968) also reviewed the literature, conducted a carefully controlled experiment with rats, and concluded that the retrograde amnesia produced in animals is permanent.

Biochemical Dysfunction Produced by ECT

Most of the studies concerning macromolecular events in the central nervous system have been conducted on rats, relatively small animals requiring a relatively significant dose of electric current in order to produce a seizure. Few of these studies have a sufficiently long follow-up to suggest the permanence of changes involved, but they do suggest a variety of changes from a massive increase in "brain free fatty acid" after one ECT (Bazan & Rakowski, 1970) to significantly increased brain weight after several (Pryor & Otis, 1969). One of the more elegant recent experiments by Colon and Notermans in 1975 found no microscopic changes in rats sacrificed two months after a course of 12 ECT, but did find significant losses in the "nuclear volume" of cells. This was diffuse throughout the entire cortex, consistent with earlier animal pathology studies showing diffuse brain changes. The authors suggest that the lack of cell loss results from the relative resistance of the rat brain to hypoxia. They conclude their findings with a statement that loss of nuclear volume "constitutes a serious warning against the use of electroconvulsive therapy and a serious indication for the suppression of epileptic manifestations."

There are many good modern reviews of the biochemical effects of ECT upon animals (Dunn et al., 1974; Essman, 1973, 1974; Lovell, 1971; McGaugh & Williams, 1974). Essman (1973) divides hundreds of studies into six overlapping categories of change following ECT: (1) cerebral electrolytes; (2) energy metabolism; (3) macromolecular events; (4) biogenic amine function and metabolism; (5) blood brain barrier permeability; and (6) cerebral spinal fluid. He finds that virtually all brain biochemistry is disrupted by ECT.

Despite this mass of data indicating severe, general biochemical dysfunction after ECT in animals, there are very few data bearing directly on permanence. Nonetheless some relevant conclusions can be drawn from the biochemical literature. Innumerable studies cited in every major review show that small doses of electric current itself can cause dramatic biochemical changes, consistent with the severe vascular and cellular changes that have already been demonstrated in the older literature. Essman pays special attention to this, drawing on the work of Hartelius as illustrative of the kind of organic deterioration that may underlie biochemical dysfunction. Like Hartelius and Alpers, he is aware that even allegedly negative experiments, such as Alexander and Lowenbach's, suggest "a strong possibility that organic physiological or physiochemical changes of the neural parenchyma[10] may be implicated in multiple ECT treatments, even with current levels utilized in man."

Essman (1974), Lovell (1971), Dunn et al. (1974), and other reviewers of the subject believe that disruptions of protein synthesis provide the ultimate explanation for the retrograde amnesia found in animal and human studies alike. Dunn et al., for example, reviewed the literature and presented new data indicating that most changes in protein synthesis are caused by the current rather than by the convulsion. They concluded that even subconvulsive currents can inhibit protein synthesis and produce amnesia:

> In summary, we have shown that electroconvulsive shock inhibits the uptake and incorporation of radioactive precursors into RNA and protein synthesis in the mouse brain. Protein synthesis is probably inhibited and the effects are not dependent on bodily convulsions.

They believe that the retrograde amnesia is permanent.

I will not review the literature on human brain metabolism and ECT, which the reader can approach through many of the reviews I have mentioned. Although hundreds of studies show multiple severe changes

---

10. *Neural parenchyma* designates the specialized cells of the brain, i.e., the nerve cells themselves, rather than the connective tissue.

within the human body, few studies have tested for the duration of these changes, or even for the relationship between these changes and mental dysfunction. This is because of the inaccessibility of human brain tissue until after death. One interesting exception is the availability of human spinal fluid. Following ECT, Spiegel-Adolf, Wilcox, and Spiegel (1948) found enzymatic substances in the cerebral spinal fluid that proved toxic to nerve cells. Overall, however, the human biochemical literature contributes little to resolving the question of the permanence or severity of changes following ECT.

In summary, there is considerable animal research linking brain damage, the disruption of protein synthesis, and permanent retrograde amnesia as a direct result of both convulsions and the passage of an electric current through the brain. The electric current is the most frequently cited culprit.

4

Human Autopsy Studies after ECT

Many textbooks and articles promoting ECT cite an infinitesimally low rate of death following ECT, but many actual reports in the literature demonstrate a more dismal picture. Similarly, some authoritative sources deny the existence of any substantial body of literature describing brain pathology following ECT, whereas several review articles and many case reports give details of pathology closely resembling that found in animals after ECT.

The most difficult task is to separate brain changes produced by ECT from those produced by unrelated disease, by complications following the ECT trauma, or by the process of death. I have not included in this review suggestive studies that in my opinion still leave such questions largely unanswered (see for example, Gralnick, 1944; Eyman & Morris, 1950; Gaitz et al., 1956). In the studies that follow the authors and/or their data clearly relate one aspect or another of the brain pathology to the electroconvulsive therapy.

Brain Death and Pathology following Unmodified ECT

In one of the first reports on fatalities associated with electroshock, Franklin Ebaugh, Professor of Psychiatry at the University of Colorado, and his colleagues found evidence of significant brain damage, including areas of cell death at autopsy (1942). The early study of ECT brain damage in rabbits by Heilbrunn and Weil (1942) was followed by a discussion of a similar autopsy finding in a human. In a subsequent report on two autopsy cases, Alpers and Hughes (1942b) described one case that offered "a clear demonstration of the fact that electrical convulsion treatment is followed at times by structural damage of the brain." The other case, an elderly man who had been subjected to only six electroshocks, showed similar but lesser pathology: degenerative changes, cell death, and bleeding "traceable directly to the effects of the convulsive treatment." Alpers and Hughes compared this to pathology reported in shocked cats from their own laboratory and in shocked rabbits by Heilbrunn and Weil. They concluded that these permanent changes could have an effect on the health and life of the person.

Ebaugh, Barnacle, and Neuberger (1943) published autopsy reports on patients who had been receiving ECT. One patient who had died after only 13 treatments displayed gross pathology similar to electrocution:

> Several small areas of devastation appeared to be entirely devoid of nerve cells or contained some ghost cells. . . . Furthermore, there was a diffuse degeneration of nerve cells in the cortex . . . degeneration of scattered nerve cells was seen. . . . Owing to these lesions, the architecture of the cortex appeared irregular in places.

Their second case had received three treatments and the brain changes were less marked, but they were nonetheless "so pronounced as to be recognized under low magnification." On microscope there were areas of dying and dead cells. The authors supported ECT, and they emphasized that "Certainly, many of the changes were reversible." This is irrelevant. In any damage to any part of the body many or most changes will be reversible, unless the person dies or loses that part of his body. With no evidence whatsoever they concluded that the brain damage was " . . . by no means likely to interfere seriously with the normal function of the central nervous system. One would not be justified in suggesting rejection of electric shock therapy."

In 1945, Meyer and Teare found hemorrhage and vascular changes as well as fat emboli in a death after only one ECT. Otto Will and his colleagues (1948) published an extensive review of previously reported cases covering 33 patients who died during or after electroshock. Among these 33 published cases of death associated with ECT, half had not been given autopsies, and in one autopsy the brain was not examined. Of the 16 whose brains had been examined, 50 percent showed brain changes attributable to the electroshock, many of them severe.

Will and his colleagues also reported on one of their own cases of ECT death, which showed obvious brain-tissue destruction resulting from the electroshock. They concluded that the treatment presents hazards of brain damage to patients receiving it.

Sprague and Taylor (1948) found an old hemorrhage attributable to six ECT. This finding of brain damage in humans after only a few shocks is not uncommon in the literature. In a 33-year-old who died after only two ECT, Riese (1948) found bleeding and severe cell changes. In an older patient he found dead and dying cells including "ghost cells." The Riese paper included a discussion by Kalinowsky and Globus who attempted to deny the validity of these findings on much the same grounds that they had denied the validity of their own similar results in animals (Globus et al., 1943; Barrerra et al., 1942). Riese responded (1948):

> What makes this picture, just like any other neuropathological picture, a significant one, is the combination of changes: in all observations of sudden death after electric shock reported so far, petechial hemorrhages, cellular changes, and some glial proliferation stand out prominently, as an almost constant whole.

In still another report a year later Riese and Fultz (1949) described the autopsy of a patient who had died after only a few electroshocks. There were "scattered areas of disruption and 'explosive' destruction" attributable to the shock. In 1949 P.A. Martin reported five deaths after ECT and concluded, "electroshock causes petechial hemorrhages in the brain in some cases." Liban et al. (1951) described extensive hemorrhage and cell degeneration in an autopsy after seven ECT, as did Larsen and Vraa-Jensen (1953) after four ECT, only one of which produced a grand mal seizure.

Not surprisingly, the autopsy literature suggests that the degree of brain damage is related to the number of ECT. Corsellis and Mayer in 1954 reported on tissue changes in the brains of two patients who died relatively uncomplicated deaths after electroshock. A young man who had been subjected to 140 treatments had diffuse degenerative changes in his brain, suggesting reactions to his previous ECT, as well as fresher damage attributable to the more recent treatments. These changes were permanent. Another patient who had been given 38 convulsions died at age 40 after receiving three ECT in a row in one day. His brain was swollen and had evidence of hemorrhage. A group of autopsy controls from the same hospital showed no such findings.

In 1956 S.P. Alexander et al. reported an ECT-related death rate of one in 1,000 in their institution, and described four autopsies, two of which showed brain damage. In the same year Madow published an extensive review in which he estimated that 40 percent of ECT deaths were caused by cerebral complications from the treatment.

> By far the most frequent alterations recorded in the brain were in the vascular system. Petechial hemorrhages were found in 17 of 38 cases; subarachnoid hemorrhages in four; and large intracerebral hemorrhages in two cases. Areas of softening were described in three patients. . . .

Madow also reported on four cases of his own—one who died after six ECT—and he summarized that they "revealed significant vascular changes in all, ranging from petechiae scattered throughout the tissue to a massive intraventricular hemorrhage." Madow compared his findings to those of Hartelius in animals, and concluded that the vascular changes were the primary cause of damage.

The last of the major studies of brain death caused by unmodified ECT was published in 1957 by Impastato. He verified an overall death rate of 1:1,000 from ECT, and a specific death rate of 1:200 in patients over 60 years of age. Impastato reviewed 214 fatalities from the literature, plus 40 previously unpublished cases. This study, in which most of the patients had undergone unmodified ECT, was lengthy and detailed, and can only be highlighted in regard to brain damage following ECT. The category "cerebral death" accounted for 66 of 235 cases in which the cause of death was known. Within this category, cardiorespiratory arrest was the main culprit (31 deaths), followed by hemorrhage, thrombosis, and necrosis[1] of the brain (16 deaths), and congestion and edema (5 deaths). In the hemorrhagic group, six cases suffered gross hemorrhages and five petechial. Patients in this group tended to die after only a few ECT. In the age group under 40, cerebral trauma was the leading cause of death. Although a staunch advocate of ECT, Impastato emphasized that ECT is a "risky" treatment not to be entered into lightly. His study confirmed that ECT can and does produce severe enough brain damage to lead to death in a significant number of cases.

Again we return to the question, "How has the myth of harmlessness remained alive?" The culminating autopsy review of unmodified ECT published by Impastato in 1957 is unmentioned in the text or bibliographies of key reviews over the following years (Kalinowsky, 1959; Kalinowsky & Hoch, 1961; Kalinowsky & Hippius, 1969). Because Impastato's other works are frequently cited, this oversight cannot be acci-

---

1. A *thrombus* is a clot within a blood vessel. *Necrosis* is cell death, in this case brought about by the clotting of the vessel.

dental. We find repeated statements that no significant autopsy findings occur in the brain following death by ECT: "Aside from symptom aggravation of brain tumors . . . neurologic complications are extremely rare" (Kalinowsky & Hippius, 1969). In reality the literature contains many examples of central nervous system death following ECT, often with postmortem findings of brain damage that mimic those in animal studies.

Brain Death and Pathology following Modified ECT

Far fewer autopsy reports appear in modern literature on modified ECT. This cannot be taken as an indication that the death rate has decreased, for investigators have observed that recent ECT modifications have increased the mortality rate, as well as other hazards, by adding the complications of pharmacologic muscle paralysis and anesthesia (Barker & Baker, 1959; Novello, 1974; Kalinowsky, 1956; Impastato, 1957). The decline in such reports may be from a general lack of interest in ECT research after 40 years of practice, or it may reflect a desire to withhold damaging evidence against the treatment as a part of the current attempt to improve its public image. I share neurologist Robert Grimm's (1978) concern in this regard:

> . . . there has been a dramatic drop in the number of published accounts of *any* problems with the practice of ECT, especially deaths. There is an eerie journal silence in a literature that hitherto was substantial and extremely useful in questions of morbidity and mortality.

Nonetheless there are reports that do confirm brain damage, especially hemorrhage, following modified ECT.

Impastato's massive review of ECT autopsy data has already been summarized in regard to cerebral disasters following unmodified ECT. A number of the patients in this series did undergo modified ECT, but they were not always differentiated from the larger group of deaths after unmodified ECT. In the cerebral death group, however, it was noted that 13 of 66 patients had been given modified ECT, and it was observed that the addition of the anesthetic seriously increased the risk of death in this group.

Two of Madow's (1956) four cases died following modified ECT. He states, "all showed definite neuropathological alterations . . . mainly vascular changes in all." The effects of modified ECT as found at autopsy did not differ from those of unmodified ECT.

Graber and McHugh (1960) reported one death after 30 modified ECT. The patient's cause of death was listed as an acute organic brain syndrome. Autopsy revealed "congestion of the cerebral vessels and petechial hemorrhages in the cerebral white matter and to some extent in the cortex," a finding consistent with autopsy reports and animal studies of unmodified ECT.

McKegney and Panzetta (1963) reported on the case of a 23-year-old man who died after one ECT. "He first manifested evidence of brain damage immediately following his first ECT and died after a progressively deteriorating course of two months." Biopsy data showed diffuse damage similar to that seen in animals, but the long period between the catastrophe and his actual death render the findings difficult to interpret. What is important, however, is that one modified ECT did cause a severe cerebral reaction leading to death. Gomez (1974) also reported prolonged coma and death following ECT. McKegney and Panzetta estimate that 10 percent of ECT-related deaths are the product of brain damage. This is much lower than found by Will et al., Impastato, and others. As McKegney and Panzetta note, " . . . most cerebral deaths or complications of ECT occur in patients without previously recognized C.N.S. pathology or even without specific pathology at autopsy."

Matthew and Constan (1964) reported four deaths following modified ECT, but the data are not very explicit. One patient, however, is clearly described as suffering from "cerebral hemorrhage" following what appears to be one ECT. The autopsy picture in this patient is similar to that in animal studies, including "multiple punctate hemorrhage" in one area of the brain.

Despite repeated claims to the contrary in standard textbooks and reviews, the psychiatric literature contains many large-scale reviews and many individual case reports of brain death and brain pathology following ECT. The reality reflected in this literature may be more serious than the reports themselves. There has been a marked decline in the number of such reports, despite indications that the mortality rate has gone up with the introduction of anesthetics. Furthermore, death due to trauma of the brain, such as a blow to the head, may leave no visible or significant pathology. Even more commonly, death due to respiratory or cardiac arrest following electrical disruption of the brain may produce no identifiable pathology. Even when pathological findings are expected, death can easily occur too soon after the trauma for these signs to develop (Hartelius, 1952). For all these reasons, many ECT deaths that show no brain damage on autopsy may involve individuals with severe or even fatal brain trauma. Indeed, most ECT deaths listed as "unknown origin" are probably related to brain dysfunction and damage. But even without these conjectures, the autopsy literature leaves no doubt that ECT can cause brain death and brain damage, often producing lesions similar to those found in animals. Because electric current has been implicated as the major culprit (see Chapter 8), it is not surprising that similar findings appear in modified and unmodified ECT.

Beyond the question of brain pathology, on which this book focuses, there remains the larger question of ECT mortality from any and all causes. Following the lead of Kalinowsky in all his reviews and textbooks, most advocates of ECT claim that the death rate associated with ECT is so slight as to be insignificant. Yet some studies indicate an overall death rate of 1:1,000 (Impastato, 1957; S.P. Alexander et al., 1956), with occasional reports of much higher or much lower death rates in individual series. In special risk groups, as the aged, the rate may reach 1 :200 (Impastato, 1957). For mortality alone, Impastato's warning about the risky nature of ECT is well taken.

5

Human Brain-Wave and Neurological Studies

As in other areas of ECT research, almost all projects that study the effect of ECT on brain waves are conducted by strong advocates of ECT, and the long-term damage produced by the treatment usually must be culled out of the fine print and the actual data rather than out of the opinions expressed by investigators. The problem is made more difficult by the fact that the electroencephalograph (EEG) is not a very sensitive instrument. It easily and frequently can fail to disclose severe brain damage. A normal EEG is therefore by no means proof of the absence of brain damage (Pacella, 1944). As Liberson (1949) and others have noted, the EEG can return to normal even after lobotomy. On the other hand, the presence of changes in brain waves in the form of increased high-voltage slow-wave activity following ECT is a certain sign of functional damage to the brain (Levy et al., 1942; Pacella et al., 1942). The high-voltage slow waves found routinely after ECT are similar to those found after other trauma and after epileptic seizures (Roth & Garside, 1962), and, like other ECT damage, are most apparent over the frontal and temporal areas.

From the earliest studies (Lowenbach & Stainbrook, 1942) it was known that the EEG registers severe brain-wave changes following one ECT. The disruption of electrical activity is very similar to that following a spontaneous convulsion, but is more severe. The response may vary depending on the type of treatment, including the intensity of the current, the location of the electrodes, and the presence of various modifications. But, with a few exceptions to be examined, EEG reports following modified and unmodified ECT are remarkably uniform.

The EEG after Unmodified ECT

Early in the history of ECT research, Grinker (in the discussion following Levy, Serota, & Grinker, 1942) noted the persistence of EEG abnormalities after ECT in the form of high-voltage slow waves, and declared that it made them "suspicious that irreparable damage to the brain had been produced."

Grinker's suspicion was immediately confirmed in a detailed study by Pacella, Barrera, and Kalinowsky (1942). They demonstrated that electroshock results in total obliteration of normal brain patterns immediately after one treatment. After five to 10 minutes the characteristic alpha waves begin to reappear, and only after 15 to 30 minutes does the EEG "approximate" normal state. Some abnormal waves fail to disappear, and the recording "remains abnormal for a number of days, even though no further treatment is administered." After six or less ECT, "abnormally slow waves completely disappeared in from one to five weeks"; after seven to 12 treatments, abnormal waves disappeared in one to three months; and after 13 to 22 treatments, abnormalities typically remained for two to six months, and many (30 percent) remained abnormal after discontinuation of the tests six months later. In the last group follow-up studies continued to find "abnormally slow potentials."

Pacella, Barrera, and Kalinowsky concluded:

> In general, the electroencephalograph abnormalities associated with electric shock treatment are for the most part "reversible" in the sense that they gradually disappear. It should be stressed that this does not necessarily imply that any concomitant functional or histopathologic[1] disturbances which may occur as a result of the treatments are also correspondingly "reversible."

In other words, even those changes that do reverse themselves in the EEG do not rule out undetected permanent damage.

Especially in the light of the overall insensitivity of the EEG in testing for brain damage, and further in the light of the pro-ECT advocacy of the investigators, this study is ominous in its findings. The phrase "for the most part 'reversible' " is an attempt to soften the results.

---

1. *Histopathologic* refers to microscopically visible disease of the brain.

The expression might have been stated more conservatively as "partially irreversible." In a later publication Pacella (1944) took the position that some degree of brain damage might represent a worthwhile sacrifice anyway.

Kalinowsky has gone further in "reinterpreting" the findings of his own study in his various books and reviews, declaring (1975b, p. 1972), "After 2 or 3 months at the latest, the electroencephalogram returns to normal in all cases." In fact, as his own work had shown, abnormalities often remain up to six months and sometimes longer, and presumably permanently. Indeed, in a follow-up study, Chusid and Pacella (1952) found that with the use of hyperventilation, abnormalities[2] comparable to those found in "Metrazol therapy, head trauma, and encephalitis" could still be found one year after ECT.

By 1945 a number of studies of EEG pathology following ECT had been published. Bagchi, Howell, and Schmale (1945) took note of these and did an extensive review of 54 patients of their own who received two to three ECT per week, with a maximum of 15. Without giving details, they reported that many changes could still be found 60 days after the last ECT, and that some (four cases) were found as long as five to nine months after treatment. The authors commented, "a definite electroencephalographic similarity between the epileptic and the shocked brain is noted." In the same year Proctor and Goodwin, in an impressionistic study, noted that some EEG abnormalities remain "for many months after electroshock therapy has been terminated," but that most clear up in 10 days or two weeks.

In 1947 Weil and Brinegar published one of the most careful reports on patients given between three and 20 treatments with unidirectional fluctuating current at the rate of three times per week (a method thought to produce less damage than ordinary current). They state, "Our figures indicate that the abnormalities in brain waves increase after 10 treatments and probably produce long-lasting disturbances of cerebral rhythm." Even those subjected to less than 10 treatments often showed persistent abnormalities; 14 days after the termination of treatment, individuals receiving less than 10 ECT displayed the following EEG records: 41 "normal," 17 "questionable," 24 "pathologic," and 17 "grossly pathologic." Even of those receiving only four to five ECT, three of seven were pathologic at 14 days and two were questionable. Those receiving more than 10 ECT displayed far more pathology. Abnormalities correlated with age as well as with the amount of ECT. People under 24 and over 45 had a higher percentage of abnormal EEGs.

---

2. *Hyperventilation* is excessively rapid, deep breathing. It can bring out or accentuate brain wave abnormalities.

Again in 1947, and again using unusually low doses of electricity and only three to six ECT, Moriarty and Siemens discovered that most EEGs recover in two weeks, but that some showed persistent "definite abnormalities" at the conclusion of the study one month after ECT.

In 1948 Taylor and Pacella studied the EEGs of individuals who had brain-wave abnormalities before treatment. Five of these 27 individuals showed persistent new changes over a prolonged follow-up of $1^{1}/_{2}$ to $9^{1}/_{2}$ months, and some showed neurological abnormalities, including two who developed convulsions and two with signs of arteriosclerosis who developed severe amnesia and confusion. This was confirmed by Impastato's (1957) autopsy findings that people who have preexisting brain damage can respond with a worsening of their condition after ECT.

Large-scale EEG studies involving 60 patients were carried out at St. Elizabeth's Hospital in Washington, D.C., to determine the degree of permanent brain wave changes following ECT. In a preliminary report in 1948 Will and his associates posited that persistent EEG changes indicated permanent brain damage. They stated,

> The re-establishment of a normal EEG pattern may not indicate a complete return to normal cortical cellular function as scattered damaged areas may become silent as healing and gliosis occur. It is our opinion at this time that organic cerebral cortical changes may be produced by electroshock, and that the reversibility of such changes has not been fully established.

The final report from St. Elizabeth's by Mosovitch and Katzenelbogen in 1948 left no doubt concerning the severity of EEG abnormalities following routine ECT at that hospital. Many patients were found to retain a severe abnormality called "cerebral dysrhythmia" at 10 months. Grossly abnormal, diffuse, high-voltage slow waves appeared for the first time during the treatment, and then failed to disappear. The authors compared these EEG abnormalities to those of severe epileptics and considered them to be very serious. Overall, 15 percent of patients receiving three to 15 treatments retained EEG abnormalities at 10 months; 50 percent receiving 16 to 42 treatments retained abnormalities at 10 months. This study was very carefully documented and included pretreatment EEG testing and monthly follow-up EEGs during the testing period.

In a discussion as part of a paper by Himwich, Kalinowsky, and Stone (1952), Katzenelbogen of St. Elizabeth's Hospital again confirmed that some changes are permanent: "In our studies we found abnormal electroencephalographic records for ten months after cessation of treatment; the electroencephalographic changes were associated with memory defects."

Simon et al. (1953) examined the EEGs of patients who received electronarcosis, a form of intensive electrical stimulation, and they found correspondingly major changes in the EEG, some up to 27 months following treatment. Specifically examining patients who had normal EEGs before therapy, they found that 11 percent showed persistent changes when tested more than six weeks after the completion of therapy.

The above studies all showed significant changes maintained long after the termination of ECT. Other studies using milder electrical stimuli also show EEG changes after ECT, but the follow-ups are not lengthy enough to render conclusions concerning permanence (Liberson, 1948; Bayles et al., 1950).

Other occasional studies have been more equivocal in regard to EEG findings. Klotz (1955), for example, noted that 82 percent of 100 patients developed EEG abnormalities but that 98 percent returned to normal within three months. The article is brief, however, and no objective criteria for normal are mentioned. For some reason, 67 more patients originally included in the study were later dropped.

It is not surprising that some EEG studies would fail to detect permanent abnormalities. What is surprising is that so many EEG studies do report changes and that these changes are frequently permanent, especially after increasing numbers of treatments. That the EEG abnormalities often clear up is not in itself very reassuring, as several investigators have noted, for severe pathology may remain in the brain without showing up on the tracings. Considering that the healing process of the brain slows down considerably a few weeks after any trauma (Anderson, 1971), it seems likely that even those brain-wave changes that fade at a few months may indicate persisting underlying pathology.

The EEG after Modified ECT

The first four studies that follow do not bear on the permanence of EEG pathology following modified ECT, but are important in documenting that acute changes occur that are similar to those in unmodified ECT.

Misurec (1965) studied the EEG patterns of patients subjected to modified ECT. He found that the typical brain-wave paroxysm lasts 1 min. 20 sec. after the electrical stimulus. This is followed by a silent (isoelectric) period of no electrical activity, an observation of importance because some proponents of modified ECT have claimed that no silent period follows this method. As in unmodified ECT, the seizure was found comparable clinically and electroencephalographically to an epileptic seizure. Slow-wave activity following the ECT was correlated with the appearance of clinical confusion and with age, indicating that "Therefore, we may interpret the presence of slow waves as a sign of increased CNS damage, probably due to hypoxia."

In a carefully reported study Stein et al. (1969) confirmed the existence of an isoelectric period in more than 70 percent of their patients, lasting from one to 55 seconds, with an average of 15.5.

Using unilateral ECT, Zamora and Kaebling (1965) ran EEGs on patients 30 to 36 hours after the last of five ECT. "EEG changes were so unmistakable and invariable on the side of electrode placement" that the electroencephalographer was able to determine which side the electrodes had been placed on from reading the brain-wave patterns. Roubicek et al. (1970) reported very similar correlations between electrode placement and brain wave abnormalities 24 hours after four to eight ECT.

From these and many other studies there can be no doubt that modified ECT, both unilateral and bilateral, profoundly affects the EEG in the immediate posttreatment period. The following studies confirm brain-wave dysfunction at the conclusion of the testing period, suggesting long-term and probably permanent brain damage. Valentine et al. in 1968 found "adverse changes" 10 days after treatment in 12 of 23 patients. Matsuda (1968) found many persistent effects 30 days after the conclusion of a course of 10 ECT at three per week. Schulz et al. in 1969 tested brain-waves after both Metrazol and ECT. They do not break down their findings, but indicate that some changes persisted as long as 3.5 years.

Turek (1972) found that EEG changes after ECT increased with the number of ECT, age, and amount of previous abnormality. He noted that he found persistent EEG changes two weeks after nine ECT. In 1974 J. Small evaluated EEGs 60 to 90 days after modified bilateral and nondominant unilateral ECT and found no permanent changes in the standard EEG; but when testing for "mean energy content," she found persistent changes in some cases at 90 days after both bilateral and unilateral ECT.

Volavka et al. reviewed the subject of EEG changes following ECT in 1972 and found them correlated with memory loss and the total number of ECT. They observed, "EEG changes may persist for several months after the termination of a course of treatment" in both bilateral and unilateral modified ECT.

Because the convulsion associated with ECT is generalized, placement of the electrodes on one side of the head or the other provides an opportunity to test the relative importance of the electrical current versus the convulsion in traumatizing the brain. As already noted, Roubicek et al. (1970) and Zamora and Kaebling (1965) found more obviously abnormal EEG readings on the side of the electrode placement. In a well-developed experiment Sutherland et al. (1974), using an "independent, double blind EEG assessment," found "considerable" changes three weeks after ECT in a large percentage of their patients: 75 percent of patients receiving bilateral, 75 percent of those receiving dominant unilateral, and 57.9 percent of those receiving unilateral nondominant. The double-blind evaluators proved extremely accurate in assessing which group had received which treatment on the basis of brain waves alone.

Not only do serious pathological brain waves usually develop shortly after the beginning of a course of ECT, many advocates of ECT believe that these pathological brain waves must be produced in order to achieve a good clinical effect. Max Fink has especially elaborated this theory and compared the ECT effect to that of lobotomy (Fink, 1957, 1958; Fink, Kahn, & Green, 1958). His views will be discussed in regard to the brain-disabling hypothesis of electroconvulsive therapy (Chapter 12).

Roth and Garside (1962) have summarized the effects of ECT on the brain waves, stating, "long courses of treatment are almost invariably associated with an obvious and sustained change in the electrical activity of the brain," which they believe is "continuous and lasting." The changes are consistent with a variety of pathological conditions:

> There is rhythmic, high voltage, bilaterally and synchronous and usually paroxysmal delta activity which shows maximal amplitude in the frontal areas. A similar EEG change is manifest in association with hyperventilation, particularly in young people, hypoglycaemia, hepatic coma, unconsciousness induced by tumours and other lesions in the neighborhood of the third ventricle. In the presence of such an abnormality there is a presumption in favor of the view that there is an alteration in the activity of the diffuse projection system responsible.

They observe that both lobotomy and electroshock have their impact independently of any specific psychiatric disorder, and hypothesize that

> . . . the similarity between the two forms of treatment might possibly be due to a common site of action upon the frontal lobes and the thalamo-frontal connections, with the difference that in the one we generate a temporary physiological disturbance, in the other a permanent anatomical lesion.

Roth and Garside are not critics of ECT, and at the end of that statement they contradicted their own observation that in long courses of ECT the EEG defect is continuous and lasting. They also overlooked a great deal of evidence that it frequently can be permanent in shorter courses as well. Overall, their viewpoint supports the hypothesis that ECT damages the brain and that it produces its effect by means of this damage, in the manner of a lobotomy. The difference of opinion concerns the permanence of the ECT-induced damage, a point on which Roth and Garside contradict themselves.

Serious Neurologic Dysfunction following ECT

I. M. Allen of New Zealand was one of the first and only physicians to show a thoroughgoing concern about the damaging effects of ECT and to relate clinical observations to animal research, autopsy reports, and EEG studies. In 1951 he reviewed the literature on brain damage from ECT with special emphasis on neurological impairment caused by ECT, then presented five new cases of his own. The following are summary interpretations after each of his five case histories.

> Thus a series of electric shock treatments was followed by extreme apathy for three months and then, at the first opportunity of submitting him to examination, by evidence of structural changes in the cortex of the left frontal lobe. That evidence was still present six months after the treatment had been completed. The essential features of the patient's condition were unchanged.

> . . . five weeks after five electric shock treatments, evidence was found of structural damage in the cortex of the left frontal lobe when it had not been there before the treatment. Clinical evidence of physical lesions had disappeared ten weeks after the treatment, but, apart from the cessation of most of the depression, the other features of his condition remained unchanged.

> . . . at least nine months after a full course of electric shock treatment, evidence was found of structural changes in the cortex of the left frontal lobe. As nine months had elapsed since the treatment, those changes and the clinical effects arising from them had to be regarded as permanent.

> . . . at least two and a half years after two full courses of electric shock treatment, evidence was found of structural changes in the cortex of the left frontal and parietal lobes. Those changes and the clinical effects arising from them had to be regarded as permanent.

> . . . Two months after a course of electric shock treatment evidence was found of structural changes in the cortex of the

left frontal lobe and of the right parietal lobe. As only two months had elapsed since the treatment it was uncertain whether those changes and their clinical effects were permanent, but with their severity and wide distribution it was probable that they would be so.

Allen concluded that ECT produced diffuse damage to the central nervous system.

In 1959 Allen again reviewed the literature, with many foreign language citations, including some concerning spontaneous seizure disorders after ECT. He reviewed 18 clinical cases of his own in which lesions of the brain were caused by ECT, 11 of which were of sufficient duration to indicate permanence. The amount of ECT was generally small, averaging less than eight per patient and less than five in two cases. He presented one case in special detail. This 53-year-old woman had been given a careful neurological examination as a work-up for depression and was found to have "no evidence of structural change in the brain." She recovered with conservative treatment, but after three years became depressed again and was treated with 15 ECT. It is not stated whether they were modified ECT. Immediately after treatment, she deteriorated mentally and neurologically:

> Her husband was startled at the deterioration in her after the treatment and said that, during the 18 months since then, she had been worse than she had been before, done no more than potter about the house and garden, and needed constant help in the home. She got lost in her own house, needed help with dressing and undressing, and had no idea what time of what day it was. The patient herself said that she had no confidence; did little; could not concentrate or remember; could not retain what she heard. . . .

Neurological examination revealed multiple sensorimotor defects and aphasia. Allen concluded,

> They indicated the presence of lesions throughout the cerebral cortex on both sides and in the brain down to the level of the substantia nigra. They followed a long course of electric shock treatment, appeared in a patient who had no evidence of structural change in the brain before, may have been progressive, and were followed by the death of the patient.

In regard to the phrase "long course of electric shock treatment," she had only 15 treatments. The findings, Allen believed, "confirmed the appearance of irreversible physical changes in the brain after and as a result of electric shock treatment."

Although by far the most comprehensive in their review of the literature and most detailed in their case presentations, both of Allen's publications are omitted from the extensive bibliographies of the best-known advocates of ECT (Kalinowsky & Hoch, 1961; Kalinowsky & Hippius, 1969; Noyes & Kolb, 1973).

With the exception of Allen's review and occasional individual reports (Taylor & Pacella, 1948), the literature on ECT before 1966 is not replete with papers drawing attention to neurological damage. That such catastrophes did take place is nonetheless documented in the autopsy literature, which describes many neurologic disasters leading to death (Chapter 4). Despite the relative paucity of any critical reports on ECT in the modified literature, there are a number of reports of neurological damage following modified ECT.

Moss-Herjanik reported in 1967 on a patient who received six ECT and developed a flaccid paralysis and coma, recovering eventually with a residue of Jacksonian seizures.[3] The article included a review of the literature on similar cases. In the same year Paulson presented six cases supporting the hypothesis that "ECT may directly accentuate underlying organic disease." Patients with tumors, central nervous system syphilis, vascular problems, and other diseases affecting the brain became markedly worse after one or more ECT. The changes were often dramatic, suggesting a significant cerebral impact from the ECT itself. One patient who had an unrecognized subdural hematoma[4] went into coma after one ECT. Another case had a spontaneous subarachnoid hemorrhage following ECT, which was not attributable to other factors. The author also noted that senile patients sometimes have "prolonged confusion" following ECT. He suggested that the pathology is brought out by edema of the brain following modified ECT.

In 1970 Cronin et al. reaffirmed the phenomenon noted by Paulson and long recognized in unmodified ECT: ECT in elderly individuals can "cause real organic confusion with marked intellectual disturbance and memory impairment which is not always temporary."

Strain and Bidder (1971) reported on a patient who was given multiple modified ECT (four in one session) and fell immediately into a coma with signs of continuous seizures for one hour. A three-week follow-up of the patient indicated that she still had a "mild" left-sided "facial weakness." The authors' use of the term "transient" in the title to describe this permanent defect is misleading, since their own follow-up ended with the finding of residual paralysis at three weeks.

Reinhart (1967) described a case of profound, permanent regression

---

3. A *Jacksonian seizure* is localized to one part or one side of the body, and is usually produced by a specific area of damage within the brain.

4. A *subdural hematoma* is a collection of blood between two of the membranes which surround the brain. It can produce severe and often life-threatening effects.

following only two modified ECT. The patient's dilapidation progressed over a period of days following the second treatment until she became incontinent and required tube feeding. She died of a myocardial infarction more than two months later, and an autopsy revealed no pathological explanation for her deterioration.

Assael et al. (1967) reported the development of grand mal epilepsy and an abnormal EEG following four ECT. They concluded, "We presume that this disorder was caused by a lesion in the brain-stem caused by ECT." They did not state whether the treatment was unmodified, but the data suggest it was.

All human EEG studies indicate that a severe disruption of the brain-wave pattern in the form of cerebral dysrhythmia typically follows one modified or unmodified ECT, with a longer-lasting development of high-potential slow waves. Many follow-ups terminating a month or less after the last ECT indicate that the slow waves often persist, and follow-ups lasting six months or a year often demonstrate that a significant percentage of patients have very long-lasting or permanent defects. The degree of abnormality and its permanence are roughly proportional to the amount of ECT. One in-depth study with a large series (Will et al., 1948; Mosovich & Katzenelbogen, 1948) found that severe dysrhythmias were frequently permanent.

Unilateral ECT tends to produce a more severe reaction on the side on which the electrodes are placed, again implicating the current as a major if not the major source of damage. This confirms that unilateral ECT tends to localize the damage, and perhaps to intensify it on one side.

Neurological reports in the literature are sparse but indicate that cerebral catastrophes do at times follow unmodified and modified ECT. The autopsy literature confirms many more such disasters in association with death, suggesting that nonfatal neurological defects following ECT may go unreported.

The EEG literature reveals that even one ECT may have a profound pathological effect on the brain. With increasing ECT treatments, the effect worsens and becomes more sustained. Routine courses of ECT sometimes produce lasting pathological brain waves, and longer courses commonly produce them. The ECT effect as reflected in the brain waves is that of a rather global, nonspecific trauma, especially to the frontal region, and perhaps reaching deeper into the frontal-thalamic projections and anterior portions of the limbic system.[5] This traumatic effect has been compared to that of a lobotomy.

---

5. The *limbic system* includes the frontal lobes of the brain, the projections from the thalamus to the frontal lobes, and other adjacent parts of the brain. While some investigators might dispute the specific usefulness of the term limbic system, there is general agreement that the area described is crucial to the higher mental functions.

6

Clinical and Research Reports Confirming Permanent Mental Dysfunction after ECT

Most proponents of ECT claim that retrograde amnesia is the *only* possible permanent defect resulting from the treatment. The global manifestations of a severe, acute organic brain syndrome are said to clear up without leaving a trace. I myself harbored the belief that amnesia in an otherwise intact intellect is the typical aftermath of ECT until I examined my own cases and the literature in greater depth.

Indeed, there is considerable clinical precedent for the possibility that amnesia can remain as the only discernible mental defect following trauma to the brain (Symonds, 1966; Seltzer & Benson, 1974; Whitty & Zangwill, 1966). Because electrodes are positioned above the anterior portion of the temporal lobes, an area critical to memory function, it seems especially likely that ECT patients might suffer from a specific, isolated memory defect. Consistent with this, ECT patients frequently complain about retrograde amnesia as their only lasting symptom. But even one ECT produces severe, general trauma, and a full course can frequently produce permanent diffuse brain damage. Therefore it is not surprising to discover that many clinical reports and some research reports demonstrate a more generalized anterograde loss of function similar to that found in four of my six cases. As Stone (1947) observed:

> However, even the most cursory psychometric examination of patients who complain of memory loss will reveal a considerable degree of impairment in ability to comprehend what is heard or read, in simple arithmetical computations, in percep-

tion of relationships, in choice reactions, and in the performance of tasks involving abstraction, classification, and arrangement of words or objects according to a specific plan.
Therefore, it would seem not only more informative but more
correct to speak of general impairment of the cognitive functions resulting from electroconvulsive shocks. . . .

Clinical Reports of Permanent Mental Dysfunction after Unmodified ECT

There has been no dispute in the psychiatric literature concerning
whether unmodified electroconvulsive therapy produces an acute organic
brain syndrome characterized by confusion, disorientation, memory
loss, emotional lability, and other signs of generalized dysfunction. One
of the first clinical studies, published by Lowenbach and Stainbrook in
1942, began with the observation, "A generalized convulsion leaves a
human being in a state in which all that is called the personality has been
extinguished." Stupor, confusion, and overall mental dysfunction was
such after only one ECT that the individual was unable to write his name
normally for 20 to 30 minutes afterward. The report described how the
patient tends to lose whatever is most recently learned and integrated
into the personality. Women came out of ECT without recall for their
married names, calling themselves by their maiden names. Persons
whose native tongue was not English began speaking in their native
tongue.

Brengelman (1959), in a book-length treatise, compared the degree
of the acute organic brain syndrome after various modifications of the
electrical stimulus and found little difference. He described how bewilderment, psychomotor depression, difficulties in concentration and
memory, disorientation, confusion, perplexity, and agitation develop
routinely after two to 10 treatments. "As a rule, the organic syndrome
has set in by the seventh shock, but seldom before the third or fourth."
This will turn out to be the reason why a typical ECT treatment sequence
usually lasts for at least four treatments (see Chapters 10-12).

Brengelman, like Lowenbach and Stainbrook and many others, felt
able to correlate the breakdown of the patient's mental function with the
deterioration of his brain wave tracing. He did not ask whether the acute
organic brain syndrome, so obvious and so ominous in its symptoms, left
a residual of permanent mental dysfunction.

The Brengelman studies suggested a fairly predictable increase in
brain dysfunction with increasing numbers of ECT, but the literature
demonstrates that there are frequently severe reactions after only one or

two treatments. Kalinowsky (1945) called these disastrous reactions organic psychotic syndromes.

> A typical delirium is not infrequent. Patients who never had hallucinations have visual hallucinatory experiences. They experience entire scenes, which are changeable and may stir their fear to panic. When treatment is continued despite such productive symptoms, these manifestations are usually replaced by simple dementia. At this stage the patient may wet and soil himself, wander around aimlessly or become underactive and pass into a vegetative existence.

Note that Kalinowsky says that these severe reactions are "not infrequent" in routine ECT programs.

Early in the history of ECT some clinicians noted that manifestations of severe and long-lasting dysfunction often followed the acute organic brain syndrome. Levy, Serota, and Grinker (1942) found that as few as four or eight treatments could make patients "slap-happy" for several weeks after treatment. "Recovery from these disturbances of cerebral function occurred in most patients in a few weeks. In the most severely affected patients evidences of impaired cerebral function sometimes lasted as long as six months." The paper itself did not explore the implications of these findings, but fortunately the discussion that took place after the presentation of the paper was recorded and published. Grinker seemed to let his hair down as he observed,

> This mechanistic approach to psychiatry is being used extensively at present; I think it can be stated unequivocally that it is fraught with *extreme danger*. There is not only an emotional but an intellectual change in the patients. Those who have seen fighters that have been in many battles know the "punch drunk" or "slap-happy" conditions and may recognize a similar state in some patients after shock therapy. This does not last long, at least in its striking form.

Another physician declared in the discussion, ". . . there is grave danger in using such procedures as Metrazol and electric shock in treatment of human beings." Still another, Norman A. Levy, confirmed that these dangers can materialize after a very few treatments. But while Grinker and his colleagues were concerned about the damaging effects of the treatment, they by no means opposed it in principle.

Given the immediate devastating effects of ECT on memory, it is not surprising that many reports have appeared in the literature confirming that full recovery of memory is not always achieved after ECT. As early as 1941 Jessner and Ryan observed that "There is frequently a complaint on the part of the patient about 'loss of memory'. . . ." They appeared to be reassuring themselves when they concluded, "certainly in the majority, memory loss is temporary."

Many reports of mental dysfunction following ECT accumulated over the years. Millet and Mosse (1944) reported lasting retrograde amnesias, as did Dedichen (1946) and Braatoy (1948). Pacella made passing references to permanent memory losses (1944). Osgood (1944) was one of the first to note the great variability in the degree of amnesia following ECT, including occasional cases of permanent retrograde amnesia. Zubin (1948) noted that a "general organic syndrome" develops after three, or four ECT, "sometimes affecting remote memories in a spotty manner," and that "There are a few instances in which it has been demonstrated that some memory losses continue for as long as a year. . . ."

Tyler and Lowenbach (1947) presented the case of a 35-year-old man who was given intensive ECT—13 treatments in 72 hours—as evidence that the treatment does not cause permanent mental impairment. But they noted, "In the third week, the patient regained most of his memory except for a period extending back almost one year." I.M. Allen (1951, 1959), in the two reports previously described, presented many cases of brain-damaged patients displaying both irreversible retrograde amnesia and severe anterograde defects.

One of the most detailed clinical follow-ups of long-term retrograde amnesia was published by Brody (1944), whose concern had been stimulated by Grinker's observations: "The following case-notes revealing memory defects lasting a year or more suggest that Grinker's apprehension may be justified." One of Brody's patients was still aware of gross losses after 18 months. She declared, "I have met one or two people who seem to know all about me and I cannot remember anything about them. I look silly at them and get frightened of meeting people."

A 48-year-old woman with only 15 treatments complained of anterograde defects as well as retrograde amnesia: "I cannot seem to remember but it comes back later on. It takes me a long time to remember. My memory seems 'slower.' It lets me down over just small things that I am doing like posting a letter." She had shown some improvement for six months, then none over the following two years. She was similar in this regard to still another case of Brody's, who improved for nine months, then leveled off with memory defects. The case descriptions are consistent with my six cases.

In selecting his five patients to report on, Brody was careful to choose people who reportedly were *doing well* following their treatment. Some of them were carrying on their routine life activities. As in four of my cases, reports of "doing well" did not by any means rule out gross brain damage and even deep despair over the damage.

Like most psychiatrists involved in ECT research, Brody was unwilling to condemn electroshock on principle. But he did warn that these memory problems caused considerable "mental strain," and that they implied "permanent, or semi-permanent, damage to the brain. . . ." He proposed that ECT should not be given to people working in professions requiring a high degree of mental and memory dexterity. Such a viewpoint belittles the spiritual or personal loss of individuals who value their minds regardless of the job requirements placed on their mental faculties.

Millet and Mosse (1944), Mather (1946), a letter writer to the *Journal of the American Medical Association* (Anon., 1948), and E. W. Anderson (1951) cited cases in which profound memory loss interfered with occupational or professional work. Pacella and Impastato (1954) also showed concern about using bilateral ECT to treat "individuals whose livelihood depends on a relatively intact memory." Similarly, Alpers (1946) described a young lawyer who had been given 50 ECT and who continued to suffer from a debilitating memory loss. Alpers observed, "It is doubtful, in my opinion, whether he will ever regain his normal memory capacity."

Miura, Okada, and Okamoto (1960) declared that "impairment of memory as a complication in electroconvulsive therapy is quite common, but cases of retrograde amnesia extending to years before the onset of the mental illness are rare." They cited reports of amnesia extending back 10 years, then gave a detailed account of a 20-year-old female given 11 ECT who lost the entire period of two years before her ECT. "The only residues left intact at the present are the names of her school, her mother and one of her teachers. She has no sense of chronological sequence." Neurological and psychological tests were negative, and the authors attributed the losses to ECT.

Medlicott (1948) sent out follow-up questionnaires to the families of patients who had been given ECT and found that 30 out of 100 of the families reported memory loss in the patient, the majority permanent. Some patients had severe memory loss reaching back several years before ECT, including one person with a six-year "blank."

Proctor and Goodwin (1945) noted that objective memory tests are relatively insensitive but that clinical observations clearly show memory loss following ECT. They discussed "complex plans" for the future with a patient before his electroshock, but afterward, "he could remember portions of the plans but was unable to piece them together."

Reviewing "Physical Methods of Treatment" for *The Medical Annual* in 1951, Anderson lent his own clinical support to studies indicating memory loss following ECT. Specifically citing Janis (1948), he commented, "Every psychiatrist has seen such amnesias last for years after treatment." He wonders about "premature aging" and other hidden dangers, and calls for "careful and detailed follow-ups over at least twenty years. . . ." His presumption is that a drastic treatment causing such acute devastation must be considered dangerous until proved otherwise, a frequently voiced presumption even in the early days of the treatment (Masserman & Jacques, 1947; Alpers & Hughes, 1942b; Will et al, 1948; and many others).

Three clinical reports concerning the effects of ECT on physician patients give striking examples of the severe mental dysfunction caused by one to five ECT. Watkins, Stainbrook, and Lowenbach (1941) reported the devastating effect of one subconvulsive electroshock (400 ma for 0.165 sec) administered to a 25-year-old physician as an experiment. Forty-one minutes after the shock, he "had lost the ability of recalling recent as well as past events, and could not retain information." He was euphoric three hours later, and forgot his regular room assignment four hours later. Fourteen hours later he awakened with a "queer" feeling and suffering an indescribable "feeling of unreality." Over the following days most of his memory gradually returned, but events prior to the shock and for 15 hours after the shock remained "completely blotted out." Throughout this, his outward behavior seemed normal to casual observers.

A French-language report by Bersot (1943) describes similar dramatic effects on a physician after two ECT. For several weeks afterward he showed a variety of symptoms, including mild euphoria, mental fatigue, difficulty with memory, and a remoteness from the past. Again, his social conduct remained relatively normal during this period. He felt that he became himself again about one month after the two treatments.

A third report (Practising Psychiatrist, 1965) deals with similar findings in a physician who received five modified ECT for depression, and will be described under clinical impressions of modified ECT (p. 000).

The damaging effects of ECT can be seen in an exaggerated form following intensive or regressive ECT in which the individual is subjected to ECT at the rate of one or more a day until a state of regression, dilapidation, and neurological collapse is produced (see Chapters 1 and 10). As Bennett (1949) has described, 50 ECT can produce "an amentia greater than that seen in lobotomized patients." Patients subjected to intensive ECT become utterly helpless and unable to take care of their most commonplace needs, such as feeding themselves or going to the bathroom. Memory is so obliterated that the patient is usually unaware that he has received any treatment (Glueck et al., 1957). Stengel (1951) evaluated the lasting effects of this form of therapy. In one case,

> She had forgotten not only the events of her whole previous life,
> but also much that she had learned from childhood. Everything
> seemed new to her. She inquired about the significance and the
> names of familiar objects like a child of three.

This women's amnesia, four years later, had gradually "shrunk to a period of three years."

Stengel found the name "annihilation therapy" (coined by Cerletti) unfortunately appropriate, and he compared its effects to that of head injury with "severe traumatic interference with brain functions." He declared that it did much harm and little good, and should be abandoned. In 1969 Kalinowsky and Hippius declared "Stengel demonstrated how the retrograde amnesia shrinks only very gradually," neglecting to mention that Stengel's case was specifically left with a three-year amnesia four years after treatment.

The long-lasting memory defects produced by routine ECT are also demonstrated by a modern but informal report on the work of Tien (1974) who, unlike most of his colleagues, continues to use unmodified ECT along with some updated behavioral techniques. Tien uses ECT to erase the patient's memory of his or her past personality before reindoctrinating the person with a new personality (see Chapter 10).

In their textbook of psychiatry Mayer-Gross, Slater, and Roth (1955) specifically addressed themselves to the dangers of permanent disability following ECT. Although not against this or any psychiatric treatment in principle, they warned that "The mistake that is most frequently made nowadays is its excessive or too indiscriminate use. The authors have seen no good results from battering the patient with more than one fit a day." They state, "It should not be forgotten that a succession of fits, even as infrequently as once a week, causes some mental impairment," and that "unexpected and severe memory loss may occur and we have seen at least one severe dysmnesic syndrome[1] lasting two months in a patient of 30 after a few convulsions."

Despite repeated statements to the contrary in the most widely read reviews and textbooks, the psychiatric literature is filled with examples of severe, permanent amnesia and more occasional anterograde mental dysfunction following unmodified ECT. When cases are presented in any detail, as in Brody's follow-ups, they closely resemble the experiences of the six cases in Chapter 2.

---

1. *Dysmnesic syndrome* means amnesia.

Research Reports of Permanent Mental Dysfunction after Unmodified ECT

Janis studied 19 patients given routine ECT (eight or more ECT at three per week) in psychiatric hospitals, and he interviewed them before and after their treatments concerning significant events in their past (1948, 1950; Janis & Astrachan, 1951). He also interviewed 11 control patients with similar diagnoses from the same hospitals at the same intervals. The posttreatment interview was administered four weeks after the termination of the treatment and was designed to test recall of personal data that the patients had been able to remember before treatment. Great care was taken to retest in a gradual and ultimately thorough manner, beginning with general questions about the past and, in the case of lost recollections, presenting a portion of former recollections in order to see if these memories could be restimulated. The results were unequivocal. The patients' ability to recall past events was devastated by ECT, but almost untouched in the control groups (1948):

> It was found that every one of the 19 patients in the electro-shock group displayed definite retroactive amnesias, as of approximately four weeks after the termination of ECT. For each case it was possible to verify many of the forgotten events as actual occurrences, on the basis of independent sources of information in the patient's case history records. Many of the patients were unable to recall from 10 to 20 life experiences which had been available to recall prior to electroshock treatments.

The control group patients were given the identical tests at the same spaced intervals, and they demonstrated none of the massive losses found among the ECT patients (1950):

> Among the control patients there were practically no convincing examples of forgetting of the sort regarded as evidence of retroactive amnesias among the ECT group. Five of the 11 control patients were able to reproduce every detail of the personal memories they had given in the first interviews; 6 of the control patients each showed a single instance of a possible recall failure but these were limited to a single detail of a personal experience which was otherwise reproduced accurately.

Janis concluded (1948): "The results show, therefore, that electric convulsive treatments, as administered in standard psychiatric practice, produce amnesias which do not clear up within four weeks after the termination of treatments."

As in the cases I have reported, the amnesias were not limited to the six-month period prior to ECT, and occasionally reached back to childhood events twenty to forty years earlier (1948, 1950). Some patients lost *all* memory for a *several-month* period before ECT, exactly as in the six cases in my presentation. More tragically, in the five cases Janis was able to follow up beyond four weeks, almost all the memory gaps remained (1950):

> *Persistence of Post-treatment Amnesias.* How long do the amnesias following ECT persist? Do they clear up rapidly or do they continue indefinitely? To obtain some preliminary information on this problem, a follow-up study was carried out on as many of the patients as were available. Altogether, 5 of the 19 ECT patients were reexamined, each of whom had completed ECT from two and one-half to three and one-half months before the follow-up interview. The follow-up recall tests were limited to those memories which each patient had failed to recall when tested approximately four weeks after the last treatment. The same questions were repeated as in the preceding post-treatment interview.
>
> It was found that most of the experiences which the patients failed to recall in the original post-treatment interview were still unavailable to recall. . . .
>
> This finding bears out . . . the general conclusion that a series of electrically induced convulsions, as administered in standard psychiatric practice, produces circumscribed amnesias for past experiences which persist beyond the usual period of recovery during which the temporary organic reactions to the treatments clear up.

According to a personal communication sent to Davies et al. (1971), Janis continued to find memory losses "at least one year following the last treatment."

Janis (1950) also carried out word tests of the patients' capacity to create and to recall word associations. He found that four weeks after electroshock there was an increase in "deviant" or irrational responses compared to before electroshock and that there were more "defective reproductions," reflecting a decreased ability to recall associations. Thus, he found anterograde as well as retrograde mental dysfunction.

Concerning the "therapeutic" effect of ECT, Janis (1950) found, as I have so often found, "Time and again ECT patients made such statements as, 'I don't exactly remember what it was that used to bother me.'"

Janis carried out his studies under the supervision of Zubin, one of the nation's best known advocates of ECT, and they were therefore well known in ECT circles. Yet the results have been ignored, or they have been reported in a most puzzling manner. Apparently referring indirectly to them, Kalinowsky (1959) wrote, "Psychological investigations by Zubin and many others have shown convincingly that the most constant psychiatric side-effect of ECT, memory impairment, is not permanent." Because he made no mention of the Janis study by name in the text, no casual reader can track down the facts. In the lengthy bibliography, however, he listed one of the four Janis studies. In Kalinowsky and Hoch (1961, p. 119) the Janis studies were mentioned in passing in the text, unaccountably placed in a misleading fashion among those used as proof that "no evidence of permanent destruction of memory traces is available:"

> Some impairment of both learning and retention was noted but both returned within three weeks after treatment to a level as good or better than the pre-treatment status. ECT affected personal memories in about the same way as implanted memories. This was also seen by Janis who tested the recall of a series of life experiences before and after the treatment. The hypothesis that the patient recovers because his memory for adverse events or situations is wiped out is hardly tenable *since no evidence of permanent destruction of memory traces is available.* (Italics added)

The placement of the last sentence immediately after the Janis study is particularly ironic because Janis specifically supported the hypothesis that the therapeutic effect of ECT is related to the wiping out of memory.

In his 1969 textbook with Hippius, Kalinowsky did list all four key Janis studies in the bibliography in the back of the book, but again mentioned Janis in the text (p. 205) in passing in the identical misleading fashion, as if Janis supported the position that ECT causes no permanent memory defects.

Schwartzman and Termansen (1967) studied the long-range effects of "depatterning" or intensive ECT as developed by Cameron (see Cameron & Pande, 1958). Schwartzman and Termansen's publication dealt with 79 patients treated between 1956 and 1963, and thus provided very long-term follow-ups. The patients—77 percent of whom had been diagnosed as schizophrenic or borderline—did very poorly following the treatment. Seventy-five percent of the sample demonstrated "unsatisfactory or impoverished social adjustment," and more than half the patients who had been employed before treatment were underemployed or unemployed at the time of follow-up.

Twenty-eight patients were given "intelligence and memory tests" many years after ECT, and they displayed "little evidence of general

intellectual or memory impairment attributable to intensive electroconvulsive therapy"; no data were provided for this statement. But although
"little evidence" of memory defects were found on psychological testing,
the authors did go on to comment, "the shorter the interval between
electroshocks, the greater was the current memory impairment as seen
on the Wechsler Memory Scale." The Rorschach test "was notably diminished" in a manner comparable to "hospitalized chronic schizophrenics." But only 15 percent of the 47 patients who could be located were
hospitalized at the time of the follow-up study, suggesting the unexam-
ined possibility that they were not chronic hospitalized schizophrenics
and that their impoverishment was the product of ECT.

Turning their attention to the reports of the patients themselves,
Schwartzman and Termansen found drastic amnesias:

> A questionnaire designed to examine memory function in detail
> was completed by 27 former patients who had received the
> intensive E.C.T. The 29 "memory" items were distributed
> among 31 questions dealing with physical and emotional health
> in order to minimize the aim of the questionnaire. The depend-
> ence on others for recall of past events is reported by 63 percent
> of the sample. A persisting amnesia retrograde to the "depat-
> terning" and ranging in time from six months to ten years is
> reported by 60 percent of the respondents. The number of
> "memory" complaints presented by the patient appeared to be
> independent of both the patient's state of health as reported by
> the patient, and his current clinical condition as judged by the
> clinician.

Note that a six-month to 10-year retrograde amnesia was reported by 60
percent of the sample, and a dependence for recall on others was reported
by 63 percent.

The authors were unwilling to take a stand on the objective reality of
this consistently reported memory loss. They suggested the possibility
that these reports reflected a subjective distress (years and years later!)
over the original acute memory loss following ECT. They also considered
the possibility that the reported losses were real, and in concluding they
took the complaints of the patients somewhat more seriously:

> The incidence of physical complications and the anxiety gener-
> ated in the patient because of real or imagined memory diffi-
> culty argue against the administration of intensive electrocon-
> vulsive shock as a standard therapeutic procedure.

Unhappily, this study has been ignored by those who continue to advocate intensive ECT, and is unmentioned and unlisted in textbooks that advocate the procedure, such as Kalinowsky & Hippius, 1969.

Stieper et al. (1951) also dealt specifically with the complaint of lost personal memories, noting that "In personal interviews, post-shock patients most frequently express concern over their personal memory defects, rather than impersonal defects." They studied a control group and 15 patients who had received between five and 25 treatments, using a personal memory inventory of 20 recent and 20 remote recollections. They found a statistically significant loss of "personal and current information" and found that "Items which appeared to be most affected were those involving their prehospitalization personal adjustments: jobs held previous to entering the hospital and recent illnesses." Patients frequently responded, "I don't know," when asked about recent memories. Stieper et al. are unmentioned and unlisted in Kalinowsky (1959), Kalinowsky and Hoch (1961), and Kalinowsky and Hippius (1969).

Other experimental studies do shed interesting sidelights on the issues. Grinker, in the discussion following the Levy, Serota, and Grinker publication of 1942, may be among the first to claim that "careful studies by means of a battery of psychological tests reveal a definite organic change in memory which does not entirely clear up." Unfortunately, he did not publish these results in detail. In another early report Mayer-Gross (1943) compared amnesia for past events after ECT to the same retrograde amnesia following head trauma, and he considered the amnesia an indicator of severity of brain damage. His study showed that after only one ECT patients were unable to recall cards that had been shown to them immediately before the ECT. The defect showed little tendency to improve over 24 hours post-ECT. Indeed, in a later commentary Mayer-Gross, Slater, and Roth (1955) warned against "unexpected and severe memory loss" following ECT. But for some unexplainable reason, Kalinowsky and Hoch (1961, p. 163) and Kalinowsky and Hippius (1969, p. 202) cite Mayer-Gross as showing "surprisingly short retrograde amnesia," using his study as proof for the temporary nature of ECT memory loss.

A. I. Rabin (1948) became concerned about the frequent use of electroshock for "quieting down" long-term state hospital patients by giving them a hundred or more treatments over a period of years. He selected six who had received individual totals of 110 to 234 treatments and gave them psychological tests and clinical interviews. The methods he used were crude, but he found that several of the patients showed gross brain damage, including one bleak case: "Fantasy is nil, and one vague affective response was produced. The record as a whole is dull, repetitive, and perseverative."

Ordinarily a study using crude testing methods on patients who were deteriorating from chronic hospitalization and who had received extraordinarily large doses of shock might not be worth emphasizing. Its importance is that ECT advocates have cited it as proving that patients are *undamaged* by massive numbers of shock. In 1959 (p. 1507), for example, Kalinowsky declared that the Rabin study (cited by name) "showed that no organic patterns remain" after massive ECT. Writing with Hoch in 1961 (p. 167), and with Hippius (1969, p. 205) he again unaccountably stated: "Rabin showed the absence of permanent organic patterns in Rorschach tests even after 100 and more treatments."

Again using patients subjected to large numbers of unmodified ECT (40 to 263), recent studies by Goldman et al. (1972) and Templer et al. (1973) found evidence for permanent brain damage. The first study used the Bender-Gestalt and the Benton tests; the second, which attempted to use partial controls, concluded, "The ECT patients' inferior Bender-Gestalt performance does suggest that ECT causes permanent brain damage." These two modern studies are omitted from both 1975 reviews by Kalinowsky.

In 1961, with Hoch, Kalinowsky made his most detailed analysis of memory loss and cited the greatest number of references. He repeated this analysis, often word for word, in 1969 (Kalinowsky & Hippius). But a direct examination of each of the references cited in these two books leads to astounding revelations. In addition to the misleading reference to Janis noted above, and citation of Rabin as proof that no dysfunction follows ECT, they listed four studies as further evidence that no permanent memory loss follows ECT (1961, p. 167; 1969, p. 205). The studies themselves are largely irrelevant, for none tests the specific complaint made by patients that they cannot recall past personal memories and experiences. Nonetheless, they are worth reviewing in the context of Kalinowsky's claim that they demonstrate the absence of permanent memory loss.

The most extensive citation by Kalinowsky and Hoch is to Zubin and Barrera (1941), a study done at Kalinowsky's own institute. To quote Kalinowsky and Hoch, and Kalinowsky and Hippius:

> The normal saving in the number of trials when material is relearned was lost after treatment. Recognition memory is hardly touched. Some impairment of both learning and retention was noted but both returned within three weeks after treatment to a level as good or better than the pretreatment status.

Kalinowsky's statements about the report bear little resemblance to it. Instead of "recognition memory is hardly touched," the authors report a statistically significant drop of 12.5 percent in recognition, although they do downplay this drop by calling it a slight interference. Most startling, however, Kalinowsky's claim that "retention" returned to "pretreatment status" or "better" is wholly without support in the article, which made no mention of any improvement in any of the several types of memory loss suffered. All in all, Kalinowsky's interpretation of this article is mysteriously benign. The study instead supported the basic contention of its authors that "One of the most striking psychological concomitants of this treatment is the characteristic impairment of the patient's memory."

The second of the four studies was by Huston and Strother (1948), who used tests with no known or validated correlation to clinical losses as described by typical patients. Ironically, the tests were given during the period when the patient was suffering from an acute organic brain syndrome, and they were so insensitive that they did not even detect abnormalities during this period when all mental processes were catastrophically disrupted.

The third citation, Sherman et al. (1941), was still more obviously inappropriate to the task of measuring mental function. In order to test recent memory the patient was told at the start of the interview, "Go to the nurses' office and call Miss W." If the patient could recall performing the task when asked about it at the end of the interview, "The reply served as a measure of recent memory." Actually, this was a crude test of anterograde mental function, and only a person devoid of any mental capacity would have failed. Again the tests were so crude that they did not detect the patient's acute organic brain syndrome.

It is hard to understand how or why Kalinowsky included a fourth citation (K. W. Wilcox, 1955) to demonstrate the "reversible nature" of memory loss following ECT. What Wilcox examined was the differential recovery rate from several severe manifestations of the acute organic brain syndrome:

> The process of becoming aware was studied by means of a group of serial questions designed to elicit information as to the patient's recognition of herself, of other persons, of the place, and of time. Recognition of place was considered acceptable if the patient could name the city, hospital, building, or ward, and recognition of person, if she could name a physician, psychologist, or nurse who had been in recent attendance.

To call this a test of the return of memory is of course highly misleading. It is a test of the return of "one's senses," defined in the most crude sense, and only fragments of one's senses at that.

But Kalinowsky's citation is doubly misleading because even in regard to these gross criteria the tests did not show anywhere near a full return of function. The patient did improve rapidly from the worst of the acute organic brain syndrome following the first ECT, but, even after this initial ECT, recovery as charted on the graph was incomplete at the end of data collection 45 minutes after awakening. The study then lumped together observations made after the first, fifth, and tenth ECT, so that there is no way to isolate and to examine the far greater losses experienced with increasing ECT. Nonetheless the losses were so great that even lumped together in this manner the patients *all* failed to return to pretreatment baseline performance in orientation to others, orientation to time, and orientation to place. They were so disoriented to place, for example, that they could name *none* of the following: the ward, the building, the hospital, or the town. They did return to pretreatment baseline in so-called orientation to self, but this involved nothing more than remembering their own names!

Cited by Kalinowsky as an example of the "reversible nature" of memory loss following ECT, this study instead proved that patients do not fully recover 45 minutes after awakening from one ECT, and that they remain grossly disoriented in most spheres during the test period after increasing ECT.

It seems astonishing that these studies have been cited by Kalinowsky for years (including Kalinowsky & Hippius in 1969) without being challenged, and that they still provide the basis for most modern ECT experts who declare that the treatment is harmless (Kolb, 1977). Almost without exception, all the studies cited by Kalinowsky as evidence for the harmlessness of ECT instead confirmed its dangerousness. Those few test protocols that showed no lasting damage were so insensitive that they could not even detect the acute organic brain syndrome documented by Wilcox.

Reports Confirming the Acute Organic Brain Syndrome after Modified ECT

My own clinical experience as reported leaves no doubt that modified ECT produces a severe acute brain syndrome identical to that in unmodified ECT. The observation is of such importance, however, that it is necessary to verify it.

In 1969 Sutherland et al. studied the organic brain syndrome following modified ECT with some of the same detailed attention that Brengelman gave to the syndrome following unmodified ECT (see p. 75). The effects of the bilateral modified ECT were greater than those of unilateral ECT to the nondominant side, but both showed substantial evidence of an acute organic brain syndrome and EEG dysfunction. Of four patients given their first bilateral modified ECT, one remained mute for 20 minutes after his physical recovery from the convulsion, and it took the other three patients five to seven minutes to remember their names and seven to 12 minutes to remember where they were. Similarly, Laurell (1970) described gross confusion lasting 40 minutes after a modified ECT in response to simple questions.

Cannicott (1962) and Cannicott and Waggoner (1967) compared the effects of unilateral and bilateral modified ECT in regard to the intensity of the acute organic brain syndrome. Cannicott reported that 13 of 87 patients receiving unilateral ECT "complained of severe post-ECT amnesia and confusion," and even more suffered from this syndrome after bilateral modified ECT. He compared the syndrome to that of a severe concussion, and illustrated the phenomenon with quotations such as "you meet people you ought to know and cannot remember names or what connections." In the follow-up study patients were tested one hour before and two hours after their fifth modified ECT, and again memory losses were detected.

Using admittedly insensitive tests—the Wechsler, Gresham, and paired words—Levy (1968) found that six hours after the sixth unilateral or bilateral modified treatment, "memory and orientation were impaired in both groups." Zung et al. (1968) found organic brain syndrome signs on a variety of tests after ECT. Similarly, Kafi et al. (1969) found a "dramatic drop in performance" on the Wechsler Memory Scale and a nonstandardized short-term memory test 24 hours after six modified ECT treatments.

As in unmodified ECT, the patient's immediate post-ECT acute organic brain syndrome is of sufficient severity to interfere with any psychological testing. Dornbush and Williams (1974) noted that most researchers find it necessary to wait at least three hours after ECT before subjecting a patient to a test protocol, and Williams (1973) found that after both bilateral and unilateral ECT "many were often still disoriented for time and place, and often were not aware of having had the treatment." Zinkin and Birtchnell (1968) reported a period of one hour of acute disorientation after only one bilateral ECT. The severe "organic-psychotic" reaction is found as an extreme response following modified ECT as well as unmodified ECT (Kalinowsky & Hippius, 1969), again confirming the crushing effects of both treatments.

Intensive modified ECT has the same devastating effect as intensive unmodified ECT. Comparing multiple ECT (MECT) to routine ECT,

Abrams in 1974 noted an "increase in undesirable side-effects with MECT (e.g., organic confusional states, increased post-ictal sleep and cognitive disorganization, status epilepticus, and pulmonary aspiration). . . . "[2] Exner and Murillo (1973) described regression following intensive modified ECT, including neurologic helplessness and collapse, much like the condition their predecessors at Stoney Lodge described following unmodified ECT (Glueck et al., 1957).

Strain (1972) warned about the typical acute organic brain syndrome following routine modified ECT:

> Members of the patient's family should be informed of the temporary amnesia and confusion that may follow treatment. In this way, they can help reassure the patient after treatment that his disorientation is only transitory. . . . Important side-effects are transient memory loss that may be apparent for several days or weeks and hypomania.[3]

As we shall see, research in which Strain himself has participated suggests that the memory defects are by no means "transient."

Most studies of the immediate post-ECT period focus on the isolated variable of memory loss rather than on the overall organic brain syndrome of which it is but a part. Nonetheless the evidence for memory defects following unilateral and bilateral ECT in the immediate post-ECT period (24 to 48 hours) is incontrovertible, and confirms that modified and unmodified ECT do not differ in frequently producing marked brain dysfunction after only one ECT and in invariably producing it after three or four ECT. Martin et al. (1965) found that after 10 bilateral modified ECT, patients could not even remember being involved in the pretreatment testing program. Costello et al. (1970); Stones (1973); Fromholt et al. (1973); Berent et al. (1975); and Hargreaves et al. (1972) have demonstrated the existence of memory dysfunction in the period shortly after modified ECT. Hargreaves confirmed Hartelius' finding in animal autopsies that dysfunction *increases* over a period of 24 hours or more after ECT, so that maximum effects are delayed a day or two.

---

2. *Organic confusional states* designates severe organic brain syndromes as described in Chapter 1. *Increased post-ictal sleep* is a prolongation of the typical deep sleep that follows any convulsion. *Status epilepticus* is a severe disorder involving a series of generalized convulsions in rapid succession. *Pulmonary aspiration* is the inhaling of gastric contents or other materials into the lungs.

3. *Hypomania* is a mild form of manic-depressive reaction, characterized by unrealistic elation, irritability, impatience, high energy, and perhaps alternating bouts of depression. When used to describe post-ECT patients, hypomania is roughly equivalent to euphoria, which is an unrealistic or exaggerated sense of well being. In psychiatry and medicine, hypomania and euphoria are both used to designate abnormal conditions.

While denying that ECT can cause any permanent mental dysfunction or memory loss, Kolb (1977) describes the severity of the acute organic brain syndrome along a wide spectrum of memory defects from a "mild tendency to forget names to a severe confusion of the Korsakoff type."[4] The memory defects can last "several weeks or a few months following the termination of the treatment."

There is a trend in the literature suggesting more memory loss from bilateral modified than from unilateral ECT, but Ashton and Hess (1976) have demonstrated that this finding results from failures to measure components of memory represented in the nondominant side of the brain. In a visual memory test conducted after confusion had cleared up following one ECT, bilateral and unilateral patients did equally poorly.

Indeed, trauma to the nondominant side on which *both* the electrodes are placed may be even greater than to either side in bilateral ECT. Impastato and Karliner (1966) did not find patients "confused and babbling" after unilateral ECT as they did after bilateral, but they did observe some transient paralyses on the affected side. Zamora and Kaebling (1965) noted that patients undergoing unilateral ECT are routinely given greater doses of electricity in order to achieve a convulsion. In a recent interview (McDonald, 1978), Kalinowsky calls unilateral ECT relatively ineffective and declares that whatever gain is achieved requires a larger number of treatments. He claims that even the originators of unilateral ECT are giving it up, and indeed it appears to have little and possibly declining usage in the United States (Asnis et al., 1978; Kalinowsky, 1978).

Modifications in current present no more hope of ameliorating the effects of ECT than do modifications in premedication, anesthetics, and oxygenation. As discussed in detail in Chapter 8, modern ECT studies often report currents of greater intensity and duration than in earlier studies, and they frequently use the more devastating wave forms. In this regard I would agree with Kalinowsky (1975b) who observed, "No convincing evidence has ever been given to prove that the memory impairment is actually reduced with these modified currents."

In discussing the brain- and mind-disabling hypothesis of ECT effect, it will be shown that modified ECT produces the same dread and fear reactions as unmodified ECT. This is because both treatments produce such devastating effects on the mind.

---

4. *Korsakoff's syndrome* or *psychosis* occurs in chronic alcoholism and other causes of vitamin B deficiency, but similar reactions may develop after other insults to the brain. The syndrome includes confusion, retrograde amnesia, and confabulation.

Research Reports of Permanent Mental Dysfunction after Modified ECT

Much as in the literature on unmodified ECT, most research reports involving modified ECT fail to detect permanent amnesia (Cronholm & Ottosson, 1960, 1961, 1963a, 1963b). But as Strain et al. (1968), Stieper et al. (1951), and McGaugh and Williams (1974) have noted, these negative reports have not measured the type of amnesia found in actual clinical examination—retrograde amnesia for life experiences. As in the unmodified ECT literature, those few studies that have measured this loss by controlled clinical studies or by objective testing do confirm the existence of permanent amnesia in a significant number of patients.

The team led by Squire (1974 et seq.), has tested for retrograde amnesia for a period of weeks following ECT, using a multiple-choice instrument involving recollections of television programs, and has found only temporary losses. However, the result merely indicates that the amnesia cannot be detected by the test; the test has not been proved to correlate with subjective complaints or with any other clinical variable. Indeed, the patient I described in Chapter 2, who had severe amnesia and brain damage confirmed in neurologic studies and a battery of psychological tests, was found to be normal when tested by Squire. But Squire and Chace (1975) did ask patients to assess their own memory loss six to nine months after ECT, and had startling results: Amnesia was reported by 63 percent of patients receiving bilateral ECT and 30 percent receiving right unilateral ECT. Fifteen members of this group were followed up by telephone one year later, and many patients who had received bilateral ECT continued to report memory losses.

Squire elaborated somewhat on these findings in 1977. Thirty-seven of 55 subjects receiving short courses of bilateral modified ECT "indicated that their memory was not as good as it used to be." Only four of 15 receiving right unilateral ECT felt impaired. These results were obtained despite the exclusion of memory loss surrounding the hospitalization.

In another recent study Squire, Chace, and Slater (1976) modified the television memory test to check recall for the yearly sequence of past television programs, and found that "temporal order is remarkably affected by ECT" for a period covering one to seven years preceding ECT. These patients were impaired in their ability to recall the order in which they had last seen the programs. Their follow-ups came six to 25 days after five to 18 ECT, and disclosed more severe and persistent memory defect for remote events than the earlier tests.

A team including Strain, Bidder, and Brunschwig (Strain et al., 1968) developed a Personal Data Sheet (PDS) to test patients' remote and recent memory before and after modified ECT:

One set of at least 25 questions, hereafter referred to as "Remote Memory," involved recall of factual information pertaining to personal experiences prior to the patient's present illness. The second set of 25 or more questions, labeled "Recent Memory," tested recall of factual memory content pertaining to events related to the period leading up to and including the present hospitalization.

In the first report on their test, they found significant drops in the PDS after six ECT; these losses were not fully recovered at the final 10-day post-ECT testing. There was no difference between unilateral and bilateral modified ECT at the 10-day post-ECT testing.

Of great importance in demonstrating the unpredictability of potential damage to patients, Strain et al. noted, "individuals differed widely in amount of memory impairment regardless of treatment mode or number of ECTs given." They stated, "It is difficult to predict with any degree of certainty . . . the probable amounts of memory loss for the individual patient." They repeated this theme in 1970 (Bidder, Strain, & Brunschwig) and described how one patient had "practically no memory loss" after 12 bilateral ECT, whereas another receiving six unilateral treatments "suffered profound memory dysfunction."

In their last report of their results Brunschwig, Strain, and Bidder (1971) included 96 patients in their double-blind experiment and tested them before and after four, six, eight, 10, and 12 treatments. Every group dropped in PDS score after treatment, and all except the 12 ECT group began a gradual but incomplete recovery over the first 10 days. The group receiving 12 ECT stabilized the PDS loss by the fourth ECT and showed no improvement 10 days after ECT. They observed, "On the PDS, impaired memory retention persisted after treatment even among patients strongly motivated to regain normal functioning."

I communicated personally with Strain and with Brunschwig in November 1976, and they reported that they had not administered the PDS beyond 10 days post-ECT. Although anterograde tests were reaching normal by that time, the PDS continued to show evidence of retrograde amnesia on a typical gradient, with more remote and more well-known data remaining more stable. Brunschwig described how a grandmother could recall the name of her granddaughter but had forgotten the child's previously well-known grade in school or her birthday. A man could recall that he owned a car but had forgotten the once-important make. The older the memories, the more likely that details would be recalled. Strain and Brunschwig are staunch advocates of ECT; they provided this unpublished information reluctantly, with the request that I emphasize that their findings do not diminish their enthusiasm for the treatment.

Small, Sharpley, and Small (1968) also have studied long-term memory loss after modified ECT. Sixty to 90 days after 10 ECT a statistically significant number of patients showed a memory defect on the often insensitive Wechsler Memory Quotient. In 1974 I.F. Small conducted a long-term follow-up of subjective memory loss in patients who had received bilateral, unilateral dominant, unilateral nondominant ECT, or inhalant-induced convulsive therapy. He found that "more than half the patients considered their memory to be worse," and "in addition, six complained of persistent memory defects for several years after convulsive therapy." The follow-ups took place two to five years after the treatment and therefore the defects could be considered permanent. Small believed that the subjective reports of the patients were unbiased, and as confirmation he noted that patients receiving bilateral ECT reported greater losses than those receiving unilateral, although they did not know which treatment they had received.

Cronin et al. (1970) evaluated patients after eight ECT at the rate of two per week and found deficits in a word-learning test at four to six weeks. From a graph it is apparent that there was no tendency to improve at the termination of the study. They did not evaluate these findings, but did comment that bilateral ECT in the elderly can "cause real organic confusion with marked intellectual disturbance and memory impairment, which is not always temporary."

Halliday et al. (1968), using a battery of tests including digit span, nonverbal learning, and delayed recall, found persistent impairments in patients with bilateral ECT three months after the treatment, including some patients who had been given only four ECT.

The last two studies dealt with anterograde function, or the loss of the ability to learn, to memorize, and recall new materials after electroshock. Tests thus far used in ECT research are not very sensitive to anterograde mental dysfunction, but these provided some confirmation of clinical observations.

Strong evidence for permanent mental disability following ECT comes from an unusual source. The National Commission for the Protection of Human Subjects of Biomedical and Behavioral Research was mandated by Congress to report on psychosurgery. As an aspect of their research, they commissioned a Massachusetts Institute of Technology research team to investigate the effects of cingulotomy[5] on selected patients (Teuber et al., 1977). Many of the patients studied by Teuber et al. had been given ECT before psychosurgery, and they were found to

---

5. *Cingulotomy* is a form of psychosurgery or psychiatric brain surgery in which electrodes are used to destroy a portion of the cingulum which lies adjacent to the frontal lobes. In intention and effect it is closely related to the original lobotomy operations, although the mental defects produced are usually less blatant (Breggin, 1972a; 1973a,c; 1975b; 1979).

perform much more poorly on a variety of tests than the controls or patients who had been given psychosurgery without previous ECT:

> We found that individuals whose prior treatments included ECT were inferior to normal control subjects and to patients who had been spared ECT, and this inferiority was apparent on the following measures: verbal and nonverbal fluency, delayed alternation performance, tactual maze learning, continuous recognition of verbal and nonverbal material, delayed recall of a complex drawing, recognition of faces and houses, and identification of famous public figures. In some cases, the degree of deficit was related to the number of ECT received, patients who had been given more than 50 ECT being significantly worse than those who had sustained fewer than 50.

Displaying a marked propsychosurgery bias, they concluded that these losses were purely ECT effect, possibly complicated by the severity of the psychiatric disorders in patients receiving ECT. But the effects described most likely result from the *combined* effects of ECT *and* cingulotomy. Perhaps a comparable ECT group without psychosurgery would have fared as well as the cingulotomy group without ECT. What can be concluded from this study is that the combined insults of ECT and cingulotomy brought out *severe* and *global* losses of mental function, including recent and remote memory and anterograde or current mental function. The investigators did not describe the method of ECT, but the treatment environment (Boston) and the time period indicates that the great majority and perhaps all received modified ECT.

The study by Teuber et al., intended as an examination of psychosurgery, demonstrates a principle that is constantly reaffirmed throughout the psychiatry literature: The best sources of experimental and clinical data concerning damage produced by a psychiatric treatment are to be found in studies attempting to validate a newer form of treatment. Mental health professionals rarely publish data that reflect poorly on an established treatment unless an attempt is being made to encourage a competing form of treatment.

The experimental literature on mental dysfunction following modified ECT is generally inadequate at the present time. With a few notable exceptions, such as Teuber et al., studies that fail to test for the kinds of loss most frequently described by ECT patients (retrograde amnesia for personal experiences) do not usually detect mental disability. But studies that measure the loss of personal memories or evaluate reports of subjective loss usually if not always confirm retrograde amnesia in a significant number of post-ECT patients.

Clinical Reports of Permanent Mental Dysfunction after Modified ECT

There are far fewer clinical reports of any kind in the modern ECT literature than in the earlier literature. The absence of clinical reports probably relates, first, to the glut of reports on ECT published in the earlier literature, and, second, to the general tendency in modern psychiatry to replace clinical observations with statistical reports and charts. Lengthy descriptions of individual lives and responses are becoming infrequent in every area of psychiatric reporting.

Nonetheless, offhand remarks in various research papers indicate that severe memory loss is still frequently seen. Stromgren (1973), Valentine et al. (1968), Zinkin and Birtchnell (1968), Dolenz (1964), and others have noted that there are dangers in giving modified ECT to individuals who must use their minds and especially their memories to earn a living. Stromgren, for example, stated that there is "no doubt" that ECT can be harmful to patients "engaged in an intellectual kind of work."

Valentine et al. (1968) cited

> . . . the amnesia which affects most patients to a degree, and some severely. Indeed, the use of electroconvulsive therapy (ECT) is usually postponed or avoided in patients where memory impairment would be a serious handicap. . . . A patient with marked E.C.T. amnesia is likely to have substantial memory loss for the sequence of events immediately prior to treatment, and also a very partial and scattered amnesia, extending backwards in time for perhaps many months. The fragmentary nature of this amnesia is striking, some areas of experiential memory being quite unimpaired, others totally lost. . . .

The authors also described a patient who had seven ECT in 12 days and who had "considerable memory loss for at least a month before treatment and also for several days after the course was completed."

> Her memory deficit was most marked for people, but also affected her memories of her daily life, routine and environment. She lost all recollection of psychotherapeutic interviews during the previous three months; much of the work she had been studying had also been forgotten, and she could not remember having used or owned the textbooks she employed in her studies.

This case closely parallels the six that I have presented.

An autobiographical anonymous report by a psychiatrist in the *British Journal of Psychiatry* (Practising Psychiatrist, 1965) described firsthand the experience of modified ECT and verified most of the phenomena experienced by my patients, except the dread and resentment of the treatment. This psychiatrist wrote the article to dispel "groundless fear" about the treatment. He himself had two very short series of ECT for depression—three treatments three years earlier and five treatments shortly before the article. He reassured the reader that he had no memory defects of any importance. He worked throughout the treatments and had "not been at all seriously hampered by memory loss or disabled in any other way." But in the next paragraph he described these effects:

> I have always had a good topographical sense and have been able to memorize maps and, for example, find my way with ease around the Underground system of London, from the schema in my head without recourse to maps. With the second course of E.C.T., though not the first, my topographical schemata have become totally disorganized. I must look at a map in order to visualize the route from A to B, and I have forgotten completely the patterns that previously have been almost second nature to me. It is with considerable effort that I am learning them again. Similarly, I have considerable difficulty in finding my way about my filing system, which previously was familiar to me through years of use, but now seems strange so that I am at a loss to know where to start searching.

Clearly he was telling the truth when he said, "One of the most celebrated effects of E.C.T. is the memory loss it induces. This can be alarming, as whole tracts of memory seem to be expunged without trace. Memory for recent events, during the week or so preceding the treatment, appears to be the most severely affected." But just as clearly he was fooling himself when he said, "Memories for events of several years ago seem to impaired hardly at all." Instead of being affected "hardly at all," his memory of the subway system and his own files—built up through "years of use"—had been wiped out. There is also a suggestion in the quotation that his ability to relearn had been impaired.

As is typical in reports from post-ECT patients, including my six cases, this doctor's recognition of past memories has become faulty and unreal in its quality. There is also a hint of euphoria:

> When an event, entirely forgotten, is brought to one's notice, it sounds completely strange, foreign and unknown. One has the feeling that a confabulation is being presented; the details of the account seem unnecessarily elaborate, as if to make the

story convincing, and the whole effect is almost laughable. Then a fragment of the story rings true; a name is recognized, for example, and a series of events or facts come suddenly to mind, in a linear sequence. One is suddenly aware of a curious faculty to "feel one's way" along this sequence, as one element leads to the next. The revelation has a marked quality of unreality, as if one is trying to convince oneself of something fictitious, and as one gropes one's way along the sequence it is as if one is looking at the remembered facts for the very first time. This feeling of alienation is very strong, even in the face of indisputable evidence of the reality of the remembered facts.

After becoming concerned about the effects of electroshock witnessed during his residency in neurology, Friedberg (1976) placed advertisements in a newspaper to obtain interviews with individuals who had reacted badly to electroshock therapy. His sample was, therefore, selective and biased, as are almost all the case reports—positive or negative—in ECT literature. Friedberg's reports are rich in verbatim descriptions of the fear and memory loss often associated with electroshock. At least four of his interviewees appear to have been given modified ECT. One of these claimed no permanent memory loss after four treatments; three described permanent memory loss. One young student revealed a severe memory loss after ECT for educational and personal experiences as well as for artistic skills reaching several years back. He also described the typical unreality associated with many memories that can be recalled:

And when I got out of the hospital my memory didn't come back. It slowly came back. It's been almost two years and chunks of my life I can't remember. And my whole past life seems much more blurred and gray. Everything is much less real, everything's more just as if things were never real. Feelings you had with other people weren't real. As if the only flowers you could ever imagine were just plastic ones. You can't remember the real, real anything.

Q. Where are the chunks missing from?

A. Well, most of the chunks are preceding, I'd say in the two or three years before that. Like my college life, which had some of the best times of my life, I can't remember. I can't remember.

Q. How do you know you can't remember?

A. Because when I went back to school I'd see people that were my friends and I can't remember them.

Q. Just didn't ring a bell?

A. I knew I knew them from somewhere—especially people I'd met from two years before that. Friends I'd had from before that I'd remember and like very close friends but I just didn't remember. Just common experiences I'd had with close friends when I was in New York or Italy I couldn't remember. You know, just inside things that friends share. If it was brought back to me I might remember but in much less detail.

Q. Was your art work affected?

A. I couldn't remember how to do art. I'd been doing it all my life, especially all the time I was in school. I didn't do art all the time I was there [the hospital]—they brought me to the point where, you know, the whole time I was there I made a belt. Here I was, working with sculptures and plastics and the technology of molds and plastics and wood and I made a belt!

Q. How about subject matter that you were taught? History of Art?

A. I couldn't remember artists that I was really into. Because I was very much interested in the gallery scene and I just couldn't remember anyone I was into. I used to have a very good memory for names and pieces of art and where they are and just the . . . you know, I could look at a painting once and remember it, and I forgot everything. It's coming back. But I don't think to the same extent. Plus kind of an organized structure of doing work, I still haven't been able to get back into it. You know, just sitting down and carrying out ideas.

Perhaps because of renewed concern about ECT, two detailed case studies have been published recently documenting severe persistent mental dysfunction following ECT. Regestein et al. (1975) described a case of "prolonged, reversible dementia" associated with "abuse of electroconvulsive therapy." The woman had been given three months of ECT at three per week, followed by one month at two per week, with more than two years of one ECT per week. During her prolonged once-a-week ECT, her husband and her psychiatrist appeared willing to "nurture a helpless wife" with ECT-induced dementia.[6] When seen in a state of

6. *Dementia* is the deterioration or loss of intellectual faculties, memory, and emotional stability as a result of organic brain disease. It is essentially a very severe organic brain syndrome. Before declaring such a serious illness "reversible," very careful clinical, psychological and neurological examinations would be called for. Such data were not provided in the report.

dementia soon after the termination of ECT, she had a "profound memory deficit" including ignorance of the existence of her daughter and ignorance of her own age. Her mental state 29 weeks later was not fully described, but it was noted that she still had "a tendency to perseverate."[7]

Another recent study of Elmore and Sugerman (1975) described three flagrant organic psychoses precipitated after courses of six, four, and three ECT. The individual given the four ECT became a suicide "several months" later, and the person given the three ECT "gradually stabilized to a condition of apathy and indifference punctuated by episodes of fearfulness without floridly psychotic symptoms." The authors noted that without an awareness of the phenomenon described by Kalinowsky and Hippius they might have failed to realize that they were dealing with an organic, ECT-induced psychosis.

I have seen a number of florid psychoses develop after ECT, including three who were not included in the six cases discussed in Chapter 2. I treated these three individuals in the space of one year in which I was affiliated with a hospital that administered modified ECT. Two were middle-aged women and one was an elderly man, and their courses varied from six to 22 bilateral modified ECT. During ECT all three developed a severe organic brain syndrome, including helplessness, dependence, and delusions, and two hallucinated. Before ECT none had shown signs of psychosis, but when they failed to recover rapidly from their acute organic brain syndromes following ECT, the obvious diagnosis of chronic organic brain syndrome was ignored. Instead, they were given functional psychotic diagnoses that disguised the iatrogenic[8] nature of their organic mental dysfunction.

It is my experience that many middle-aged women are given ECT for problems originally diagnosed as "reactive depression," only to have their diagnoses changed to "involutional melancholia" or "paranoid schizophrenia" when their problems became complicated by a persisting organic brain syndrome following ECT.[9] Thus devastating reactions to ECT often are disguised as "psychoses" allegedly uncovered or "un-

---

7. *Perseveration* is the involuntary, pathologic repetition of words or activities. It is a sign of organic brain damage and would most likely appear in association with other indications of mental dysfunction.

8. An *iatrogenic* disorder is one produced by the physician, or by his method of treatment.

9. A *reactive depression* is neurotic rather than psychotic, and presumably originates as a psychological reaction to inner conflicts and life stresses. *Involutional melancholia* is a psychotic disorder characterized by severe depression and often complicated by paranoid ideas, delusions, and other symptoms. It is often presumed to originate from some as yet undiscovered biological infirmity. A depressed person who has the added difficulty of an ECT-induced organic brain syndrome would often mimic the clinical picture of involutional melancholia.

masked" by ECT (Bennett, 1949), when in reality they are chronic organic brain syndromes reflecting severe brain damage.

I have already examined the manner in which Kalinowsky and others have reviewed the literature on unmodified ECT to give the false impression that it contains no evidence that ECT produces permanent amnesia and mental dysfunction. In the 1970s, however, ECT advocates took a new approach. Gone were the lengthy bibliographies of the past, and instead assertions concerning the harmlessness of ECT were made as if they were established truths requiring no proofs, no logic, and few citations (Kalinowsky, 1975a, b; Noyes & Kolb, 1973; Kolb, 1977). Kalinowsky's earlier reviews with Hoch (1961) and with Hippius (1969) remain the bulwark of the modern advocates' defense of ECT.

7

Are the Patients Lying?

Pro-ECT articles and books often acknowledge frequent complaints about memory loss from their patients, but they dismiss or rationalize them as manifestations of "mental illness" and especially "neuroticism." As in so many other aspects of justifying ECT, Kalinowsky has led the way in dismissing patient complaints about the treatment. In 1959 he wrote:

> More insistent complaints of memory impairment are some-
> times heard from neurotic patients who are overconcerned with
> all side effects of the treatment, and many complain of forget-
> fulness long after tests have shown a return to normal memory
> function.

Kalinowsky has repeated this viewpoint throughout the era of modi-fied ECT (see Kalinowsky & Hoch, 1961; Kalinowsky & Hippius, 1969). In the 1975 edition of *The American Handbook of Psychiatry* he again called the complainers "neurotics" and said, "Many complain of forget-fulness long after tests have shown a return of normal memory func-tion." In the same year in the *Comprehensive Textbook of Psychiatry,* he took the position that "Some patients complain more than others, and neurotics are often overconcerned with these temporary memory difficulties."

Perhaps the most revealing statement in all the electroshock litera-ture was made by Kalinowsky and Hoch in the 1952 edition of their textbook when they wrote," "All patients who remain unimproved after ECT are inclined to complain bitterly about their memory difficulties" (p. 139). The sentence (one of the few edited out of later editions) merits careful reading. The authors said that *all* patients who remain unimproved complain about amnesia and, furthermore, they admitted that these people complain *bitterly*. How then could Kalinowsky and Hoch argue, on the same page, "No evidence has been brought forward to indicate that permanent mental sequelae are caused by the treatment"? In order to make this claim they must disregard the report of *every patient* who does not respond to ECT in their prescribed manner. These patients are "unimproved" or "neurotic" and therefore cannot be trusted. Why *all* such patients complain *bitterly* about memory loss is left to the imagination. Is there some inexplicable ECT effect that always brings about a subjective feeling of memory loss in patients whom it fails to help, although it never does so in the patients whom it succeeds in helping? Instead, could it be that those patients who complain about memory loss are labeled "unimproved" or "neurotic" in order to invalidate their opinions, while all those patients who make no complaints are labeled "improved" or "cured"?

Refusing to accept that so many consistent complaints must be taken seriously, other apologists for ECT have suggested variations on the theme that patients who complain about memory loss are irresponsible and "mentally ill," whereas patients who don't complain are "trustworthy" and "improved." Schwartzman and Termansen (1967) concluded from their research that patients are so upset about "subjective" memory loss that intensive ECT should be largely abandoned, yet they raised the possibility that these complaints have no basis in reality. Squire (1977) concluded from his own systematic follow-up studies that, "it seems quite clear that individuals judged clinically appropriate for bilateral ECT do have memory complaints long after ECT"; then he went on to suggest that memory loss is an "illusion."

Faced with insurmountable evidence that patients complain about memory loss years after ECT, the American Psychiatric Association Task Force on ECT (1978), with Squire as its research consultant, rallied around the suggestion that former ECT patients are suffering a "persistent illusion of memory impairment" (p. 68). The theory states that bilateral modified ECT (but not unilateral, nondominant ECT) does produce a "lingering sense of memory impairment," which then causes "some individuals to be more sensitive to subsequent failures in recall, even if they occur at a normal frequency." This is not ascribed to neuroticism in the patients, but to the treatment itself, so that the "illusion" of memory loss can occur "with or without psychiatric illness." This is the final suggestion made by the Task Force at the conclusion of its skimpy review of the literature on mental dysfunction following ECT.

But why would patients experience this illusion following bilateral modified ECT but not following nondominant unilateral ECT? The advocates of this theory must claim that nondominant unilateral ECT does not produce an acute organic brain syndrome and acute memory loss, a position wholly at odds with the literature and clinical observation. The position also seems faulty as a defense against liability; should not a patient be able to sue a psychiatrist for using a treatment that commonly produces an emotionally upsetting and disabling "illusion"? The advocates of the illusion theory seem to be hoping for a switch from bilateral to unilateral ECT, accompanied by a new cycle of claims that this form of ECT is harmless.

The illusion theory was stated in a less elaborated form by Noyes and Kolb (1973) and by Kolb (1977) in recent editions of *Modern Clinical Psychiatry*. The patients, they said, cannot be "trusted" in evaluating their own memory loss. Their thrust was clear: the patients unaccountably *exaggerate* their losses. Noyes and Kolb cited a study by Cronholm and Ottosson (1963a) to support their assertion that the patients cannot be trusted. But, on reading the Cronholm and Ottosson study, we find to the contrary that the patients who have the *most memory loss tend to complain the least*. This is why they cannot be trusted—they tend to *deny* the degree of damage they have suffered. Gomez (1975) found in regard to the treatment period that "those who remembered least of this period complained least of memory loss."

This denial of mental impairment is exactly what can be expected and what typically is found after brain damage. Instead of exaggerating their mental defects after brain damage, patients *almost always* tend to deny or to downplay them. They do this out of fear and shame over their mental condition (Goldstein, 1975). The phenomenon of denying mental dysfunction after brain damage is so commonplace that it has a name: confabulation. If post-ECT patients cannot be trusted in evaluating their mental function, it is because they do not wish to acknowledge their impairments. Confabulation is such a well-known phenomenon in clinical neurology and psychiatry that it is usually discussed, in separate chapters, in the very books in which it is claimed that ECT patients, for some unaccountable reason, *like to exaggerate* their mental losses and dysfunction.

In the 1959 edition of the *American Handbook of Psychiatry*, in which Kalinowsky claimed that patients who complain about memory defects after ECT are "neurotic," two excellent discussions of confabulation were presented in other chapters (Brosin; Weinstein & Kahn). Both chapters made clear that patients with brain trauma, including ECT, tend to deny or hide the extent of their brain dysfunction. As Weinstein and Kahn put it, the confabulations are "seemingly designed to amplify the denial, minimize the traumatic implications of the illness, and explain away the manifestations." Weinstein and Kahn went so far as to relate the confabulations and euphoria to the alleged "improvement" seen in post-ECT patients—a subject that will receive further attention in regard to the brain-disabling hypothesis (Chapters 11 and 12).

Weinstein and Kahn made clear the difference between retrograde amnesia based on brain disease and fake or neurotic amnesia. Retrograde amnesia following brain trauma is general and rubs out a broad spectrum of memories, both trivial and significant, without regard for their symbolic importance to the individual. Fake amnesia is usually highly symbolic. Typically, a painful loss or traumatic event is forgotten, such as the death of a comrade in battle. Global memory will be unaffected and the amnesia will not be retrograde. The patient forgets what he *wishes* to forget. But in memory loss following damage to the brain, the person cannot remember things he wishes to remember. As described in my six cases and in the psychiatric literature, post-ECT patients have very global losses that follow the classic pattern of true retrograde amnesia, with the greatest losses occurring nearest to the trauma. Rarely if ever do such patients report symbolic losses.

Weinstein and Kahn also described another well-known diagnostic difference between real, or retrograde, amnesias and fake, or neurotic, amnesias. The patient who is consciously or unconsciously faking wishes to forget his forgotten memories, so he rarely displays eagerness to recover them. When he is reminded of his forgotten memories, he is rather indifferent to the revelation. By contrast, the individual with retrograde amnesia is very upset about his losses and often works very hard, much as my cases, in order to recover them. When Kalinowsky admits that his patients complain "bitterly" about their losses, he adds validity to their complaints.

Brosin's chapter (1959) confirms the observations of Weinstein and Kahn. He described the Korsakoff-like syndrome that develops after trauma to the brain, pointed out that it can occur after lobotomy and electroshock, and emphasized the confabulation and euphoria with which patients try to cover up or to deny their defects.

> Questions designed to reveal the functions of mental status, such as perception, recent memory, orientation, attention, ability to handle abstractions, arithmetic, and proverbs, will usually reveal marked defects. This may be true in other acute brain disorders, including patients operated on for brain tumor, lobotomy, and post-electric shock. In the Korsakoff syndrome we often have the opportunity to see many of the psychodynamic defenses described by Goldstein and some of the psychoanalysts. As in other organic cerebral disorders, the patient

> is unconsciously, if not consciously, aware of many of his de-
> fects and tries to overcome them, compensate for them, or avoid
> them in many ways. . . . Some patients are placid and even
> euphoric, but the delicately defensive nature of this facade can
> usually be quickly proved by questions.

Brosin's observations help destroy the hypothesis that the patients are
exaggerating their defects.

The reality that most brain-damaged people cannot bear to acknowledge or face their deficits was portrayed in various ways by each of
my six patients. Their losses were almost always greater than they were
willing to admit. While all acknowledged some degree of retrograde
amnesia, they were especially reluctant to talk about any ongoing mental
disabilities, such as difficulties remembering new material or a lack of
mental dexterity. One patient denied any ongoing mental defects despite
a long course of ECT treatment, until I mentioned his good fortune off-
handedly a year after we had gotten to know each other. Only then did
he confess with great shame that he felt less able to think and learn. He
was very guarded and very embarrassed about this, and I chose for lack
of information or confirmation not to include him in the group of four of
six patients having anterograde defects. He is listed in my study as
suffering from retrograde amnesia alone. In long-term relationships with
three of the six post-ECT patients I had begun to assume that their lack
of complaints about ongoing dsyfunction meant a full recovery, only to
realize from the expressions on their faces and from subsequent discussions that they were hiding their dysfunctions out of shame and frustration. As further confirmation of the confabulation in the six cases, the
two most obviously damaged individuals were the ones who most ada-
mantly and strenuously denied any losses other than retrograde amnesia. In one case I too was misled, and only realized the degree of confabulation when the neurologic tests and psychological tests were returned
with significant defects.

I am not the only investigator who has discovered that ECT patients, however much they complain of memory loss, are nonetheless
hiding many of their deficits. In his painstaking and elegant research,
Janis (1948) came to the same conclusion. Here is his classic illustration
of confabulation in a post-ECT patient:

> Sometimes a patient will deny that a given event or series of
> events has occurred, and he will fill in the amnesic gap, as in
> the following example. The patient, a 37-year-old borderline
> schizophrenic, reported in the pretreatment interview that he
> had been unable to work for several months before coming to
> the hospital, during which period he would spend his time

riding around in subways, wandering about the city, sitting in churches, etc. (These facts were confirmed by information from members of the family in the patient's case history record.) Four weeks after a series of 12 electroshock treatments, the patient was unable to recall this period of unemployment and claimed: "I worked right up till I came to this hospital." After many detailed questions, the patient was finally told about his former statement and he replied: "I don't recall that. My wife would know because she has to take care of the bills. You could ask her. It might have been for a few days . . . There are some things I can't remember. But I think I did support the family right up till I came to this hospital" (elipses in original).

Other clinicians have made similar observations. Dedichen (1946) was aware that patients "often do not spontaneously complain" of amnesia. He believed the complaint is withheld because the patient "interprets this defect as an aftermath of the psychosis from which he has just suffered and not as a sequel to the treatment." Indeed, as Kalinowsky exemplifies, the *doctor* is likely to attribute any such complaint to mental illness, or to a failure to improve. The complaining patient may be forced to receive more treatment because her complaints "show" she is unimproved. This could very well encourage a patient to withhold complaints out of fear.

To whatever degree patients do confuse their ECT brain-damage with psychosis, they are most likely to make this error in regard to anterograde dysfunction, such as difficulties in thinking rapidly, concentrating, or learning. Similarly, their physicians will more easily dismiss these ongoing symptoms as manifestations of "mental illness" rather than consider them organic illness. This may be the main reason why clinical reports concerning post-ECT effects rarely mention continuing mental dysfunction. Even "Practising Psychiatrist" (1965) had difficulty in interpreting his own post-ECT dysfunction. He described unpleasant olfactory sensations and could not determine if they were caused by his depression or by ECT.

Addressing himself to "the marked impairment of memory in a large number of patients after shock treatment," Braatoy (1948) summed up the problem accurately:

It seems to be generally agreed that this deficiency can be detected in ordinary clinical examination in some patients for a couple of months after the conclusion of the treatment. (N.B.: The examination must then be made with a special view to this matter. Many of these patients will, like other persons with impaired memory, be somewhat reserved in conversation and therefore the defect may easily be overlooked on cursory in-

spection, just as all psychiatrists and neurologists know that
presenile dementia may advance remarkably far without any
changes being noted by the patient's associates—precisely because the person affected seeks to evade test situations.)

Fink (1957, 1958), Fink, Kahn & Green (1958), and others have
described the frequency with which post-ECT patients use denial as a
mechanism of defense. This further verifies the probability that these
patients are denying their brain damage as well as their psychological
problems. The euphoria described by Fink, Kalinowsky, and dozens of
others as a frequent sequela of the treatment is in itself a form of denial.
It is entirely consistent with a refusal to admit mental defects of any
kind. Euphoria is most common in the face of catastrophic losses, such
as severe, general central nervous system disease, or lobotomy and ECT.
As already noted, euphoria is defined in medical dictionaries and medical
usage as an abnormal state in which the individual exaggerates his state
of well being, or conversely, denies his state of ill health. In the earlier
electroshock literature (see for example, Levy et al., 1942), it was openly
recognized that euphoria was a serious indication of brain damage and
dysfunction. Only in the hands of modern advocates of ECT has an
abnormal reaction been redefined as an indicator of improvement (see
Chapters 11 and 12).

Because detailed case reports are rarely presented in the ECT literature, it is usually impossible to judge for oneself the actual losses of
patients presented as proof of the harmlessness of ECT. One especially
detailed self-report was offered anonymously by "Practising Psychiatrist" (1965) and, as already described, his claim to no significant memory loss was in sharp contrast to his actual description of labored attempts to relearn the subway system and his filing cabinets, despite
years of familiarity with them before ECT. Similarly, Watkins, Stainbrook, and Lowenbach (1941) described the disastrous reaction of another physician to one subconvulsive ECT and reported that those who
knew him were largely unaware of his impairment. As Dedichen (1946)
originally observed, it is not only easy for the patient to hide his defects,
it is easy for others to overlook them.

ECT and Psychological Testing

I have already noted that no reputable neurologist would rule out the
existence of brain damage, even *severe* brain damage, on the grounds
that psychological tests failed to detect any objective evidence. Because
this question is so crucial, I want to return to it again. The question is

this: If post-ECT patients report classic symptoms of permanent retrograde amnesia, can negative psychological tests be used to invalidate their claims or even to cast doubt about them?

As in one of my six cases, psychological tests are occasionally useful in documenting serious organic defects, especially in the presence of more objective physical findings. But they are not reliable or sensitive enough to rule out serious organic defects. In other words, the tests are useful when they find something definitive, but they are not meaningful when they fail in this task. In his discussion of trauma to the brain Brosin (1959) addressed himself to the question of psychological testing, noting that a great deal of evidence had been generated pertaining to its usefulness in regard to measuring organic brain damage. He observed that "the high hopes which existed from 1920 to 1945" concerning the development of reliable and sensitive objective tests had failed to materialize. He affirmed the position taken by all experts on psychological testing—that objective psychological tests "have not provided the clinician with readily available, reliable measures of loss of cortical function owing to brain-tissue damage." In his own detailed analysis of the mental effects of brain damage, Brosin relied almost wholly on clinical evaluations of the patient's subjective reports.

Neurologist Robert Grimm (1978) has addressed himself specifically to the matter of psychological testing for amnesia following electroshock therapy.

> Experimentalists who find no significant lasting changes in ECT memory studies must be concerned with the question of whether or not their measures are sensitive enough or aimed in the right direction. . . .
>
> In addition to losses of familiar recall items, it is the small, intermittent, or subtle changes in memory or its processes that may be at risk, intrinsic events which go undetected to external observers or formal testing. . . .
>
> In personal matters, small lacunae in memory can be very consequential. After the fact, recalling a missed appointment ordinarily engenders elaborate social responses to repair the situation. But not to know that a memory has been dropped is infinitely more troublesome to those embarrassed by the event and puzzled as how to respond.
>
> In memory as in intellect, it is the "little things" that count. Given the current lack of data, it is inappropriate to be blithe or argumentative about a patient's concern over alleged memory troubles or to be too comfortable with experimental findings that fail to reveal losses.

In the light of these generally accepted medical truths, it is dismaying that advocates of ECT use negative psychological tests to invalidate the patient's symptoms, and even more dismaying that they often use tests of their own creation with no known relevance to any clinical manifestations of brain disease.

The Lessons of Lobotomy

In animal studies, human autopsies, and EEG reports, the frontal lobes take the brunt of the damage inflicted by ECT. This is consistent with the placement of the electrodes and the flow of electric current. We have noted comparisons between ECT and lobotomy effects in the clinical literature, and in the following chapters we will find this comparison made more systematically, especially in regard to intensive ECT. We can therefore gain further insight into the question "Are the patients lying?" by examining the reaction of lobotomy patients to their deficits.

All lobotomized patients tend to underestimate their losses; none tends to exaggerate them. Lobotomy patients do distort a great deal, but wholly in the interest of denying their massive, overwhelming psychological deficits. Though obviously damaged, they often label themselves "better than ever," and frequently deny that they have been operated on, even when confronted with their surgical scars (Freeman & Watts, 1950; Tow, 1954).

A clinical experience cruelly illustrates both the losses and the process of denial. A man in his 30s had been lobotomized in the 1950s at the age of 20 and twice again in the mid-1960s. He and his mother brought a malpractice suit against the surgeon, not only because of the patient's mental deficits, but because of a partial paralysis following the third operation. He denied any impairment of intellectual function and believed that his IQ was higher than ever. He confabulated about reading the newspapers and staying abreast of current events. On clinical examination he had massive losses in abstract reasoning, judgment, insight, and planning for the future. He could not initiate simple activities and had to be supervised in his self-care, such as dressing and eating. He was apathetic and his emotions were shallow and almost nonexistent, except for occasional displays of inappropriate levity. However, after hearing me testify in court about his psychological deficits, he approached me during recess and in hesitant, broken sentences thanked me for my efforts. He agreed for the first time that his mind had been impaired by the surgery and he reported that he felt very sad, although his face remained stiff and emotionless. I asked him if he felt like crying, and he said with unusual firmness, "I am crying," though his eyes remained dry and his face masklike. After this very short exchange, he retreated again into apathy and denial.

The lobotomy studies not only confirm the denial and confabulation typical of individuals with frontal lobe damage, but they also suggest the direction in which to search for post-ECT mental deficits. The most comprehensive clinical analyses of postlobotomy patients were reported by Freeman (Freeman & Watts, 1944, 1950), and the most thorough psychological studies were provided by Tow (1954). The two reports are wholly in agreement. The patients suffer global psychological losses in all the higher human functions: abstract reasoning, judgment, insight, imagination, creativity, emotional sensitivity, moral awareness. The losses are not always obvious on a standard IQ test, which may show an artifactual improvement when previously rebellious and unruly patients become more willing to sit down and to follow instructions following lobotomy. But the losses will show up grossly when the patients are asked to demonstrate initiative, autonomy, or spontaneously generated activity. When the patients are asked to perform fully unstructured and self-determined tasks, such as writing a brief autobiography, a rich and sensitive prelobotomy production will be replaced by a sterile, mechanical, and sometimes more grossly psychotic postlobotomy production (Tow, 1954). Freeman & Watts, and Tow, strong advocates of the treatment, reported that the patients do best in structured, supervised and simplified environments after surgery. Tow (1954) observed, "One generalization which is fairly consistently true is that his performance is considerably better in a structured situation." He elaborated:

> Where the test is completely unstructured for him as in the autobiographies, the verbal fluency tests and abstract words, the deterioration in performance of the frontal subject was so gross as to be obvious without quantitative comparison. Where the situation is structured for him so that he only has to perform to a certain set pattern, within certain narrow limits, his performance approximates more nearly to his pre-operative.

Similar observations were made in the modern era of psychosurgery by Andersen (1972), who found that amygdalotomy[1] produced more docile, tractable individuals requiring a supervised environment:

> Typically the patient tends to become more inert, and shows less zest and intensity of emotions. His spontaneous activity appears to be reduced, and he becomes less capable of creative

---

1. *Amygdalotomy* is a psychosurgical operation that damages or destroys the amygdala, a portion of the temporal lobe which plays a key role in the regulation of emotion. It lies close to the heaviest concentration of electric current during ECT.

productivity, which is independent of the intelligence level. . . .
With these changes in initiative and control of behavior, our
patients resemble those with frontal lesions. . . . Presumably he
will make the most of this gain in well-structured situations of
a somewhat monotonous and simple character.

A similar lack of self-determination, initiative, and spontaneity becomes grossly apparent during the acute brain syndrome that develops
routinely after three or four ECT. This phenomenon is usually called
apathy. That this reaction can last for months was demonstrated by the
extensive use of ECT to subdue or quiet difficult, unruly, or uncooperative mental patients on a large scale in the state mental hospitals in the
1940s and 1950s (see Chapter 10). Two of my six cases, one in the short-
course group, described a permanent loss of initiative, spontaneity, and
overall energy years after ECT. A third was unsure if ECT caused this
same feeling, since he had suffered a similar psychological reaction prior
to ECT. A fourth felt he had more energy than ever, but he had a long
course of ECT, showed clinical signs of an organic brain syndrome, and
confabulated. His energy level seemed to reflect an ineffective, irrational
euphoria. Finally, two patients in the short-course group felt and displayed no loss in this area, although one did have demonstrable brain
damage.

The typical ECT patient suffers less damage to the frontal lobes
than the typical lobotomy patient, and so we would expect to find a less
severe clinical reaction. But any loss of self-determination, initiative, or
spontaneity in a human being is a significant loss. Difficult to define
subjectively and almost impossible to measure objectively except in
grossly disordered cases, this loss is nonetheless of very great importance. It is therefore surprising that no ECT research study or textbook
has raised the possibility of such a defect following ECT, even though
many clinical studies indirectly describe the defect when reporting on the
use of ECT to pacify or calm state mental hospital wards.

Throughout the United States and around the world today, former
psychiatric patients have begun to organize to publicize their concern
about the damaging and humiliating treatment they have received in
psychiatric hospitals (Frank, 1978). Much of their energy has been devoted to describing the devastating effects of electroconvulsive therapy.
What they have to say about the treatment corresponds exactly to the
cases I have reported and to the many clinical and research studies in the
literature. Are we to believe with Kalinowsky that these people—one and
all—are "neurotics" who have not been helped by their ECT? Because
the existence of brain damage following ECT is also confirmed through

animal research, autopsy reports, brain-wave studies, neurological examinations, and systematic psychological research, it is both rational and imperative to acknowledge that ECT frequently produces severe mental dysfunction in the form of both retrograde amnesia and ongoing mental disabilities. In the next chapter the mechanism of damage in ECT will be summarized and reviewed.

8

The Mechanism of Brain Damage in ECT

There are two separate origins of brain damage in electroconvulsive therapy—the electrical current and the convulsion. Most ECT researchers believe that the current is the main source of damage, but some disagree. Perhaps the most extreme position is taken by Kalinowsky (1975a, p. 533) who believes that "there is no harm in applying too large an amount of current."

Electric Current as the Cause of Damage

In the section concerning biochemical dysfunction following ECT (Chapter 3) it was noted that although convulsions of all kinds can cause biochemical disturbances in the brain, experienced researchers in the field believe that a case has been made for the electrical current as the main culprit (McGaugh & Alpern, 1966; Dunn et al., 1974; Essman, 1968). Many of these studies involve deductions made from studying the effects of varying electrical and convulsive stimuli on brain tissue extracts.

Other evidence confirms the damaging effects of the current. Electrical stimulation without convulsion can produce damage and dysfunction. Subconvulsive currents can cause severe acute brain dysfunction in humans, as reflected in clinical reports (Watkins et al., 1941; Jaffe et al., 1960) and demonstrated in controlled studies of subconvulsive shock in modified ECT (Pulver & Jacobs, 1961; Larsen & Vraa-Jensen, 1953). Electric currents without convulsion have produced retrograde amnesia in animals (Chevalier, 1965; Essman, 1968; McGaugh & Alpern, 1966), as well as marked metabolic changes in animal brain chemistry (Dunn et al., 1974; McGaugh & Williams, 1974; McGaugh, 1974; Lovell, 1971). Severe electrical assaults on the human and animal can cause severe damage to the brain without the production of a convulsion, and this damage often mimics ECT effects (Morrison et al., 1930; Langworthy, 1930; Hassin, 1933).

Methods of applying the current also may affect the degree of the damage. Varying the amount of energy delivered or the wave form has been reported to bring about significant changes in the amount of subsequent mental dysfunction (Cronholm & Ottosson, 1963b; Liberson, 1948). However, this has not been a unanimous finding (Kalinowsky, 1975a; Brengelman, 1959; Strain et al., 1968); Hartelius (1952) found no difference varying the wave form in his animal studies. Varying the strength of the electrical impulse may affect the length of the apnea (Marshall & Dobbs, 1959). Many studies show that lateralizing the current to one side of the head or the other produces a corresponding brain-wave change, even though the convulsion is generalized (see Chapter 5). Unilateral ECT also produces clinical changes associated with lateralization[1] (Cannicott & Waggoner, 1967; Levy, 1968; Dornbush & Williams, 1974; Valentine et al., 1968; Ottosson, 1961). Shifting the electrodes forward on the head in bilateral ECT produces a convulsion but much less memory loss, implicating the placement of the electrodes over the anterior temporal lobe and therefore current intensity as a source of damage to the memory centers in that region (Abrams & Taylor, 1974).

Several studies have elucidated the mechanism of current damage and have related it to pathologic findings after ECT. Hayes (1950), at the Yerkes Laboratory of Primate Biology, used implanted electrodes to demonstrate that "The current flow through the brain is very diffuse" during ECT. He hypothesized that the skull acts as a resistor and that the electrical charge that builds up around the surface of the skull then breaks through the thinnest parts. Reviewing additional foreign-language studies, Hartelius (1952) came to the same conclusions as Hayes:

> Broadly speaking, the existing experimental data warrant the conclusion that, with the doses of current applied in ECT, the

---

1. *Lateralization* refers to the localization of an abnormality on one side of the body, indicating a corresponding organic defect in the opposite cerebral hemisphere which controls that portion of the body. Thus when unilateral ECT is applied to the left side of the head, transient or permanent paralyses may appear on the right side of the body.

current is distributed relatively evenly over the whole brain, with a moderate increase in the direct path between the electrodes. In other words, the brain behaves as a relatively homogeneous conductor.

Hartelius also cited foreign-language studies demonstrating a corresponding diffuse action of the current on the cerebral blood vessels. This analysis of the mechanism of diffuse damage is extremely important because so many advocates of ECT have dismissed findings of diffuse brain damage in animal studies and human autopsies on the grounds that the current passes between the electrodes across the front of the brain. This analysis also invalidates the criticism made of some animal studies on the grounds that the electrodes used were too large in proportion to the animal's head. Because the passage of current is diffuse, electrode size makes no difference. Hartelius confirmed this experimentally.

A series of studies deals with the direct visualization of the brain vasculature during electrical stimulation. The first of these was published by Echlin in 1942. Using 30 cats, one dog, and four monkeys, he carried out the first attempts to produce artificial cerebral ischemia[2] with electrical current. He applied very small subconvulsive electrical stimuli to the blood vessels passing through the meninges of the brain and discovered that arteries, arterioles, and capillaries promptly constricted. The strength of the weak unipolar current was no greater than that routinely used in surgery for the electrical stimulation of the motor cortex, but blood flow was completely stopped in the affected vessels.

No ischemia was produced by this localized stimulus because of alternative routes of blood flow to the tissue. Echlin theorized that ischemia would follow a more generalized constriction of the vessels, and tested this hypothesis by applying a convulsive electrical stimulus (110 v; 1 to 3 sec) to the head during direct observation by means of craniotomy. He found that the pial vessels constricted exactly as they did during direct stimulation with the small electrical currents. They were completely obliterated and sometimes remained closed for up to *three minutes*. The greatest degree of effect was achieved on the side where the current was applied, again implicating the current rather than the convulsion.

Echlin's findings concerning the direct effect of current on the brain were confirmed by Alexander and Lowenbach's (1944) study, in which they found "a fleeting period of vasoconstriction and blanching of the capillary bed within the path of the current within the range of amperage

---

2. *Ischemia* is a local impairment of blood supply due to obstruction or constriction of the blood vessels. It can lead to cell death and gross tissue destruction.

employed in treatment in man."[3] In one example they sacrificed an animal four minutes after a 300 ma dose of electricity, and found blanching. They also saw vascular damage in the form of increased vessel wall permeability to dye during relatively mild electrical stimulation.

Aware of the diffuse nature of ECT-related brain damage and aware of the diffuse spread of the current through the brain during ECT, Halpern and Peyser in 1953 attempted to explore further the mechanism of ECT brain damage. They used angiography to observe the cranial vessels during ECT applied to animals in the human therapeutic dose range (100 to 120v; 0.2 to 0.3 sec). They found such severe vasoconstriction during the convulsion that in some instances only "large arteries" filled with blood. They concluded,

> With regard to the occurrence of reversible or irreversible vascular damage following convulsive therapy it has to be assumed, in accordance with the results of our experiments, that structurally inferior vessels may be further damaged during convulsions and lead to additional brain lesions, even if therapeutic limits of convulsive treatment are not exceeded.

In another attempt to elaborate the mechanism of diffuse brain damage found in animal experiments and human autopsy studies, Aird and his colleagues in 1956 gave 12 ECT to cats over a 22-day period, again using currents in the human clinical dose range (400 ma; 0.2 sec). They injected tracer substances and found increased permeability of the blood brain barrier.[4] They concluded that once within the brain the current follows the vascular tree, breaks down the blood brain barrier, and thereby produces diffuse changes in the brain such as those reported in animals and humans.

In still another attempt to clarify the mechanism of ECT brain damage, Lee and Olszewski in 1961 subjected cats and rabbits to large numbers of ECT (40 to 55). They found an increase in the blood brain barrier permeability, which they also attributed to the passage of current down the vascular tree. These changes were found with the use of both *modified* and unmodified ECT.

A great controversy has surrounded one particular mechanism of damage—general cerebral anoxia produced by the convulsion (Meyer & Ericsson, 1972). Proponents of ECT have argued that modified ECT produces no general cerebral anoxia and hence no damage. Those who

---

3. *Vasoconstriction* is a narrowing of blood vessels that produces ischemia. *Blanching* is the loss of color associated with ischemia.

4. The *blood brain barrier* is the functional barrier between the smallest blood vessels of the brain and the brain tissue. It controls the passage of substances from the blood to the brain.

believe that modified ECT would not produce general anoxia base their thinking on two mechanisms: first, that the tonic-clonic movements of the musculature cause excess oxygen consumption, hastening anoxia, and second, that the apnea associated with the seizure reduces oxygenation of the blood. On this theory, paralyzing the musculature and artificially breathing the individual during his apnea (modified ECT) should reduce overall cerebral anoxia.

Matsuba et al. (1968), Posner et al. (1969), and Broderson et al. (1973) tested this hypothesis by a variety of complex methods, and their tests indicate that general cerebral anoxia is greatly reduced and perhaps eliminated by modification of the ECT. J.W. Lovett Doust et al. (1974) showed an increased blood flow to the brain during modified ECT, indicating another compensatory mechanism that may be at work to relieve cerebral anoxia.

These studies only suggest that general cerebral anoxia is alleviated by ECT modification. They in no way controvert the mass of evidence indicating brain damage following modified ECT. Furthermore, the studies in no way support the hypothesis that the mechanism of ECT damage is general anoxia. In this regard, one of the investigatory teams, Posner et al., stated that, "At some point during repeated seizures, depletion of cerebral substances might become irreversible and permanent brain damage ensue." Thus this research is of theoretical interest, but does not bear on the question: Does modified ECT produce brain damage?

These studies specifically disregard the possibility of local anoxia in sensitive parts of the brain. Broderson et al. did in fact find an increased lactate[5] production of unknown origin despite the absence of general hypoxemia,[6] suggesting that local portions of the brain might have become anoxic. A careful reading of Matsuda et al. also indicates an unexplained, slight increase in lactate, on which the authors do not remark. Lee and Olszewski (1961) also concluded, on the basis of their own experiments with modified ECT, that the breakdown of vascular permeability was a local tissue reaction independent of any respiratory modifications.

Ottosson (1974), by no means a critic of ECT, directly confronted the issue of these studies. He observed that ECT in clinical practice is not given under such controlled conditions, and more important that, "some parts of the brain, e.g., the hippocampus, have a higher oxygen consumption than other parts, which may give rise to local cerebral anoxia."

---

5. *Lactate* is a salt of lactic acid produced during metabolic processes that take place in the absence of oxygen.

6. *Hypoxemia* or hypoxia is a deficiency of oxygen.

The hippocampus of the temporal lobe is intimately involved in memory, and lies close to the point of electrode application (Penfield & Mathieson, 1974).

It should also be noted that some studies have confirmed an isoelectric period in the EEG following modified as well as unmodified ECT (Misurec, 1965; Stein et al., 1969). This period of absent brain waves may reflect a shutdown of brain metabolism in association with anoxia or depletion of energy sources leading to brain damage (Meyer & Ericsson 1972). This isoelectric period follows spontaneous convulsions and is therefore independent of the electrical current, although it may be increased by it.

Even if massive evidence were unavailable, common sense and rational analysis would immediately suggest the enormous hazard involved in passing an electric current through the brain, especially through the anterior portion of the temporal lobe. Neurologist John Friedberg (1977a) has summarized the hazards of such an assault:

> The electrodes, whether applied over the temples or limited to one side of the head, discharge through the very sensitive temporal lobes. The squamous plate of the temporal lobe is the thinnest in the cranium—thus, where resistance is lowest, the current is greatest. Just beneath lie the temporal lobes containing the least stable cortex by EEG criteria. On their mesial aspects are found the hippocampal formations, so indispensable to memory that their destruction—by lobotomy and encephalitis, sclerosis from birth injury and hamartomas, impairment by posterior circulation insufficiency, or loss through thiamine deficiency—leads to the densest amnesias known to medicine. The hippocampal formations, moreover, have the lowest seizure thresholds and the greatest propensity to epileptic kindling in the entire brain. It is here that the cellular damage caused by ECT wreaks the greatest havoc.[7]

Because the current, more than the convulsion, appears to be involved in ECT-induced brain damage, it is important to document that many clinical applications of ECT at the present time use electric stimuli at least as strong as those originally employed by Cerletti and much stronger than many or most of ECT experiments. No one has fully

---

7. Defining the various medical terms in this paragraph is beyond the scope of a footnote. The meaning should be apparent, however: the portion of the brain that lies immediately beneath the electrodes during ECT is subjected to an especially intense current, not only due to the proximity of the electrodes, but due to the thinness of the skull at this point. In addition, this portion of the brain is particularly susceptible to electrical disruption, and damage to it is known to produce extremely severe memory loss.

evaluated the various aspects of the administration of electricity that influence the amount of damage done, but they include wave form (A.C. producing more damage than D.C., and higher peaks producing more damage than flatter curves), total electrical energy administered, peak electrical energy administered, and duration of administration (Chusid & Pacella, 1952; Bayles et al., 1950; Liberson, 1949; Voris, 1962). The typical measurement quoted in the literature is voltage, but this is a poor indicator. The next most frequent variable mentioned is amperage, which is a far better but imperfect indicator. All this is complicated by the fact that most studies give the manufacturer's specifications, which may not be accurate (Davies et al., 1971).

Cerletti (1954) used a sinusoidal alternating current of 110 v—approximately house current—for 0.2 sec to produce the first recorded ECT. It is estimated that these early machines delivered between 450 and 800 ma of current (D. Goldman, 1961). Kalinowsky and Hippius (1969) and Volavka (1972) have confirmed that the technology of many of the machines has changed little over the years. Indeed, over the years Kalinowsky, in his major reviews, has seen little advantage in modern electrical modification. An examination of earlier and later editions of other ECT textbooks confirms that the basic electrical stimulus in many clinical projects has not changed much since Cerletti's day (Kolb, 1977). Kalinowsky (1975a) continues to advocate an alternating current of 70 to 130 v for 0.1 to 0.5 sec, and Kalinowsky and Hippius (1969), as well as Hurwitz (1974), confirm that the intensity of the stimulus remains in the same wide range of 200 to 1,600 ma.

A further scanning of individual studies in the literature indicates that many of the most modern ones exceed the voltage, amperage, and duration of stimulus in earlier studies. Here are some typical recent voltage and duration figures that exceed the range estimated by Kalinowsky: I. F. Small (1974), 110 to 150 v, 0.3 to 0.6 sec; Squire, Slater, and Chace (1975), 140 to 160 v, 0.5 to 0.75 sec; Bridenbaugh et al. (1972), 140 v, 1.0 sec; Berent et al. (1975) 150 v, 0.3 to 0.6 sec. Amperage figures also appear in the same range as older clinical studies, with durations considerably beyond: Squire, Slater, and Chace (1975), 400 to 500 ma, 2 to 3 sec; Cronin et al. (1970), 400 ma, 2.5 sec; Strain et al. (1968), 500 to 600 ma, 2.0 sec; d'Elia and Raotma (1975), 800 ma, 2 to 6 sec; Stromgren (1973), 500 to 800 ma, up to 8 sec.

Davies et al. (1971) examined and tested two commonly used ECT machines, the Reuben Reiter MOL-AC II and the Medicraft Model B 24. The *minimum* deliverable stimulus with the Reuben Reiter was 360 ma for 0.750 sec. The voltage could be varied from 110 to 195. They noted that the use of a manual button to control the current duration made it exceedingly difficult to deliver a stimulus of short duration. On the other hand, the Medicraft Model B 24 could deliver a stimulus as low as 200 ma for 0.08 sec, but 500 ma for 0.1 second was required to produce a convulsion. The voltage varied from 70 to 170. There was no reason to believe that the machines were typically used in clinical practice at the extreme bottom of their range of stimulus intensity. Furthermore, one of the machines did not meet the manufacturer's specifications, but delivered a higher current (also see *Psychiatric News*, 1971).

The Food and Drug Administration of the U. S. Department of Health, Education and Welfare sponsored a study by the Utah Biomedical Test Laboratory (Grahn et al., 1977) to ascertain the safety and performance of ECT machines in current use (also see summary of these findings in Leflar and Wolfe, 1979, a report from Nader's Health Research Group). The Utah survey of existing machines found that up to 90 percent of the devices currently sold utilize the same 60 Hz sinewave as the original Cerletti ECT machine (p. 55). While the percentage of patients treated with these machines was not determined, it was found that some of the most frequently employed ECT devices were among those using the original and most damaging wave form. The Utah survey also found that many of the machines actually in use are obsolete, homemade, or lacking an important control apparatus found on the earlier machines. The report also noted that some machines depend upon an extremely difficult to control manual push button rather than an automatic timer for determining the duration of the electrical stimulus. The recent survey by the American Psychiatric Association (1978) disclosed that 69 percent of the psychiatrists administering ECT use the same electrical wave form as that produced by the original 1938 Cerletti device, a 60 Hz. bipolar sinewave.

Not only is the amount of electrical energy being delivered in modern clinical studies equal to or in excess of that delivered in the older clinical studies, but the amount of electrical energy delivered in modern times almost always exceeds that delivered in the animal research that has demonstrated brain damage from ECT. Using both voltage and amperage as criteria, the following typical animal studies fall below routine clinical doses: Alpers and Hughes (1942a), 110 v, 150 to 200 ma; Heilbrunn and Weil (1942), 60 to 150 v, 65 to 300 ma; Neuburger et al. (1942), 80 v, 200 ma; Ferraro, Roizen, and Helford (1946), 70 to 90 v, 102 to 400 ma. Hartelius (1952) also used electrical doses in the low range.

The majority of modern research and clinical projects employ electrical energies very similar to that delivered by the earliest ECT machines in clinical and animal research, and modern projects vary the stimulus within or above the duration employed in the earliest studies. One reason the increased current is required in modern ECT is the use of barbiturates, which raise the seizure threshold (Salzman et al., 1955; Kalinowsky, 1975b, p. 1971).

Convulsion as the Cause of Damage

Spontaneous major seizures as well as major seizures induced by artificial means cause an acute organic brain syndrome with residual amnesia qualitatively similar to ECT (Jessner & Ryan, 1941; Tooth & Blackburn, 1939). In addition, seizures induced by Metrazol and other early convulsive agents have been found to cause brain pathology similar to that produced by ECT (Jessner & Ryan, 1941; Cobb, 1938; Arieti, 1941). Furthermore, seizures induced by means other than electricity can produce widespread biochemical changes in the brain similar to those found after ECT (Essman, 1973; Lovell, 1971). EEG experts have compared the chronic brain wave changes after repeated ECT to those after repeated spontaneous convulsions in epileptics (D. Goldman, 1961; Bagchi et al. 1945; Weil & Brinegar, 1947; Mosovitch & Katzenelbogen, 1948; Roth & Garside, 1962; H. Goldman et al., 1972; Assael et al., 1967). Finally, eliminating the seizure while applying the same electrical stimulus can reduce some of the amnesic effects of ECT in animals (McGaugh, 1974; Hunt, 1965). All this evidence indicates that the seizure plays a significant role in producing damage and dysfunction with ECT.

Some evidence does suggest that the damage associated with inhalant-induced convulsions is less than that associated with ECT (Kafi et al., 1969; Fromholt et al., 1973; I.F. Small, 1974). Kalinowsky and Hippius (1969) strongly disagree with this position, however, claiming that post-ictal confusion is "at least as pronounced" after inhalant-induced seizures. Artificially induced seizures in Metrazol therapy and insulin coma treatment have been documented to produce even more severe damage than ECT (Arieti, 1941; Cobb, 1938; Jessner & Ryan, 1941).

Thus there is considerable evidence implicating the role of the seizure in producing the damage and dysfunction associated with ECT. But this evidence is less substantial and more difficult to interpret than evidence implicating the current. Spontaneous seizures by themselves are no longer believed to produce the kind or amount of brain damage seen following either traumatic electrical assaults on the brain or ECT and other psychiatrically induced seizures.

A vast literature did accumulate over the years suggesting that spontaneous convulsions cause brain damage, and some authorities still believe that this relates specifically to the damage done by ECT (Portnov & Fedotov, 1969). But modern expert opinion (Strauss, 1959; Merritt, 1973) and carefully conducted research (Hirsch & Martin, 1971; Sutherland et al., 1974), indicate that spontaneous convulsions in epileptics rarely if ever produce visible pathologic brain changes.

Some advocates of modified ECT believe that ECT damage is produced by the apnea and the subsequent lack of oxygenation to the brain, especially when vigorous convulsive movements of the body put an additional strain on oxygen stores and the cardiovascular system. Modifications of ECT, including artificial respiration and paralysis of the musculature, may reduce this form of oxygen deprivation and stress, but there is no reason to believe that apnea is the main source of stress or trauma. If apnea were a major cause, then epileptics, who frequently endure apnea, would display brain damage. Indeed, these modifications were not developed in order to reduce apnea and anoxia of the brain, which many, many ECT advocates regard favorably as a component of the ECT effect (see Chapter 9). These modifications were developed to reduce fractures during the muscular spasms (Salzman et al., 1955). Some well-known advocates of ECT continue to use unmodified ECT (Tien, 1974) without incurring censure within the community of electroshock proponents.

The severe electrical storm associated with major convulsions of all origins may be closely linked with the mechanism of damage (Meyer & Ericsson, 1972; Hartelius, 1952). This storm may deplete the energy stores of the brain to such a low point that brain cells deteriorate, and the isoelectric period of electrical inactivity that follows the convulsion may reflect such a point of deterioration. The convulsion also may produce areas of local vasoconstriction, reducing the supply of nutrients and oxygen.

Neurologist Robert Grimm has shown a particular concern about the effects of the convulsion during ECT. Even in the absence of empirical data, he has warned, clinicians should be loath to produce convulsions as a means of therapy. He finds it ironic that psychiatrists are willing to induce multiple convulsions in their patients while neurologists struggle to prevent even one spontaneous convulsion from taking place in an epileptic (1978):

> How is it that one group in medicine works to protect patients from fits, while another programs fits as therapy? Can both groups be right? Neurologists are trained from a literature and experience based on clinical and model epilepsy, none of which recommends breaching the intrinsic inhibitory mechanisms of brain with transcortical currents sufficient to trigger a convul-

sion. Instead, all therapeutic effort is aimed at protecting patients from spontaneous or evoked seizures for a combination of clinical, social, and practical reasons. To those who have had training in the complexity and differentiation of neuronal machinery, it hardly seems wise to drive brain above its convulsive threshold, and to do so crudely and repeatedly and on schedule. The organ gives every indication, in its acute biochemical and electrical response to ECT, that such evoked seizures are clearly traumatic and that a number of behavioral changes follow as a consequence.

As I conclude this section on the role of convulsions in producing brain damage during ECT, I find myself thinking about a young woman in my own practice who experienced a single spontaneous convulsion. With minimal evidence of a seizure disorder on EEG, respected neurologists immediately placed her on long-term medication in order to prevent a recurrence of even one convulsion. It is indeed ironic, as Grimm suggests, that one portion of the medical community treats a single spontaneous convulsion as a catastrophic occurrence while another segment of the medical community subjects patients to much more dangerous electrically induced convulsions with disregard for their harmful effects.

9

The Efficacy of ECT
in Depression and Suicide

Although there are hundreds of articles in the literature written in support of ECT by its advocates, there are very few studies that pass any kind of scientific muster. As in the literature already examined concerning brain damage and memory loss, literature cited in support of the effectiveness of the treatment often discredits it instead. Scholarly "reviews" that describe the efficacy of ECT in detail often fail to mention *any* corroborating studies, thus wholly relying on the authority of the writer (see Kalinowsky in *The American Handbook of Psychiatry*, 1959, 1975a).

In general the advocates of ECT focus on two indications for ECT: (1) serious depression (involutional melancholia or psychotic depression and manic-depressive disorder, depressed phase); and (2) potential suicide. Many advocates of ECT still would agree with Newton Bigelow (1959) in his analysis of "The Involutional Psychoses," when he averred, "electric shock therapy has transformed the entire outlook (and therapeutic plan) for this disorder." He claimed a 90 percent remission rate for ECT in severe depression, and stated that it had vastly decreased the threat of suicide.

Those who claim great efficacy for the treatment in regard to other disorders, such as schizophrenia, are on controversial ground even among ECT advocates. Therefore, in order to give ECT the benefit of the doubt, I will focus on the two most highly recommended uses of ECT: depression and suicide. In this section I will not deal with questions such as, "What is efficacy?" or "On what basis do we evaluate psychiatric treatment?" That will require a separate analysis of what I call mind-disabling therapy. Here I will evaluate the major ECT studies within their own value system and viewpoint to see if they prove their case in their own terms.

The two most widely quoted studies indicating the efficacy of ECT took place in the United States and in Great Britain. Milton Greenblatt, the senior author of the American study, summarized the American and English studies in 1977 as if they unequivocally had demonstrated the value and efficacy of ECT.

The American study was published in a series of articles, and data varied somewhat from publication to publication. It consisted of more than 200 patients, predominantly women by a ratio of 3:1. The investigators attempted to establish a double-blind,[1] but admittedly could not disguise which patients were receiving ECT (Greenblatt et al., 1966), so that evaluator bias could not be counted out. What was remarkable, however, was not the inadequacy of the study, but the data, which indicated that the safest, most remarkable therapy in psychiatry is not ECT but *placebo*. In 1964, using "marked improvement" as a standard, ECT was rated as 80 percent effective and placebo as 50 percent effective (Greenblatt et al., 1964). In 1977 Greenblatt used lower standards, and the figures for improvement were 92.9 percent for ECT and 64.2 percent for placebo.

Even if the differences were real, the safer, cheaper placebo proved to be the treatment of choice, at least initially. But a number of more startling facts appeared in the 1966 data. Using discharge and successful functioning outside the hospital as the criteria for "marked improvement," the study showed that placebo did statistically as well as two of the most commonly used antidepressants, and outperformed a third. In overall performance, according to clinical ratings, it ran behind ECT, 76.1 percent to 44.4 percent. When the figures are broken down for men and women, however, an interesting fact emerges. The ECT-placebo gap closed for men, with only 74 percent of the men "markedly improved" after ECT, and 56 percent after placebo. The implication was clear: when a true double blind was at work in comparing the four "pills"—placebo and the three antidepressants—placebo performed as well or better than the usual psychiatric treatments. When no true control was possible,

---

1. A *double-blind* experiment or clinical investigation attempts to prevent the subjects and the investigators from knowing which kind of treatment is being given each subject. The purpose is to avoid bias on the part of both subject and investigator. Obviously, it is impossible to hide from the ECT patient that he or she is undergoing a drastic therapeutic intervention expected to have a great impact. It is also impossible to hide from the investigator which patient is receiving ECT if the investigator has direct contact with the patient. The acute organic brain syndrome is an immediate giveaway.

clinical evaluations by psychiatrists gave ECT something of an edge over placebo.

The edge, however, was not overwhelming. Although ECT was found somewhat more effective in an overall statistical analysis based on the evaluations of the psychiatrists, when the study is broken down by diagnostic categories, ECT and placebo were *equally effective* in *all* diagnostic categories, including manic-depressive and involutional psychotic disorders. That is, the advantage of ECT over placebo was so slight that it disappeared when compared category by category.

Overall it can be said that in the double-blind portion of the project —using the criteria of marked improvement—placebo was as good as or better than any antidepressant, and in comparison to ECT it ran close overall and was just as good when compared by individual diagnostic categories.

In his review, Greenblatt warned about tardive dyskinesia[2] following even short-term phenothiazine administration, and he encouraged greater use of ECT. Considering that ECT can cause fatalities, brain damage, and other serious side effects, he should rather have encouraged greater use of *placebos*!

The second most frequently cited study was developed by a select committee and published in the *British Medical Journal* in 1965 (Clinical Psychiatric Committee). Typically, it included 169 women and 81 men. As in the American series, the impressive data relate to the ECT-placebo comparison. For women ECT outperformed placebo by a wide margin, but for men ECT and placebo *were equally effective.* Forty-one percent of the men were discharged after treatment with placebo, 38 percent after ECT. The authors promoted the study as a whole-hearted endorsement for ECT, without commenting on its inability to outperform placebo in depressed men. If the study is to be taken seriously, it must be used only as proof that ECT is effective for women but not effective for men.

The American Psychiatric Association report (1978) freely admits that there is a lack of controlled studies of ECT and cites the Greenblatt and the Clinical Psychiatric Committee investigations as the best and most important in the literature. It makes important omissions in summarizing these studies: for example, it fails to report the marvelous performance of placebo in the Greenblatt studies and fails to report that

---

2. *Tardive dyskinesia* is a serious, iatrogenic neurologic disorder consisting of various tics and spasms, which may follow the administration of the so-called major tranquilizers or phenothiazines. Most, if not all, cases are irreversible. While the major tranquilizers are considered more specific for schizophrenia than for depression, they are in reality given to most psychiatric in-patients, regardless of diagnosis (Breggin, 1979), and therefore are frequently used in cases of depression that Greenblatt believes would better be treated with ECT.

ECT was wholly ineffective in men in the Clinical Psychiatric Committee study.

The American Psychiatric Association report does admit one grave conclusion from the ECT literature:

> In addition, data are sparse in several areas including long-term effects of ECT on natural history and maintenance studies. In regard to the former, little evidence was found to suggest that ECT alters the long-term course, or natural history of affective illness. Like the antidepressant medications, its effect appears limited to a reduction of symptoms of the illness. (pp. 18–19)

In other words, the treatment has no effect on either the recurrence of depression or upon the underlying disorder itself. The essential "illness" or the depression itself is unaffected, and only the "symptoms" or the apparent signs of the disorder are temporarily modified, while the "long-term course" remains unchanged. Considering the controversy surrounding the treatment, and the evidence that it produces brain damage, this is a remarkable admission from a group whose purpose is advocacy of the treatment.

Beyond these two major studies, we must choose somewhat haphazardly among dozens of studies of varying quality that are cited as evidence for the effectiveness of ECT. None possesses much scientific merit.

Ziskind et al. (1945) published one of the earliest reports cited in the modern literature as evidence that ECT prevents suicide. Fink (1977) has summarized it as follows: "Another study reported nine deaths in 109 patients treated by psychotherapy alone compared with one death in 88 patients treated with ECT." Fink's description is wholly in error. Only 30 patients were treated with ECT; the remaining 58 patients received Metrazol therapy. Because no distinction was made in the findings between the ECT group and the Metrazol group, which had almost twice as many patients, there is no way to use this study to prove *anything* about ECT. Furthermore, the control group with the high suicide rate received *no treatment,* not psychotherapy. Still more important, the control was not a control; it was made up of individuals who were too physically ill to receive ECT or Metrazol and individuals who refused or were deemed inappropriate candidates for ECT or Metrazol. Whereas all the ECT- and Metrazol-treated patients were in the hospital, 30 percent of the alleged controls were not even hospitalized, and thus had greater opportunity to attempt suicide. There is no basis whatsoever for assuming the suicide rate in the two groups would have been comparable without ECT.

The control group showed more improvement than the treated group. The authors of the study did take the control group seriously, and therefore concluded that ECT has no effect on depression, but only on suicide. All in all, this is a relatively useless study except for one point. The 88 treated patients had one death by suicide and two deaths directly attributable to the convulsive therapy, for a death rate of more than 3 percent. This study may be an indictment of the dangerousness of "convulsive therapy," but tells us nothing specific about ECT.

Another well-known early study, published by Huston and Locher in 1948, compared a group of patients treated with ECT between 1941 and 1943 with a group of "controls" treated in the hospital between 1930 and 1938, before the advent of ECT. There is no way to compare groups from such different periods of time. Merely considering the changes in psychiatric hospital environment brought about by Metrazol, insulin, ECT, and lobotomy during that time rules out any comparison. Furthermore, the control group was about evenly mixed between men and women, whereas the ECT group had almost twice as many women. Because women much more often than men are evaluated as improved after electroconvulsive treatment, there was a serious bias to the experimental group. Nonetheless, the authors were forced to conclude, "the rate for complete recovery in the shock group was about the same as that for the spontaneous recovery in the control group" with figures of 88 percent and 79 percent. Why then has the study been cited as evidence of the efficacy of ECT (Allen, 1978)? It is cited because the experimental group allegedly had a shorter depression, nine months versus 15 months. Even if such a comparison could be made objectively with a retrospective "control" group, the vast differences in psychiatric hospitalization between 1930 to 1938 and 1941 to 1943 could certainly account for such a difference. So could any number of other unknown factors that may have intervened over the years, for more than a decade separated the hospital admissions of some of the controls and some of the ECT patients. These variables would be especially important in regard to one other factor for which this study is cited—the greater suicide rate in the control population than the ECT population. No mention is made of the difference in the suicide rate in the general population between the periods 1930 to 1938 and 1941 to 1943, brought about by the effect of the Great Depression on the suicide rate compared to the more prosperous, wartime 1940s (Henry and Short, 1954). All that can be truly said of this study is that it used controls that were wholly inadequate, and that under those conditions ECT was no better than no treatment at all.

Still in the era of unmodified ECT, Miller and Clancy (1953) published another frequently cited study. This study used a control group and did demonstrate that by certain criteria the ECT patients were "better": They were more cooperative and manageable on the ward. But their psychotic symptoms worsened, and "all 30 were demonstrably hallucinating at the end of the experiment." ECT made the patients more manageable but much more psychotic. The authors noted that ECT drastically frightened the patients, suggesting a possible reason why the patients became easier to manage.

Ulett et al. (1956) attempted to provide satisfactory controls for a study of unmodified ECT, including simulated ECT with sedation. But the major improvements were seen with a unique convulsive combination of photoelectric and chemical stimulation no longer in use. The regular ECT group showed only 33.3 percent marked improvement, compared to 23.8 percent for the controls. A further breakdown of the data shows that of the seven markedly improved ECT patients, two relapsed and two "regressed somewhat," whereas of the five markedly improved control-group patients the four who could be located remained fully recovered. On this basis the control group literally outperformed the ECT group on follow-up. As in so many other ECT studies, one must look beyond the authorities who cite the study (Fink, 1977) and even beyond the conclusions of the investigators.

Probably the best-controlled study of ECT in the modern era was published by Brill et al. in 1959. It compared the effects of four treatments: unmodified ECT, modified ECT, ECT with a sedative, and nitrous oxide. The study also included a "simulated ECT" group whose members were rendered unconscious with sedative alone and no other treatment. Multiple batteries of psychological tests were used to evaluate the outcomes, as well as psychiatric evaluations and ratings. The results of this best-controlled study were startling. The tests and clinical evaluations indicated that all treatment modalities, including simulated ECT, brought about an improvement, and all were equal in effectiveness, including simulated ECT. One-third of the patients in the study were diagnosed depressed, $2/3$ schizophrenic, and no difference in improvement rate was noted between those diagnosed as schizophrenic or depressed. The study clearly disproved claims for the efficacy of ECT for schizophrenia and depression.

Another relatively well-controlled study in the modern era is frequently cited in support of ECT (Allen, 1978; Fink, 1977), and indeed the authors' summary and conclusions seem to support the claim. Avery and Winokur (1976) followed 519 ECT patients from 1959 through 1969 and discovered that they had a lower "mortality rate" than a group treated with antidepressants and an untreated group. In particular, the ECT group had far fewer deaths from myocardial infarction. This is indeed an interesting but unexplained finding. Few cardiologists would leap to the conclusion that ECT should be administered prophylactically for the prevention of heart disease. Data more relevant to the ECT controversy are virtually ignored. The project also examined the suicide rate; the authors noted, almost in passing, "In the present study, treatment was not shown to affect the suicide rate." The study *disproved* the hypothesis that ECT reduces suicide.

Given that Avery and Winokur specifically demonstrated that ECT has *no effect on the suicide rate,* one wonders how a modern advocate of ECT managed to represent the study in exactly the opposite fashion in the opening paragraph of a lengthy article (Allen, 1978): ". . . Avery and Winokur showed that *suicide mortality* in patients afflicted with psychotic depression was lower in patients treated with ECT than in those who were not" (italics added). Perhaps it was wishful thinking. Perhaps it came from reliance on other authorities such as Fink (1977), who cited the study immediately after a paragraph on suicide without specifically stating that a lower "fatality" rate did not mean a lower *suicide* rate. The misleading nature of Fink's citation was recently confirmed when an advocate of ECT in a radio discussion with me cited Avery and Winokur as proof that ECT lowers the suicide rate. When challenged on whether he had read the study himself, he admitted that he was basing his citation of the study wholly on Fink's article.

Advocates of ECT often write as if ECT has proven efficacy in regard to suicide. With the exception of a couple of very inadequate studies dating back to the 1940s, there is *no evidence at all* that ECT reduces the suicide rate. Instead, as Eastwood and Peakcocke (1976) noted in a recent epidemiological study, ". . . the effect of ECT upon the suicide rate has not been demonstrated although ECT has existed for almost forty years."

Costello et al. (1970) also failed to demonstrate a therapeutic effect following ECT, and noted that changes reported by others were insubstantial or explicable in other terms: "These changes might simply occur with the passage of time. One certainly has to be suspicious about the claim that ECT has therapeutic value. . . ." Their conclusion is as appropriate today as it was in 1970:

> It is a pity that despite the clinical conviction of the therapeutic
> efficacy of ECT there are no sound data to substantiate this
> conviction. Mental health professionals would appear to have a
> serious responsibility to evaluate this method of treatment
> properly if its continued use is intended.

Regardless of the data, ECT advocates nonetheless remain staunchly adamant that the abandonment of ECT would withdraw a lifesaving intervention from the suicidal patient. The argument falls apart not only for lack of data, but for lack of support in the experience of those many psychiatrists and hospitals that never use ECT. As discussed in detail in Chapter 1, many large state hospitals with desperately unhappy and suicidal patients *never* use ECT. To justify their claims, ECT advocates must find an explanation for why their fears have not proved true in institutions that never use ECT and among psychiatrists who never refer patients for the treatment, or they must prove that these institutions and these psychiatrists do indeed have higher suicide rates (also see Chapter 13).

The average practitioner of ECT undoubtedly relies on "clinical impressions" to justify its usage, regardless of the presence or absence of scientific research to support the position. Clinical impressions have been the main justification for most somatic therapies in psychiatry throughout history, from the straightforward assaults to the body throughout the first 300 years (Kraepelin, 1962) to the more sophisticated techniques for disrupting the brain developed during the 1930s, including Metrazol convulsions, insulin coma, ECT, and lobotomy.

The notorious unreliability of clinical impressions brings to mind two reports dealing with the placebo effect in psychiatry. In the first report (Guido & Jones, 1961) the placebo effect was active in regard to the patient only, but in the second (Jones, 1974) it was active in regard to *everyone* involved in the treatment.

Guido and Jones described the effect of sham ECT on a patient who came to the hospital demanding the treatment. He was thought to be a poor candidate for ECT, and was eventually given succinylcholine to cause muscle paralysis, oxygen and a minimal nonconvulsive, nontraumatic current of 15 v, 5 ma. Awake throughout the treatment, he mimicked the convulsions he'd seen in other patients and even faked some aspects of the acute organic brain syndrome, becoming progressively more confused after each treatment. Finally he asked for an end to the treatment and for release from the hospital. On follow-up, he was doing well.

The second, more informal, report deals with a truly "double-blind" experiment—one conducted by accident without the knowledge of any of the participants that anything unusual was taking place. Jones described in *World Medicine* in 1974 how a new ECT machine had been used for *two years* before it was discovered by chance that it was nonfunctional. During that two-year period nothing unusual was noticed by the doctors, the nurses, or anyone else on the ward. Even the referring doctors made no complaints about the procedure. Here is Jones' somewhat theatrical description of this ludicrous and yet enlightening occurrence:

> We started treatment, the patient did not twitch, although the red light went on and the needle moved, "Isn't it working?" I said.

"Yes, it is," said the nurse, "this sort doesn't give any reaction—it's in the instructions."

I duly read the instructions and indeed "there should be minimal signs of any seizure with this apparatus."

We used the apparatus for two years with no complaints from the patients and although I did not actually see any consultants, apparently they were satisfied with my work.

But on a never-to-be-forgotten day a new charge nurse appeared. After the third treatment, he said, "It's not working."

"Oh yes it is, this kind does not cause any twitching."

"Look, I've just come from a hospital with one just like this and they twitch all right."

We examined this one closely . . . he was right. All the patients had been getting for two years was thiopentone and a shot of Scoline—and no one had noticed.

By conventional standards it is not difficult to criticize the ECT literature cited in support of its efficacy. One must merely list a few reasonable criteria for scientific research—control groups, unbiased observers and reporters, an intelligent consideration of all alternatives, a fair presentation of the data—and nearly all the studies fail. Even taking major studies at face value, they give more support to harmless placebo than to risky ECT!

It is also important to reaffirm that most and probably all the positive ECT studies have been conducted by psychiatrists who have spent much of their professional lives publicizing and defending the somatic treatments, including insulin coma, lobotomy, and ECT. This bias appears throughout their papers, even in the presentation of their data. The best-known American study, by Greenblatt and his colleagues (1966), summarized their own data in an awkward, difficult-to-follow fashion, carefully concealing the conclusion that the harmless, inexpensive placebo was the hero of the day. Similarly, in describing the English study, Greenblatt (1977) reported that women did better than men, without specifically pointing out that the men did not do well at all—no better on ECT than on placebo. The English study itself (Clinical Psychiatric Committee, 1965) distorted its true meaning in its conclusions, failing to mention that the study would have supported the use of ECT for women while negating its use for men.

Considering the well-known bias of most of the investigators, it is astonishing that the studies have produced no better results than they have. It is impossible to use adequate double-blind techniques, because ECT patients suffer from an acute organic brain syndrome, giving full play to subjective interpretation of the results; yet, even under these conditions, ECT has proved itself anything but the 90 to 100 percent miracle cure for depression described by its advocates.

Positive studies have failed to consider the full importance of suggestion and spontaneous cure. It is well known that depression tends to cure spontaneously, as several of the controlled studies prove. It is also well known that any interest and attention shown to depressed patients is likely to perk them up. In this regard the relative advantage of ECT over placebo in some studies easily could be accounted for in terms of ECT as the "more powerful placebo." A patient being given ECT knows that something potent has been done to him! Yet sugar pills worked nearly as well or as well in several studies.

These studies also failed to consider the importance of fear and intimidation, although several mentioned that the patients were terrified of the treatment. Ulett et al. (1956) tried to discount fear on the grounds that the patients were sedated before treatment and therefore unafraid, but, as Chapter 11 will show, the fear develops independently of all modifications. Because the criterion for "improvement" is leaving the hospital, one might postulate a far higher success rate if the patients had simply been informed, "If you don't get well and leave, we will give you ECT." In reality, just such a factor does operate in hospitals in which some of the doctors are against the treatment. When staff meetings or administrators who favor ECT begin pushing for it, the doctors who are against it urge their patients to leave (Breggin, 1964; Pollack & Fink, 1961). Almost all patients on ECT grow terrified of it, so it is no wonder that they want to leave. I believe they would leave faster if the treatment did not so thoroughly disrupt initiative (Chapter 10).

The studies also failed to account for two extremely provocative facts, first, that women are the main target population by 2:1 or 3:1, and, second, that women are usually judged to benefit more than men from ECT (see Chapter 12).

Finally, it should be recalled that the data I have been examining have focused largely on ECT with severe (usually psychotic) depression and suicide. The case for ECT with individuals diagnosed as schizo-phrenic or neurotic is even weaker, so much so that many advocates of ECT do not recommend it in such cases. Yet large numbers of individuals with these diagnoses are given ECT (see Chapter 1).

I believe that ECT has a very specific and powerful effect on the individual, one that reaches beyond placebo and beyond intimidation. The effect is physiological in origin but has vast psychological and ethi-cal implications. It is of such importance that I want to examine it in depth under the rubric of "mind-disabling therapy" in the following chapters.

10

ECT as Brain-Disabling Therapy: Historical Perspective

Psychiatrists who advocate the use of convulsive and shock therapies have discussed the question "Why do they work?" from the earliest days, when spontaneous convulsions were thought to have an ameliorating effect on schizophrenia. Although that theory has been discarded, no other has consistently replaced it. Brain damage was thought to be a crucial component of the therapy by many pioneer authorities, but most advocates of ECT now take the position that it causes no harm to the brain and that the treatment is purely empirical with no known scientific or theoretical relationale (E. Miller, 1967; Kalinowsky & Hippius, 1969). They fail to confront the reality that ECT causes such significant brain dysfunction and damage that this impairment must logically constitute its overwhelming effect. This is what I call the brain-disabling hypothesis—that ECT produces its primary effect precisely through the dysfunction and damage it inflicts on the normal brain and hence on the mind.

An organically disabled person is a more *helpless* person. As such he is often less troublesome to others. He usually but not always complains less about himself and his life situation; in many instances, the acute organic brain syndrome may include an irrational euphoria that masquerades as "improvement." Ultimately the brain-disabled person is more manageable, docile, or tractable.

When focusing on the brain-damaging aspect of somatic therapy, I will speak of the brain-disabling hypothesis, and when focusing on the mental consequences of this incapacitation, I will speak of the mind-disabling hypothesis. The two are inextricably linked, however, and the choice of one or another term largely depends on the type of phenomenon being examined—physical or mental, organic or psychological. Often I will use one or the other to refer to both.

Somatic Treatment and the Mental Hospital

Throughout the western world in the 1930s the state mental hospitals were becoming increasingly crowded and difficult to manage. Conditions were comparable to concentration camps, with hundreds of difficult, unruly inmates jammed into the narrow corridors of state hospital wards (Bockoven, 1963; Deutsch, 1949, 1948; Kraepelin, 1962). Even for individuals with considerably more personal strength than the typical mental patient, physical and moral survival in these prison-like institutions would have been difficult. Violence was commonplace, privacy was unheard of, occupational or recreational opportunities were almost unknown, a normal sexual life was impossible, basic sanitary provisions were neglected, and the diet was often insufficient to ward off vitamin-deficiency diseases. The very low-paid ward personnel who dealt with the patients were frequently frustrated and brutal, but even had they been moral giants they would have been hard pressed to deal with such a situation without inuring themselves to the use of violence. Indeed, the imposition of police control was the overriding concern of the administrators (Bockoven, 1963, Breggin, 1974, 1975c).

Because of conditions in these institutions, the people admitted to them usually deteriorated over the years, much as did the inmates of concentration camps. Increasing admissions to the hospitals were not compensated for by increasing discharges. The result was disastrous, as facilities and people alike continued to deteriorate from year to year.

The psychiatrists in charge of the institutions meanwhile rationalized the state of their patients by theorizing that they suffered from degenerative diseases that brought about their dilapidation and often their premature demise while confined (Bockoven, 1963). Given such oppressive conditions and such a bleak theory, it became easy to justify a variety of physically damaging interventions to compel the patients to conform to institutional life (Breggin, 1974, 1975c). Against this background the psychiatric technologies of the 1930s were developed—the convulsive therapies and lobotomy. It was against this *continuing* background in the 1950s that the major tranquilizers were developed (Breggin, 1979).

Psychiatrists had used a variety of aggressive measures to control mental patients during the three centuries of the state mental hospital system; but the 1930s saw a new approach in technology. In previous years assaults on the patients had been largely directed at the whole body rather than the brain. Patients were whipped, strapped into spinning chairs, dunked into cold water, poisoned with toxic agents, bled, placed in straitjackets, and thrown into solitary confinement (Kraepelin, 1962). But with the third decade of the twentieth century, psychiatrists discovered it was more efficient to attack the brain directly. The major breakthrough took place in 1928, when Sakel (1938), the inventor of insulin coma therapy, first discovered that addicts accidentally overdosed with insulin became more docile and more manageable. The widespread acceptance of insulin coma therapy in the 1930s paved the way for a variety of brain-damaging convulsive therapies, and ultimately for direct surgical destruction of the highest centers of the brain (lobotomy).

"Shock" as Brain-Disabling Therapy

Before the advent of ECT, two other so-called shock therapies dominated hospital treatment: Metrazol therapy, in which convulsions are produced by the injection of a highly toxic central nervous system stimulant, and insulin coma therapy, in which coma and often convulsions are produced by lowering the blood sugar.* By 1941 the definitive text, Jessner and Ryan's *Shock Treatment in Psychiatry,* observed that both therapies often produced central nervous system death or permanent brain damage. The authors took the view "It is possible that a certain amount of brain damage is of therapeutic value."

Hans Hoff (1959), an international advocate of insulin coma therapy, believed that insulin shock therapy "has to be done by the destruction of cells."

> . . . cells that are sick, and new cells which are potentially sick have to be destroyed. Otherwise relapses will come. This means that one of the most important things is to see that really every cell which is affected is really destroyed.

Meduna, the inventor of Metrazol injection as a convulsive therapy, openly admitted that he first demonstrated the severely toxic effect of convulsants on the brain tissue of guinea pigs before he began treating human beings (1939). Arieti (1941) confirmed severe pathological changes in a variety of human organs following Metrazol therapy, with

---

* I have a firsthand report in 1979 that at least one group of psychiatrists in a major city in the United States continues to use insulin coma. There is no way to know how many others may also be doing so on a clandestine basis.

the qualification that such changes were not "always" present in the brain.

By 1938, the year in which Bini and Cerletti first used electric current to produce convulsions in human beings, psychiatric authorities throughout the world openly recognized that the most modern psychiatric treatments—the convulsive therapies—frequently produced brain damage. Stanley Cobb (1938), Bullard professor of neuropathology emeritus at Harvard and former psychiatrist-in-chief at the Massachusetts General Hospital, wrote about insulin and Metrazol shock in the *Archives of Internal Medicine:*

> Many, although not all, animal experiments have shown that extensive damage, usually accompanied by multiple areas of hemorrhage, may occur with both types of therapy; and in a certain number of patients dying from these treatments, comparable lesions have been observed.

Cobb concluded, "Such evidence makes me believe that the therapeutic effect of insulin and Metrazol may be due to the destruction of great numbers of nerve cells in the cerebral cortex. This destruction is irreparable." He warned against the excessive use of these therapies, without condemning them, and he advocated experimental biopsy of the brains of mental patients to test the damaging effects of convulsive therapy. He justified this by judging biopsy to be less harmful than the therapy:

> . . . there is no reason to suppose that removal of biopsy specimens from the cortex does any harm to cerebral function. In fact, I think it is a less harmful procedure than the production of one therapeutic convulsion.

The tenor of the times was illustrated in an unsigned report in *Science News Letter* in 1938 entitled "Shocks of Many Kinds Are Useful Against Mental Ills," in which the director of the New York Psychiatric Institute, N. D. C. Lewis, was cited as believing, "Shock appears to be a cure for dementia praecox in some cases regardless of the agent producing the disturbance to the nervous system." Lewis had reported a cure in one patient who nearly died of snake bite, and in another who recovered consciousness and sanity after "a terrific blow over the head with an ax handle." This brief but pithy report concludes "scientists cannot afford to overlook a single avenue of approach."

Still in the year in which ECT was invented, psychiatric historian Diethelm (1938) examined the many precedents for employing physically damaging and toxic therapies in psychiatry, including the use of bleeding, bromide intoxication, and cyanide poisoning. He was somewhat critical of these measures, but praised experimentation with newer techniques aimed at producing coma and convulsion, including carbon dioxide inhalation to the point of extreme hypoxia and collapse, and insulin shock. He looked forward to the development of a "superior method of producing anoxemia," or anoxia. He did show relief that one treatment had been abandoned: cold water immersion and "extraordinary therapeutic exposure to excessive temperature changes." But as a direct result of enthusiasm over the shock and convulsive therapies, the freezing of mental patients for experimental purposes and as a shock therapy would soon be resumed.

In keeping with Diethelm's expectations, a wide variety of extreme measures were being used to reduce patients to a state of neurological collapse on the grounds that shock and anoxia were good for mental patients. H.E. Himwich was among the leaders in this field. In 1938 he and his colleagues described repeatedly inducing "intense" anoxia in mental patients by forcing them to breathe nitrogen until they collapsed in a state of cyanotic asphyxia with "opisthotonos,[1] convulsive jerkings and extension and torsion spasms. . . ." As late as 1952, Himwich, Kalinowsky, and Stone continued to promote anoxia as therapy, and a discussant, Warren S. McCulloch, described "a series of over sixty patients whom we decerebrated[2] ten times with sodium cyanide."

So-called "heroic" experiments in producing anoxia, coma, and convulsion flourished into the 1940s (Bowman, 1942). Many of them seemed far more radical and dangerous than ECT and helped maintain an attitude of indifference or even enthusiasm toward ECT-induced brain damage. Perhaps the most startling experiments involved the freezing of mental patients into a state of nearly fatal coma by packing them in ice or more modern refrigerants. The innovators in this field, Harvard psychiatrists Talbott and Tillotson, introduced their research in 1941 by relating it directly to the precedent of producing "profound alterations" in the nervous system of mental patients by means of shock treatment:

> We have become accustomed in recent years to think of the treatment of mental disorders in terms of procedures which produce profound alterations of the internal environment of the body. Insulin and metrazol therapy are examples which have contributed to the establishment of an unequivocal precedent.

---

1. *Opisthotonus* is a total body spasm in which the upper and lower portions of the body arch backward. It indicates severe neurologic dysfunction and is totally incapacitating.

2. *Decerebration* is literally removal of the brain from its functional relationship to the body, as by severing the nerve connections between brain and body. It is done for experimental purposes in animal research. That McCulloch decerebrated his patients probably means that he poisoned them until their obliterated cerebral function mimicked laboratory animals with nonfunctional brains.

Both are classified as shock treatments, in part at least, because
they are accompanied by demonstrable morphologic changes in
the central nervous system, as well as in other parts of the
body. . . .

The patients were refrigerated to lower their body temperatures
from 10 to 20 degrees, with the production of deep coma. One patient
died, but the therapy was highly recommended. Their patients had become "less combative" and "more cooperative" after the experience.

Goldman and Murray (1943) followed with research involving 16
patients. Two died of pneumonia and another of an undetermined cause,
and the investigators concluded that the therapy should be abandoned.
Spradly and Martin-Foucher nonetheless continued freezing experiments
in 1949 in Trenton State Hospital, noting that Talbott and Tillotson had
originally used the treatment on "mute, aggressive, combative and uncooperative patients." Although they lamented the corresponding Nazi
research as inhumane, they nonetheless drew on classified Nuremberg
documents on Nazi freezing experiments in the development of their own
work. Surprisingly, perhaps, reports on freezing mental patients continued to appear in 1957 (Hoen, Morello, & O'Neil) and in 1960 (Fisher &
Greiner).

ECT as Brain-Disabling Therapy

Given the commonly held theory that severe brain dysfunction and even
damage provided the therapeutic effect in the various shock and convulsive therapies, it is not surprising that the co-inventor of ECT, Bini,
espoused the brain-disabling hypothesis in 1938 in the very first English-
language publication concerning the use of electricity in inducing convulsions in animals. This report was widely available through its presentation at an international psychiatric congress and through its publication
in a supplement to *The American Journal of Psychiatry,* so it is surprising that modern-day advocates of ECT claim that Bini and Cerletti first
proved the harmlessness of ECT in animals before applying it to humans. As Bini carefully documented, he and Cerletti had experimented
with oral-anal electrode placement in dogs. Although Cerletti (1950)
later explained that this method produced milder damage than the usual
bilateral head electrode placement, Bini reported that they found
"widespread and severe" and "reversible and irreversible" alterations in
the nervous system. Bini asserted, "the importance of the alterations we
have met with thus far in our animals does not permit us to exclude the
possibility of applying these physical methods in human therapy." He

pointed out that animals subjected to insulin coma had the same "very severe and irreversible" pathology, and that, "These very alterations may be responsible for the favorable transformation of the morbid picture of schizophrenia." In other words, Bini was *encouraged* by the finding of severe, permanent brain damage in electrically convulsed dogs, because it mimicked the effect of insulin coma and was consistent with the prevalent concept that brain damage was the therapeutic agent in the convulsive therapies.

Still early in the history of ECT, A. Kennedy (1940) reviewed evidence indicating that the convulsive therapies killed brain cells. Displaying no qualms about utilizing such a treatment, he suggested:

> The question thus arises as to whether the patient secures his re-adaptation to normal life at the expense of a permanent lowering of functional efficiency. He may, in the language of chess, be sacrificing a piece to win the game.

Kennedy's analogy to chess utterly disregarded the further question, "Who makes this decision?" implying by default that it was up to the medical expert to evaluate the appropriateness of this sacrifice for the patient.

A year later, in Jessner and Ryan's *Shock Treatment in Psychiatry* (1941), Harry Solomon's introduction acknowledged that convulsive treatments produced memory loss and brain wave changes in humans, and evidence of "cerebral cellular damage and vascular injury" in animals. He directly connected the relief of depression with signs of an acute organic brain syndrome: "Following convulsive therapy, depressed patients become euphoric and mildly hypomanic." Long before the most definitive research, the textbook itself cited evidence that ECT produced severe changes in the central nervous system, including "capillary hemorrhage, ganglion cell changes, consisting of swelling and shrinkage, satellitosis, gliosis and demyelinization." Authorities were quoted who correlated brain damage with the cure.

Throughout his long career, which spanned the 1930s to the early 1970s, Walter Freeman advocated the thesis that brain damage and reduced mental function are good for mental patients. His books and articles are replete with vivid, detailed discussions of how psychosurgery brings about its therapeutic effect by "smashing the fantasy life," blunting the emotions, destroying abstract reasoning, and rendering the individual more robot-like and controllable. That his views were not considered bizarre is reflected in his position as professor at the George Washington University Medical School and as president of the District of Columbia Medical Society. In 1941, during the era in which electroshock was achieving its popularity, Freeman was given space in *Diseases of the Nervous System* to publish an editorial comment whose title, "Brain-Damaging Therapeutics," might have been chosen for this book as well. In his opening paragraph, Freeman observed, "Among the explanations advanced to account for the success of the various shock methods of therapy in the psychoses, that of actual damage to the brain has not received adequate attention."

Freeman's concluding comments are worth careful reading, for, appearing as they did in a widely read psychiatric journal, they indicate the degree to which the "brain damage is good" thesis was acceptable to the psychiatric community:

> Before the shock methods were introduced, occasional satisfactory therapeutic results were obtained by the use of barbital narcosis, sodium amytal injections, and carbon dioxide inhalations. All of these substances have been found to reduce the oxidative processes in brain tissue. Most spectacular was the original observation of Lorenz and Loevenhart that, upon intravenous injection of sodium cyanide into a catatonic patient, the individual awakened from his trance-like state and talked for the first time in months.
>
> All of the above-mentioned methods are damaging to the brain, but for the most part, the damage is either slight or temporary. *The apparent paradox develops, however, that the greater the damage, the more likely the remission of psychotic symptoms.* Surpassing the shock methods in terms of demonstrable injury is the Egas Moniz operation of pre-frontal lobotomy where the subcortical nerve fibers are destroyed surgically. Immediate arousal from catatonic and depressive states has been reported, and the results are often permanent.
>
> It has been said that if we don't think correctly, it is because we haven't "brains enough." *Maybe it will be shown that a mentally ill patient can think more clearly and more constructively with less brain in actual operation.* (italics added)

One of America's most respected psychiatrists, Abraham Myerson, was also among those who frankly promoted the theory that ECT-induced brain damage was good (in Ebaugh et al., 1942):

> I believe there have to be organic changes or organic disturbance in the physiology of the brain for the cure to take place. I think the disturbance in memory is probably an integral part of the recovery process. I think it may be true that these people have for the time being at any rate more intelligence than they

can handle and that the reduction of intelligence is an important factor in the curative process. I say this without cynicism. *The fact is that some of the very best cures that one gets are in those individuals whom one reduces almost to amentia.*[3] (italics added)

In 1944, L.C. Cook again elaborated the position that ECT and lobotomy share a common effect, the destruction or disabling of brain cells:

The weight of evidence and opinions heavily leans towards the viewpoint that the convulsions exert their effect by putting groups of cerebral neurones out of action, whether by anoxaemia or other means. The correlation between leucotomy[4] and convulsion therapy strongly supports this view. Leucotomy, which certainly cuts out large groups of cells, is most effective in the same types of case most favourable to convulsion therapy, Golla (1943), in fact, regarding ECT as a temporary leucotomy.

Paul Hoch, another director of the New York Psychiatric Institute, compared lobotomy to electroshock in regard to its across-the-board relief of tension and anxiety in patients, "regardless of the diagnostic groupings to which they may belong" (1948). He raised the question, "Is a certain amount of brain damage not necessary in this type of treatment?" He stated that lobotomy had proved the value of brain damage as therapy.

Writing a "Review of Psychiatric Progress," Joseph Wortis (1943) noted that animal research had demonstrated that electroshock treatments "are not innocuous," but that this had not discouraged him. He found a correlation in the treatment between "clinical improvement" and the appearance of abnormal brain waves, a viewpoint repeated throughout the literature.

In reviewing evidence for permanent memory loss and for long-term brain wave abnormalities following ECT, Pacella (1944) noted the possibility that ECT might be producing permanent pathology. Without taking the specific position that brain damage was in itself good, Pacella echoed Kennedy's position that it might reflect a worthwhile sacrifice: "Of course one could always argue that a normal clinical status or at

---

3. *Amentia* is literally a lack of development of the intellectual capacity, typically congenital. Myerson probably means "severe dementia" rather than amentia in its exact meaning.

4. *Leucotomy* is the British term for lobotomy.

least a socially adaptable individual with a little brain pathology is preferable to a psychotic patient with no demonstrable brain changes."

Consistent with others who directly advocated brain damage as therapy, Pacella did not raise the question, "Preferable to whom?" He did not suggest that the *patient* choose between possessing a normal brain and becoming more "socially adaptable."

The vast majority of psychiatrists who have acknowledged in print that ECT can cause severe brain damage have done so in the context of approving ECT. There have been a few exceptions to this. Braatoy (1948) remarked that "convulsions may be accompanied by cerebral changes of irreversible nature," and that authorities on epilepsy believed that convulsions "should as far as possible be avoided." He then reviewed evidence that ECT produced irreversible brain damage, acknowledged that some psychiatrists endorsed a brain-damage theory of ECT action, and warned that ECT produced a lobotomy: "The shock treatment must then be characterized as a diffuse, fortuitously localized leucotomy."

As evidence for brain damage following ECT was mounting in the form of human and animal autopsy reports, brain-wave studies, and clinical observations, the psychiatrists who pioneered the treatments were showing no inclination to restrain their enthusiasm. B.J. Alpers, a neurologist whose research had demonstrated brain damage in animals following ECT, reacted to this situation during a discussion following a research report linking ECT to brain damage (Ebaugh et al., 1942):

> I think it is fair to point out that discussion of these different pathologic changes comes pretty close to being academic, because regardless of what we conclude about the changes in the brain, there is no doubt that we will continue to use electrical shock treatment.

The orientation to brain damage as therapy was so prevalent that one psychiatrist complained (Wilcox, 1946):

> There is a prevailing assumption that therapy of certain types of mental disease must or can be accomplished only by destroying brain cells. . . .
>
> This belief has become sufficiently current so that it is not unusual to hear prominent psychiatrists and neurologists express the opinion that improvement from any of the shock therapies in certain mental conditions must necessarily depend upon brain tissue destruction.

Within a few years after Wilcox's observations a transformation took place in the stated attitudes of ECT advocates. The change was initiated by a 1947 report by the Group for the Advancement of Psychiatry (GAP), criticizing many "widespread" abuses of ECT. In an unprecedented move this committee of the nation's most prestigious psychiatrists called for a "campaign of professional education in the limits of this technique," and, more extraordinarily, suggested that "certain measures of control" might be required (Chapter 1). This caused grave concern among ECT advocates. Within three years the Group for the Advancement of Psychiatry was influenced to present a follow-up report tempering some of its conclusions, particularly those suggesting an educational campaign and the institution of controls.

Following this dramatic confrontation with criticism from the highest places within the profession, ECT advocates began to present a wholly different viewpoint in both their professional and their public commentaries. The mountain of evidence indicating brain damage in human and animal studies was virtually eradicated from review articles and textbooks; the position was taken that no such evidence ever existed (Kalinowsky, 1959; Kalinowsky & Hoch, 1961; Kalinowsky & Hippius, 1969; Noyes & Kolb, 1973; Fink, 1977; Arnot, 1975).

Was this new picture of ECT wholly cosmetic? Had the facts changed? To the contrary, during the period of the transformation the most damaging evidence against electroshock was being published. In 1948, one year after the first report by the Group for the Advancement of Psychiatry, Otto Will and his associates at the world-renowned St. Elizabeth's Hospital issued the most detailed review of autopsy data in humans, indicating brain damage as a frequent result of ECT. In the same year Mosovich and Katzenelbogen, from the same institution followed with an impressive, long-term EEG study indicating permanent, severe brain-wave pathology in many patients. In 1949 Ferraro and Roizen, at Columbia, published the definitive American study indicating brain cell death in monkeys subjected to clinical ECT, and in 1952 Hartelius followed with a book-length review and a controlled investigation proving severe vascular changes and brain-cell death in cats given small numbers of treatments. From 1948 to 1951 I.L. Janis at Yale published a series of articles containing the most definitive, detailed, and controlled examination of severe, permanent memory loss in patients receiving routine ECT. These studies were omitted from the most widely read reviews and textbooks during and after this period, and when they were mentioned occasionally, they were misrepresented as indicating little or no permanent disability following ECT.

In the 25 years following the two critical GAP reports, references to evidence for brain damage following ECT have been made by occasional critics of ECT (Gregory, 1968), or by individuals promoting alternative forms of treatment. For example, in defense of lobotomy in an interview in 1974, nationally known psychiatrist Karl Pribram declared that he would rather have a lobotomy than electroshock: "I just know what the brain looks like after a series of shocks—and it's not very pleasant to look at." In a similar vein in 1972, psychosurgeon William Scoville defended psychosurgery, including limited lobotomy (his technique of orbital undercutting), on the ground that it was less destructive than ECT: "It [ECT] may well be more destructive than limited surgery procedures if given too often. As proof, the author wishes to point out the similarity between the memory loss and confusion following electroshock therapy and head injuries."

I showed grave concern about Scoville's remarks about the relative dangers of lobotomy and ECT (Breggin, 1972a) because I feared that such a comparison might further encourage the burgeoning resurgence of lobotomy as a treatment for depression. At a conference of psychosurgeons in Philadelphia in 1972, psychiatrist Heinz Lehmann took me to task for showing this concern, and in the process confirmed Scoville's view that ECT can cause more brain damage than a limited lobotomy:

> Breggin refers as "dangerous" to one of Scoville's statements, to the effect that several courses of electroconvulsive therapy may cause more diffuse brain damage than the newer fractional lobotomies. One wonders how much experience Breggin has had with multiple electroconvulsive therapy courses, because many experienced clinicians would probably agree with Scoville, particularly in the case of older persons.

My point, of course, was not to defend ECT but to warn against using the dangers of ECT as a justification for the renewed use of lobotomy.

ECT as Mind-Disabling Therapy

The distinction between ECT as brain-disabling therapy and ECT as mind-disabling therapy is obviously somewhat arbitrary. In the previous section, however, I have shown how pioneers in the various shock therapies were often keenly aware that they achieved a clinical effect by damaging the brain. In this section, I will focus upon their awareness of the mental manifestations of this brain damage. The most obvious of these effects is a global disruption of all mental processes, leading to helplessness, passivity, and docility. In later sections, more subtle aspects of mental disability will be examined.

From the earliest beginnings of the convulsive therapies it was appreciated that the brain dysfunction and damage produced by shock treatments severely affected the patient's mind, rendering him more helpless and more tractable. Describing the effects of insulin overdose, Sakel (1938) wrote "Patients with extreme egoism and an egocentric disposition bordering on autism became extroverts, extremely accessible and dependent on others after accidental hypoglycemic shock." He recognized the destructive effect of his treatment on brain tissue and on personality, and writing much as the lobotomists would be writing, he stated, ". . . hypoglycemia abolishes or subdues principally probably first all the parts of the psychic life which have been most active and, so to speak, most vital." Sakel thus supported the mind-disabling concept of therapy.

In a similar fashion, Jessner and Ryan (1941) described the helpless tractability of the patient coming out of an insulin coma:

> The patient becomes more and more conscious, and usually then is in good spirits and of warm affectivity. One is frequently surprised by the patient's changed attitude immediately on wakening: He asks for help, is friendly, accessible, interested in his comfort and in the little things of daily life, especially food.

Jessner and Ryan were describing a person who had been starved nearly to death by means of an insulin overdose. Food for such a person would hardly be one of "the little things of daily life."

It was well known from the beginning that ECT also subdued animals and human beings, and that this reaction to compromised brain function was independent of any psychiatric disorder. As Jessner and Ryan (1941) indicated, even animals responded in this manner:

> Utilizing 4.5 milliampere current through the intact brain it was found that after five to ten convulsions rats become extremely passive, inactive and submissive, while after receiving fifty convulsions they were about 65% as active as control animals.

Pacella, Piotrowski and Lewis (1947) described the patients' reaction to ECT in lobotomy-like terms: "They were emotionally calmer and less sensitive. At the same time they appeared emotionally duller."

Anyone who has witnessed this response in otherwise normal human beings following a spontaneous seizure cannot doubt its reality. A person who has had a spontaneous seizure typically awakens from his post-ictal sleep with a feeling of bewilderment and helplessness that makes him understandably dependent and tractable. The additional trauma of electric current can only add to this pacifying effect.

Many early observers confirmed that ECT was specifically used to pacify, calm, or subdue mental patients in crowded, oppressive state hospitals. Rabin (1948) noted,

> It was and is frequently used as a short-range means of "quieting down" the patient, even though temporarily, with no prolonged effects of recovery expected. Thus, over a period of years, some patients of state hospital "back wards" have received numerous treatments, sometimes in the hundreds.

In the nation's most popular psychiatric textbook in 1948, Noyes suggested, "Experience has shown that the employment of maintenance [ECT] treatment on chronic wards has greatly simplified their management." Or, as Jessner and Ryan put it in their textbook (1941), ECT "quieted the noisy patients in the disturbed wards."

Otto Will and his colleagues (1948) at St. Elizabeth's Hospital in Washington, D.C., were deeply concerned about the brain-disabling effects of ECT and lamented its use as an "efficient" replacement for medical and nursing care and psychotherapy in state mental hospitals:

> A portion of the present enthusiasm over the use of electroshock probably arises from the observation that it seems ideal for application to large numbers of patients in crowded hospitals where medical and nursing aid are deficient in number and where any individual psychotherapy is not possible.

The criteria used to rate improvement in studies of ECT also confirmed its importance as an "enforcer" on the state hospital wards. Miller and Clancy (1953), for example, noted that studies of ECT used "wetting, soiling, destructiveness and noisiness" as assessment criteria for improvement, without even bothering to evaluate the effect of the ECT on the patient's actual mental status. Their patients did become more cooperative and easier to manage after ECT.

The role of ECT in producing docility and manageability appears most blatantly in research describing intensive ECT, which has been aptly called regressive, depatterning, or annihilation ECT. As amplified in dozens of articles in the literature, two or more ECT given daily for a total dose of 15 or more treatments eventually and invariably produces a state of nearly total neurological deterioration, disabling brain and mind alike. Glueck and his colleagues (1957) at a private hospital, Stoney

Lodge, in Ossining, New York, described the degree of regression following three ECT a day for a total of 17 to 64 treatments:

> Regression is assumed to be complete when the patient manifests a majority of the following signs: There are memory loss, marked confusion, disorientation, lack of verbal spontaneity, slurring of speech to the point of complete dysarthria[5] or muteness, and utter apathy. The patient behaves like a helpless infant, is incontinent of both bowel and bladder functions, requires spoon feeding and at times, tube-feeding. Frequently, he holds his food in his mouth as if unaware that he should swallow it—permitting it to flow out of the mouth.

A week to 10 days after their last treatment, "The majority emerge into awareness in a placid, benign manner. . . . Some are aware of having given the personnel a difficult time and are duly apologetic." During this period the psychiatrist visited the patient two or three times a day, "acting as his lost memory and as a reassuring, stable figure on whom a helpless person may depend."

In contrast to the "success" stories, however, "In a vocal minority there is much anxiety; increased restlessness to the point of belligerence." The resentful patients were subjected to *more* treatment.

Some patients also complained bitterly about their memory loss. "In spite of general return of memory, they emphasize the gaps which they do not recall; or they express their hostility about 'what the doctor did to them'." The protests of these patients were considered "intellectual defenses," and the doctors handled the patients by ignoring their complaints, "lest the individual fix his attention on his memory gap." They also discounted those relatives who complained about the patient's apathy and other possible ECT side-effects on the grounds that these symptoms are the result of "mental illness" rather than ECT. ECT thus fits into a systematic program of subduing patients with disregard for the complaints raised by these patients or their families. Regressive ECT, formerly called REST, is enjoying a renewed application at Stoney Lodge with a new acronym—MEST (Exner & Murillo, 1973).

Citing wartime experiences using ECT to control assaultive military personnel on ships, Brussel and Schneider (1951) described the value of what they called blitz electric shock therapy (acronym BEST) to control "rampaging psychotics" on navy vessels toward the end of the war:

---

5. *Dysarthria* is impairment of the ability to speak due to any disorder, including brain damage, affecting the tongue or speech muscles.

Purely on an empirical basis, it was discovered that the usual
electric shock therapy application, administered in the morning
and afternoon of *two* successive days, worked nothing less than
miracles in converting wildly disturbed patients into quiet,
tractable, cooperative, and *often improved* individuals. Port
military authorities were frequently amazed to receive a ship-
ment of docile and manageable patients about whom a prior
radio message had been sent describing them as "disturbed."
(italics added)

The authors frankly related these anecdotes to the problems they
faced in controlling the wards at Willard State Hospital while trying to
rely on conventional methods such as "sedation, individual nursing care,
restraint and/or seclusion. . . ." Blitz electric shock proved far more
effective. Brussel and Schneider picked the 50 most "disturbed" women
in the hospital. In reality they were the 50 most "disturbing" or rebellious women, for they were characterized by "noisiness, assaultiveness,
destructiveness, untidiness, resistiveness. . . ." The treatment effect was
dramatic. Rebellious behavior as characterized above was largely sup-
pressed by a course of regressive ECT, and when it did recur, the treatment was repeated. Maintenance ECT, administered whenever patients
got out of hand, then replaced the use of the camisole (straitjacket) and
seclusion as methods of control.

The "exhausted and pessimistic employees" on the wards were especially grateful for the pacification program.

Perhaps the unscientific comment of one attendant sums up the
judging of results when she came upon one patient who had
been sadistically assaultive, destructive and profane . . . now
neat and tidy, quiet, and knitting a muffler in occupational
therapy classroom. The amazed employee gaped and muttered,
"I'll be damned!"

The treatment was recommended for patients who "cannot be controlled
by such means as restraint and sedation."

Sharp, Gabriel, and Impastato (1953) also specifically advocated
intensive ECT (twice daily) to suppress difficult mental patients.

During the past eleven years, in our work with electroshock
therapy (E.S.T.) at Bellevue Psychiatric Hospital and elsewhere, we have on numerous occasions observed that acute
disturbed patients become quiet and cooperative after a few
shock treatments. In view of these observations, we decided to
administer E.S.T. as a "sedative" to selected patients on the
disturbed wards of Bellevue Hospital. The patients chosen for

treatment were those who were grossly uncooperative, assaultive or refused food.

According to the authors, "The treatment schedule followed was to administer one treatment in the morning and one in the afternoon until the patient became cooperative, and then to control him with one or two treatments daily if he relapsed." Frankly calling it "sedation," the authors concluded that "the wards are quieter and more acceptable to all patients." The authors reviewed the literature and felt they were on firm ground using ECT to replace more offensive means of control such as the camisole. The article is an explicit advocacy of assault on the brain as a replacement for less elegant methods of suppression.

Perhaps the most explicit espousal of ECT as a suppressive agent was published in 1950 by Shoor and Adams. The authors declared:

> Our goals were not curative; they were limited to the level of improved ward behavior. We had in mind the management of chronic disturbed psychotic patients, free of restraint, seclusion, and sedation. . . . Patients were selected for intensive maintenance electric shock treatment on the basis of ward behavior. This meant, in general, disturbed, aggressive behavior. . . .

The experiment was carried out on a chronic female ward with an average duration of hospitalization of 5.9 years. Although most of the patients were diagnosed as functionally psychotic, the ward also included "mental defectives, epileptics, old parenchymatous luetics, as well as postlobotomy patients,"[6] and probably many geriatric patients. With a daily census of 112 patients, 34 treatments were given per day, that is, to nearly one-third of the patients. Patients were selected without regard for "age or cardiovascular status," and "Routine pre- and post-shock laboratory examinations were not performed." The typical patient was given one treatment a day, but more might be administered to especially unmanageable ones, including one epileptic who was subjected to "6 induced grand mal seizures within one hour." Each patient was given ECT six days a week until she stopped being unmanageable and became cooperative. It was immediately resumed if uncooperativeness resurfaced. Some patients responded after only two or three ECT, others after 20 to 40. Some received over 100 treatments during the ongoing program.

---

6. *Old parenchymatous luetics* refers to individuals suffering from the last stages of syphilis, in which the brain is attacked. In each of these diagnostic categories, ECT-induced brain damage is being added to a preexisting brain disorder.

The program was extremely effective by the standards of the authors:

> Within 2 weeks from the beginning of our intensive electric shock treatment the character of the ward changed radically from that of a chronic disturbed ward to that of a quiet chronic ward. Combative behavior of the patients diminished dramatically. Physical labor of the attendants was cut in half. . . . Patients in general became better "ward citizens," and in the words of one attendant, "began to act like human beings."

The authors observed, "We are impressed with the resemblence that some of our patients who receive large amounts of electric shock treatment daily for many weeks bear to the lobotomized patient."

This publication appeared without editorial criticism in the *Journal of the American Psychiatric Association* three years after the Group for the Advancement of Psychiatry's initial electroshock report in which it condemned the indiscriminate use of ECT.

Surveys and reviews in the literature demonstrate that ECT was gaining popularity at a rapid rate in the 1940s at exactly the time that animal and human research was confirming brain damage following ECT and psychiatric authorities were proposing the mind-disabling hypothesis. By 1942, Kolb and Vogel's survey showed that ECT was being used in 93.8 percent of state hospitals sampled, 79.4 percent of federal facilities, and 74 percent of private hospitals. This partially complete national survey indicated that 75,000 patients had been electroshocked in a three-year period. In 1943 a panel chaired by Noyes reported more than 2,500 cases from five Philadelphia hospitals and 1,333 at Trenton State. In the following years, reports of more than 2,000 patients receiving ECT in individual state mental hospitals would not be uncommon (Moore, 1947; P.H. Wilcox, 1947). Individual patients would often accumulate massive numbers, frequently more than 100 (Rabin, 1948; Perlson, 1945).

With the development of the major tranquilizers in the mid-1950s, ECT lost its place as the most efficient force in the control of difficult patients on the wards of state mental hospitals. Private hospitals and general hospitals became the main users of the treatment (Chapter 1), and with that, studies of its application as a pacifier became relatively infrequent in the literature. A hospital such as Stoney Lodge (Glueck et al., 1957), which originally brought forth studies abounding with details of the pacification of patients, has continued the use of ECT, but more modern reports from the same institution have been aseptic by comparison (Exner & Murillo, 1973).

It should also be realized that while ECT is used less frequently at present in state hospitals, it nonetheless is used in some of these facilities. The recent New York State survey described in Chapter 1 (Morrissey et at., 1979) found that 11.7 percent of all treatments were carried out in state hospitals and that the facilities using them were "relatively older and larger hospitals which have a proportionately much larger chronic patient caseload." This strongly suggests that when ECT is used in New York State facilities, its purpose is the control of chronic patients in overcrowded, poorly staffed institutions. Furthermore, the growing realization that the major tranquilizers can cause brain damage may encourage a renewed use of ECT as an alternative in these institutions in the future.

Although there are patients who request ECT or who agree to it when suggested, in my own series of six clinical cases, the three patients receiving large courses of ECT (45 or more) had been held against their wishes in three different well-known private hospitals. In each of the three cases the record clearly indicated that the patient was given ECT until no longer able to complain about being held against his or her will. In two cases the doctors specifically used complaints against being hospitalized as the primary indication for ECT treatment, and used "no longer resists treatment" or "no longer shows resentment about treatment" as the major criteria for improvement. By contrast, the three patients receiving routine courses of ECT originally sought psychiatric treatment of their own free will, but once begun on ECT begged to have it ended. In two cases it is clear that ECT was continued against the specific wishes and even frantic demands of the patient, and in the third the record is incomplete on this question.

Thus ECT is less frequently used in recent years as a major pacifying agent on the wards in the state mental hospital system, but it is often used in private and in general hospitals to thwart the desires and efforts of patients who resist or resent treatment, and once begun, the mind-disabling effect of ECT is used to overcome the protests of the patient receiving it (see Chapter 13).

In the several hospitals in which I regularly observed or participated in the administration of ECT during my educational and training period, I on *no occasion* saw the treatment terminated when the patient protested vigorously against it, even when the patient ostensibly enjoyed voluntary status. Instead the treatment was routinely continued until the acute organic brain syndrome rendered the patient unable to protest, or even to recall his or her protests. The period in which I was exposed directly to the use of ECT spanned 1954 to 1958 as a volunteer in a large state mental hospital, and 1958 to 1966 as a medical student or physician in smaller, university hospital settings. My more recent exposure through forensic psychiatry, visits to mental hospitals, and other sources has confirmed my original experience.

The philosophy of brain- or mind-disabling therapy and the willingness to put it into action against vast numbers of hospitalized patients raises a broader possibility—its use for the control of dissident citizens in a totalitarian nation. Although a very enthusiastic promoter of the "miracle" of ECT, Robert Peck (1974) nonetheless worried about this potential political application. In doing so he inadvertently confirmed that ECT does indeed control individuals by producing apathy:

> It has become abundantly clear by now the extreme power that is potential in shock treatment. Surely there is also potential for misuse. I do not know of any formal use of it in brain washing, but it seems possible it could be so used. One can conjure up an image of large groups of dissidents in a police state being kept in a contented state of apathy by repeated shock treatments.

Peck failed to realize that ECT in reality had always been used in the "police state" of the mental hospital for the purpose of producing apathy and docility in rebellious, troublesome mental patients. But it probably cannot be used with any effectiveness to control people who are not incarcerated in what Goffman (1961) has called total institutions. In order to keep a person in a more or less permanent state of docility with ECT, the person must be brain-disabled by the treatment. No political authority can tolerate large numbers of disabled persons within the society at large. They reflect shame on the political authorities, and they are too costly and even difficult to support. Contrary to Peck's description, their apathy is not "contented," but anguished, and they are often resentful. Projects that have tried to maintain discharged patients on ECT have found it difficult to get patients to return willingly (Geoghegan & Stevenson, 1949), and without regular repetitions of the treatment the individual tends to recover some of his spirited resentment. ECT as a fully suppressive agent is therefore only effective within the confines of a supervised, controlled environment such as a mental hospital.

There are, of course, some individuals who do voluntarily return for ECT. This is in no way inconsistent with the brain- and mind-disabling hypothesis, for throughout history individuals have sought brain-destructive means for ending their personal anguish and personal responsibility. I have examined this phenomenon in "Why we consent to oppression" (1977a). The individual who seeks repeated insults to the integrity of his brain—whether by sniffing glue or intoxicating himself with alcohol—is attempting to diminish his capacity to think, to feel, and take responsibility for himself.

More Subtle Aspects of ECT-Induced Tractability

The mind-disabling effect of ECT has more subtle implications than making more docile and tractable patients. As suggested in some of the above-cited studies, a patient whose brain has been rendered relatively nonfunctional often becomes dependent and suggestible in more subtle ways, enabling the psychiatrist to establish an authoritarian relationship with the relatively helpless, subdued person. A number of advocates of ECT have been very explicit about this aim.

Lowenbach and Stainbrook (1942), in their analysis of the effects of routinely administered unmodified ECT, noted the crushing mental effects of the treatment, including the terror and the guilt with which many patients responded. The authors advocated making use of this dependence:

> . . . if the patient becomes almost immediately his preshock self, then the therapeutic procedure has been in vain. If, however, he displays some kind of confusion and disorientation, he needs help to find his points of reference again. This is the time during which psychotherapeutic contact can be established with him and in which new associations can be formed and a remission set off.

In 1961 Arnold and Hoff described and compared the use of electroshock, insulin shock, and an experimental phenothiazine, Majeptil, which produced a severe state of Parkinsonism, as well as tetanic or torsion spasms.[7]

> Invariably the treatment methods we have outlined constitute major insults to the total personality of the patient; electroshock, insulin shock and Majeptil, furthermore, produce considerable, if temporary, brain damage; patients undergoing these treatments must therefore do so under the strictest supervision.

The authors then described how the patient might be influenced at this time by a combination of two different therapists, the "disciplinarian" and a "benign and friendly counsellor." They stressed the imposition of authority:

---

7. In addition to producing a permanent neurologic disorder called *tardive dyskinesia*, the major tranquilizers more frequently produce a variety of severe but reversible neurologic disorders. Parkinsonian symptoms, including a rigid face, shuffling gait, and tremors, are the most frequent, and tend to occur to some degree as soon as the clinical dose range is achieved. More severe and very painful spasms may infrequently occur. The common brain-damaging effect of the major psychiatric treatments is not coincidental (Breggin, 1979).

Also of great importance at this stage of massive personality disintegration is the temporary substitution—for normal inherent personality regulation—of rules imposed upon the patient from the outside, which are easy to grasp, to understand, and to follow.

Kennedy and Anchel (1948) described the typical regressive effects of intensive ECT, and observed that it rendered the patient more suggestible and amenable to psychotherapy:

We considered a patient had regressed sufficiently when he wet and soiled, or acted and talked like a child of four. These patients became confused, could not take care of their physical needs and lost weight—despite eating, in some cases, as much as usual. Frequently, they had to be spoon-fed. . . .

Sometimes the confusion passes rapidly and patients act as if they had awakened from dreaming; their minds seem like clean slates upon which we can write. They are usually co-operative and very suggestible, and thus amenable to psychotherapy.

Those patients who failed to become cooperative were called "paranoid" and subjected to further treatment.

Cameron and Pande (1958) explicitly described the use of "psychotherapy" following intensive ECT and sedation. First the patients were subjected to "depatterning" or regressive ECT producing a state of utter mental dilapidation: "He answers simple questions but does not recognize anyone, has no idea where he is and is not troubled by that fact. He usually shows urinary incontinence and has difficulty in performing quite simple motor skills." The patient was then kept sedated for several days, and as he awakened in his state of severe brain dysfunction, he was found to be cooperative and amenable to influence.

The therapist takes every opportunity to strengthen this relationship, particularly during the period immediately after prolonged sleep when the patient is attempting to reorient himself and is gradually recovering from the period of helplessness engendered by his prolonged sleep and electroshock therapy.

In addition to the helplessness imposed through mental disability, the medical aura surrounding the treatment also enhances the doctor's authority and control. Jessner and Ryan (1941) recognized that the medical authority established through these treatments facilitated the psychiatrist's ability to influence the patient, a process they called "psychotherapy":

> The psychotherapeutic approach is important and it is some-
> what facilitated by the fact that the psychiatrist takes on, in the
> patient's mind, the characteristics of a "real doctor" in that he
> is able to apply and to utilize a physical method of treatment.

Kalinowsky (1957) devoted an article to examining "Problems of Psychotherapy and Transference in Shock Treatments and Psychosurgery," and discussed at length making use of the patient's helplessness and dependence to build a powerful relationship with him. " . . . the fact that the same physician induces a state of unconsciousness from which he later brings the patient to life and normal awareness, produces a favorable psychotherapeutic situation. . . ." Kalinowsky also promotes brain damage as therapy when he sees "the euphorization of the patient" as therapeutically helpful.

One of the most systematic attempts to combine the effects of ECT with reprogramming was carried on by Tien (1974; Also see *Frontiers in Psychiatry,* 1972a, b) who combined 10 treatments of unmodified ECT with what he called "family counseling." During the period immediately after the convulsive therapy the patient was bottle fed by another family member and "reprogrammed" with an improved or new personality:

> In this routine the patient is psychotherapeutically repro-
> grammed with the help of a relative according to a blueprint of
> a goal-directed personality, which was worked out prior to the
> session by the patient. In fact, sometimes a patient chooses a
> new name for his or her new personality so that he or she will
> be known by a new name in real life.

Tien believes that the patient's amenability to indoctrination stems from "memory loosening" as well as the "infantile" state that the treatment brings about. After the convulsive treatment, "the patient is receptive to psychotherapy, reprogramming and curative integration. . . ." Verbatim dialogues involving Tien and a married couple, (from *Frontiers in Psychiatry,* 1972a-b) dramatized the case of a young woman who clearly stated before treatment that she wanted to divorce her husband, whom she did not love, who was never home, and who allegedly beat her in front of the children. Under the threat that her husband would try to gain custody of the children, she agreed to undergo the therapy. After each unmodified ECT, she was "reprogrammed" by her bottle-feeding husband to believe that her previous personality was "bad" and that her new, more docile personality was good. Tien calls his therapy ELT (1974): "E stands for Electricity, L stands for Love, and E + L = T, therapy!"

11

Fear and Other Psychological Reactions to ECT

As described in the preceding chapters, all persons subjected to ECT become disabled at least for a time and are made relatively helpless and tractable, usually for the duration of their hospitalization and often longer. I want to turn now from the most important primary effect of ECT to an important psychological reaction—the production of fear and panic in the patient during and after ECT.

A patient's terror of ECT may have developed from stories heard about ECT and may be compounded by an understandable fear of being subjected to electrical currents and convulsions. Surely these factors influence many patients, but, more importantly, a typical panic state develops as the patient experiences the actual destructive effects of the treatment on his mind. The fear often overcomes any original desire for the treatment, and unless quickly rendered apathetic or euphoric by brain damage, the patient frequently goes through a period in which he begs and pleads to be removed from the treatment. Sometimes he will even fight physically against it.

To those unfamiliar with the experience of seeing numbers of patients subjected to ECT, it may seem daring and radical to assert that patients grow terrified of the treatment and often beg to be "saved" from it. Yet all these phenomena are openly described by some of the most widely read advocates of the treatment.

The Historical Role of Fear in Psychiatry

In explaining why brain-disabling therapies were introduced in state mental hospitals I described briefly how they became justified by the need to control thousands of hapless individuals crammed into concentration-camp-like conditions, then how they ultimately became rationalized as "treatments" for "mental illnesses." The same analysis applies to the use of terror and intimidation in psychiatric hospitals.

Terror and intimidation have a long tradition as methods of controlling psychiatric inmates. The reader interested in acquainting himself with this grisly history can do no better than to consult one of the greatest names in psychiatry, Emil Kraepelin, whose *One Hundred Years of Psychiatry* (1962) presents a page-by-page recounting of relentless assault on the mental patient by means of torture and trauma. Here are a few samples from Kraepelin's descriptions of the "treatment methods" espoused by some of the most famous names in the history of psychiatry.

> We must give the old alienists credit for having exhibited both sincerity and inventiveness in putting into practice the therapeutic principles which they considered sound. Advice given by Neumann suggests the course of treatment that might have been prescribed for a new patient in a state of agitation: "They bring the patient to the restraining chair, bleed him, put ten or twelve leeches on his head, cover him with cold, wet towels, pour about fifty buckets of cold water over his head and let him eat thin soup, drink water and take Glauber salts." The same picture is suggested by Heinroth's account of the treatment for frenzied states: blood-letting to the point of syncope, repetition of the same process, administering cold showers, douching the head after it had been shaven, putting a crown of leeches around the head, scarifying the skin and sprinkling catharides in the open cuts, massaging with tartar emetic to induce vomiting, ... and using the rack (to be discussed later) in certain instances to control rage. (pp. 82-83)

> Restraining devices were now used to repress symptoms associated with particular mental conditions just as they had once been used for security reasons. Their number was augmented by a series of newer developments. Typical are the swaddling basket which Heinroth recommended especially for women, the coffin and the English booth or clockcase in which the recalcitrant or delirious patient was imprisoned with only his face exposed. The latter was to be used, according to Nos-

tiz, only in rare cases in which the restless behavior of the patient stemmed from a bad will or from open defiance rather than from his illness. Schneider added to his description a characteristic statement: "We must at the same time do everything possible to prevent the patient from opening it, for if he should, his rage would know no bounds."

The same purpose was served by Horn's invention—a long, wide bag reinforced with oilcloth. The bag was pulled over the patient's head and tied beneath his feet. "It restrains the patient," explained Horn. "It shocks him by making him aware of his confinement and causes him to suspect or realize the fruitlessness of any attempt to stir up troubles." (pp. 85-86)

A second group of devices for handling mental patients derived from an idea advanced by Erasmus Darwin and perfected by Cox—revolving machines. In these the patient was either turned on his own axis while seated in a chair or tied to a bed with his head pointed outward and describing a circle. The effects, especially those produced by the revolving bed, were extraordinary. Centrifugal force drove the blood to the brain, and this caused intense anxiety, false sensations, fear of suffocation, nausea, vertigo, vomiting, urination and defecation, and finally bleeding under the conjunctiva tunica. Healthy persons usually begged for the machine to be stopped before two minutes had passed, yet many mental patients endured the experience for as long as 4 minutes. This contrivance was used for delirious, melancholic, obstinate, and uncooperative mental patients to train them to submit to discipline, to live according to prescribed regulations, and above all, to be obedient. It was also used for patients with suicidal tendencies, for those who refuse to eat, for silent, passive, unco-operative patients, for epileptics and for "general madness." "If this does not help," said Heinroth, "nothing will." (pp. 87-88).

The "Father of American Psychiatry," Benjamin Rush, whose likeness appears on the seal of the American Psychiatric Association, was himself an open advocate of terror and torture (Rush, 1835; Rush, 1973). In the following excerpt from this famous textbook (1835, p. 127), Rush described taking advantage of a patient's suicidal desires by agreeing to kill him. He conspired to carry out a fake murder, which ultimately terrorized the patient. When the patient complained that he was being killed, he was bled until he stopped complaining.

In the year 1803, I visited a young gentleman in our Hospital, who became deranged from remorse of conscience in consequence of killing a friend in a duel. His only cry was, for a pistol, that he might put an end to his life. I told him, the firing of a pistol would disturb the patients in the neighbouring cells, and that the wound made by it would probably cover his cell with blood, but that I could take away his life in a more easy and delicate way, by bleeding him to death, from a vein in his arm, and retaining his blood in a large bowl. He consented at once to my proposal. I then requested Dr. Hartshorn, the resident physician and apothecary to the hospital, to tie up his arm, and bleed him to death. The Doctor instantly feigned a compliance with this request. After losing nearly twenty ounces of blood, he fainted, became calm, and slept soundly the ensuing night. The next day when I visited him, he was still unhappy, not from despair and a hatred of life, but from the dread of death; for he now complained only, that several persons in the hospital had conspired to kill him. By the continuance of depleting remedies, this error was removed, and he was soon afterwards discharged from the hospital. (pp. 127-128)

Sometimes Rush and his colleagues used more direct methods of terrorizing his patients:

Terror once cured, for a while, a patient of mine, of a belief that he had been poisoned by taking arsenic as a medicine, and that it had eaten out his bowels. A student of medicine, to whom he told his tale, attempted to convince him of his error, upon which he begged him to open him, and to satisfy himself by examining the cavity of his belly. After some preparation, the student laid him upon a table, and drew the back of a knife from one extremity of his belly to the other. "Stop, stop," said my patient, "I've got guts," and suddenly escaped from the hands of his operator. His cure would probably have been durable, after the use of this remedy, had not real distress, from another cause, brought back that which was imaginary. (1835, pp. 106–107)

A maniac in the Pennsylvania Hospital some years ago, expressed a strong desire to drown himself. Mr. Higgins, the present steward of the hospital, seemed to favour this wish, and prepared water for the purpose. The distressed man stripped himself and eagerly jumped into it. Mr. Higgins endeavoured to plunge his head under the water, in order, he said, to hasten his death. The maniac resisted, and declared he would prefer being burnt to death. "You shall be gratified," said Mr. Higgins, and instantly applied a lighted candle to his flesh. "Stop, stop," said he, "I will not die now;" and never afterwards attempted to destroy himself, nor even expressed a wish for death. (p. 128)

This most revered psychiatrist in the history of the United States also invented the "tranquilizer chair." According to Kraepelin (p. 17),

> Extensive use was made of the "tranquilizer" introduced by Rush. This restraining chair was equipped with supports to which the body, legs, and arms could be lashed. In a few hours . . . it would make the most stubborn and irascible patient gentle and submissive.

Knowing the reality of how Rush actually treated patients, we must wonder about Deutch's 1949 defense of Rush:

> Kind treatment of mental patients was a rule in Rush's practice. From the first he insisted that the cells and persons of patients be kept as neat and clean as possible. If he advocated terror as a therapeutic agent, he also taught that the insane should generally be approached with respect and deference. . . .

The avowed use of terror as treatment continued into the era in which electroconvulsive therapy was developed. Meduna, who pioneered camphor and Metrazol convulsions, was aware that these treatments produced an abject state of terror in the patient as the injected central nervous system toxin drove his or her brain into a state of convulsion. Meduna believed that this terror was an unfortunate side effect of the treatment, and he wrote in *The Journal of the American Medical Association* (Meduna & Friedman, 1939):

> Almost since the beginning of the application of convulsive therapy to the psychoses, it has come *frequently* to our attention that the therapy ought to be *widely applied* to the field of psychopathology as an agent to "frighten the patient to his senses" or to "scare the devil out of him." To the scientific minded this expression harks back to medieval times and ought not to be employed in scientific discussions. (italics added)

But Meduna's protests against the use of his therapy to terrorize patients disregarded the reality that the physician's *intentions* do not change the *patient's experience*. If Meduna gave the treatment to "cure illness," while other psychiatrists used it to torture their patients, *all patients* must nonetheless endure the same terrifying experience. Like it or not, Meduna tortured his patients in exactly the same fashion as the psychiatrists about whom he complained.

The individuals who pioneered ECT and the other somatic treatments were well aware of the historical precedents they followed. I have already described how Hans Hoff, a world-renowned advocate of somatic therapies, openly advocated the use of insulin coma as a method of killing brain cells. He was well aware that "shock therapy" in general followed in the tradition of trauma and terror as a means of therapy. In 1959 he wrote:

> Already towards the end of the Middle Ages and the beginning of the new period an interest developed in attempting to treat schizophrenics by some form of shock. In Switzerland at this time schizophrenics were put into nets and lowered into lakes until they were almost drowned and then pulled out again. Sometimes short-lasting remissions were witnessed. In other countries patients were hit with chairs and whips. Some of these patients died. But again there were impressive recoveries and remissions.

In 1938 Diethelm presented an extensive discussion of "Fear as a therapeutic agent" at a psychiatric conference. He stressed the importance of fear in the shock therapies, although the discussants disagreed with him. In a paper entitled "An historical view of somatic treatment in psychiatry" in 1939, he again made a direct connection between the various torture and terror techniques of the past and the modern shock therapies. He told us perhaps more than he wished when he compared psychiatrists of the past to modern-day ones:

> It is unfair to speak, as is customary, of the barbaric treatment of mental patients at the beginning of the nineteenth century. The physicians who proposed and used the swivel chair of Cox and the tranquilizer of Rush to produce nausea and resulting fatigue and sleep were probably as humanitarian as the psychiatrists of today.

Stainbrook (1946) similarly related the evolving shock therapies to past treatment with branding, dunking, and terrorizing patients. Although a staunch defender of establishment psychiatry, he made a most remarkable suggestion—that the use of these therapies might be motivated by the psychiatrist's "infantile" frustration and anger with his patients:

> The enumeration of these historical forerunners of contemporary shock treatment, however, does not assume any necessary continuity or similarity of motivation in the use of shock treatment, unless one may speculate upon the possible common presence of the less consciously defined motivation of *aggression against the patient* evoked in the physician by the inadequately met challenge of the etiological and therapeutical de-

mands of the patient's illness, and one may perhaps also tentatively consider the incidental motivational importance of the residual in the therapist's personality of *child-like attitudes of expectancy of sudden, miraculous magic resolution of puzzling barriers.* (italics added)

My purpose is not to appeal to the passions of my reader. As in elaborating the historic precedent for inflicting brain damage as therapy, my goal here is to demonstrate the context in which ECT developed. Psychiatrists were not only aware that they frequently used terror to control their patients,they often advocated it openly. Nor were they primarily motivated, as Stainbrook suggested, by infantile outrage and violence. They were motivated, then as now, by a desire to manage, control, and influence their patients by whatever means possible.

Fear and Terror Associated with ECT

Despite sentiments that supported brain-damaging and terrorizing therapies in the 1930s, the coinventor of ECT, Ugo Cerletti, wrote that his initial intention to develop ECT was greeted with dismay and fear by his colleagues in 1938 (1954): "However, the idea of submitting man to convulsant electric charges was considered utopian, barbaric, and dangerous; in everyone's mind was the spectre of the 'electric chair'!"

Not only did some of his colleagues greet the treatment with dismay, so did the first patient whom he subjected involuntarily to ECT (Cerletti, 1973; also see Cerletti, 1950 and 1954). The first dose was inadvertently subconvulsive, and the still conscious patient rose to protest: "All at once, the patient, who evidently had been following our conversation, said clearly and solemnly, without his usual gibberish: 'Not another one! It's deadly!' " Cerletti observed;

> I confess that such explicit admonition under such circumstances, and so emphatic and commanding, coming from a person whose enigmatic jargon had until then been difficult to understand, shook my determination to carry on with the experiment. But it was just this fear of yielding to a superstitious notion that caused me to make up my mind. The electrodes were applied again, and a 110-volt discharge was applied for 0.2 seconds.

Describing his experience in *The American Journal of Psychiatry* (1950), Cerletti gave further insight into the motivation behind his abrupt decision to go on with the treatment despite the patient's protests. His colleagues were also about to protest!

The situation was such, weighted as it was with responsibility, that this warning, explicit and unequivocal, shook the persons present to the extent that some began to insist upon the suspension of the proceedings. Anxiety lest something that amounted to superstition should interfere with my decision urged me on to action. I had the electrodes applied. . . .

Thus ECT was born as it lives today: amid controversy and protest, applied to the patient wholly against his will while others stood by aghast but unwilling to take action against the psychiatrist's authority.

Not only was the treatment surrounded with fear and terror from the beginning, its regular use quickly provoked a far more important kind of fear. As individual patients actually *experienced* ECT, they typically grew still *more* afraid of it. Cerletti (1954) called this "the 'after fear' which we observe in many subjects following a few applications of electroshock; they hate to continue the treatment and regard it with a dismayed sensation of fear."

One of the most astonishing oversights in the history of psychiatry is the failure of psychiatry in general to realize that such criteria for improvement as "discharge from the hospital" might be influenced very directly by the patient's obvious fear and hatred of the treatment. Would not anyone except the most extreme masochist feel motivated to seek "discharge" from an institution in which he or she was being subjected to a treatment that was feared and hated? Such an oversight can only be understood in the context of psychiatry as an institution long inured to trauma and terror as means of "treatment."

Lowenbach and Stainbrook (1942), in their pioneering analysis of the effects of ECT, were equally aware of what they called the "terror-manifesting reactions" of the patient in response to ECT. Again, these reactions were not part of a "superstitious" fear in anticipation of ECT. They were responses to the effects of the first convulsion. On awakening, the patient is both confused and terrorized:

He may ask if this is the jail . . . and if he has committed a crime . . . and then will insist that he did not intend to do it. But any question as to what crime he thinks he committed and why he thinks he is in jail or if this would be Hell or if this could be a hospital, is first answered by "I don't know." (serial dots in the original)

Gallinek (1956) devoted an entire article to the subject of the fear produced by ECT. He noted,

Patients undergoing electroconvulsive therapy (ECT) frequently exhibit marked fear of the treatment. While many medical procedures except the most innocuous ones are accompanied by fear on the part of the patient, the fear of ECT far exceeds that of other medical procedures including surgical ones.

Even patients who have been reassured that the treatment is harmless nonetheless develop fear as they experience it (Gallinek, 1956):

> I hate to have lost my memory when I wake up. When I wake up I do not know where I am and that worries me. Falling asleep and not recognizing anybody, I get frightened. . . . When you wake up it is the most terrible feeling like if you were an idiot.

In the discussion following Gallinek's paper, Kalinowsky focused on the problem of making the patient continue on with the therapy despite his terror.

Bennett (1949) noted that patients become so frightened of ECT that "the patient may require reassurance that he is not losing his mind" as a result of the mental dysfunction produced by the treatment. He also warned that patients who are already suffering from "anxiety states" may be worse, "causing increased panic states."

Sagebiel (1961) frankly described the terror produced by intensive or regressive ECT. It appeared routinely in the early stages of the treatment:

> This took many forms, such as the patient pleading to go home, or finding excuses why he should go home with negative attitudes toward the treatment. This might progress all the way to violent resistance to the treatment. Many times the patient would frankly admit a fear of EST.

Patients often continue to experience terror even though the ECT has been modified to render them unconscious during the actual treatment procedure. In a study comparing modified and unmodified ECT Brill et al. (1959) described this terror in as graphic a manner as any of the earlier unmodified literature:

> When patients are questioned concerning their feelings about shock treatment, there is little doubt that they see it as a threat to their lives, judging from their comparing it to "going to the electric chair" or fearing "that they'll be burned to a crisp" or "never wake up." To some, it may fulfill desires for punishment, and to others, the hope for death and rejuvenation; and to others it may mobilize ego defenses and increased attention

to reality in the face of a treatment that is perceived as a threat
to the patient's very existence, or the desire to be the passive
receiver of treatment. These subtle psychological variables, difficult to elucidate though they are, should receive more research
attention.

Amid all these subtle interpretations of ECT effect, they failed to acknowledge one of the most obvious—the intimidation of the patient.

In nearly every review he has written on the subject throughout the
eras of unmodified and modified ECT, Kalinowsky has made note of the
terror ECT produces in patients. Writing with Hippius in 1969 (p. 200),
he specifically stated, "In spite of some statements to the contrary, it is
our experience that the use of anesthesia techniques has not diminished
this problem, and the fear increases with each subsequent treatment."
The fear was attributed to many possible factors, chief among them "the
agonizing experience of the shattered self." This was believed to be the
"most convincing explanation" because of the appearance of the fear
after the start of the treatment itself. In the *Comprehensive Textbook of
Psychiatry* in 1975 Kalinowsky continued to acknowledge the importance of the fear, and described in detail its origin in the patient's experience of the damaging effects of the treatment:

> A most vexing psychopathological phenomenon is the fear the
> patient has of the treatment. Before the first treatment the fear
> is probably due to the name "shock" treatment and anything
> he may have heard about it. He is relieved of this fear after the
> first treatment, when he realizes that he did not have any dis-
> comfort during the treatment. However, after several treat-
> ments another type of fear sets in which does not leave the
> patient until he has finished the series. He remains aware of the
> fear, although he cannot give a reason for it, and it recurs when
> he has to undergo treatment again even after years. This fear
> seems to be a result of the unpleasant experience of waking up
> after the treatment and not knowing who he is and where he is.
> This loss of his identity is usually not given by the patient as
> the reason for his fear, but the fact that it is first realized a week
> or so after the first treatment, when the amnesia for the inci-
> dents surrounding the first treatment have [sic] subsided, sug-
> gests that this does explain the treatment fear of almost all
> patients.

A particularly terrifying ECT technique is the administration of
modified ECT without prior sedation to render the patient unconscious.
If the patient is not unconscious at the time of the injection of the neuromuscular blocking agent, he remains awake while unable to move a

muscle or to breathe immediately before being knocked out by the electric current. The extreme fear and dread produced was noted in the earliest reports. Salzman et al. (1955) quoted a patient as saying, "I feel as if I were buried alive." More recently, the technique of paralyzing prisoners in this manner as a means of punishment became a prison scandal in California (Mitford, 1973, p. 123). Kalinowsky and Hippius (1969, p. 177) noted the especially frightening effects of this technique and observed that "most psychiatrists" take care to make sure the sedative is given separately before the neuromuscular blocking agent. Nonetheless, within the last few years I have come across two cases in which patients in well-known private hospitals were given modified ECT without first rendering them unconscious. One patient died as a result of ECT, and no subjective report of his experience was available. The other patient is included among my six cases, and despite only fragmentary recall for the experience of ECT, this person vividly recalled a horrible sensation of suffocating or drowning just before losing consciousness during ECT.

Although the majority of psychiatrists who use ECT have denied that it achieves any of its effect through terror or torture, a number of others have disagreed. They have argued that the main effect of the treatment is the punishment it inflicts, and they have therefore advocated inflicting the electric current on patients without bothering to induce a convulsion. Berkwitz (1939) at the University of Minnesota School of Medicine was one of the first modern psychiatrists to openly support fear and terror as a means of psychiatric treatment. He quoted Jacobs as stating, "Whatever benumbs the power of judgment and resistance, whether it be fear, passionate excitement or a strong hypnotic will, enhances the use of suggestion." Berkwitz also warned that convulsive ECT could cause severe brain damage, citing the work of Bini and Cerletti. He therefore advocated a powerful nonconvulsive electric shock to the head, applied 10 to 20 times a day, to produce pain and fear. He vividly described how "The patient's eyelids and facial muscles twitch, the head jerks, and evidence of fear and panic is exhibited." It is not surprising that Berkwitz was able to provide illustrations of how patients stopped complaining and asked for discharge after a few treatments.

Although it never gained a great following, Berkwitz's use of nonconvulsive painful electrical shocks to the head did gather sufficient support to be advocated in psychiatric publications and to be reviewed in the standard textbooks as a legitimate psychiatric treatment. Kalinowsky and Hippius (1969, p. 187), for example, reviewed the subject and described how one study "states frankly that no cures were obtained but that the treatment sometimes controlled destructiveness." They discussed the possibility that such favorable effects on some patients are "due to the associated discomfort." Kalinowsky and Hippius express no concern about the use of torture as treatment, and discuss it as one more treatment alternative.

Those psychiatrists who claim that ECT somehow eradicates or improves the "symptoms" of the patient have seldom attempted to find out if the patient were simply hiding his or her symptoms out of fear of further treatment. When Rush's patient stopped expressing a desire to die after his doctors threatened to kill him, was he "cured" of suicide, or had he learned to dissemble? Pacella, Piotrowski, and Lewis (1947) did notice that psychological testing of their post-ECT patients indicated that they were hiding their symptoms:

> From the Rorschach evidence at least, the impression was gained that one of the effects of a successful ECT was the improved capacity of the patient to be on his guard in disclosing his personality deficiencies. . . .
>
> The basic personality defects are still largely retained but *successful treatment* enabled the patient to be more prudent in manifesting these defects even to his physician. (italics added)

This is a guarded statement, calculated to avoid self-censure for giving ECT. But they *were* saying that the patient learned his or her lesson after ECT and hid complaints from the doctors.

Physical Resistance to ECT

Given that patients fear and dread ECT, it is not surprising that some choose to resist it physically. Indeed, this is very common in psychiatric hospitals, although the resistance is quickly overcome by the apathy or euphoria that sets in after a few treatments, or by simultaneous medication with stupifying tranquilizers.

Kalinowsky has tried to invalidate this resistance to ECT by describing it in diagnostic terms that make it appear as a physiological response to the convulsion. Immediately after describing how patients awaken severely disoriented after ECT, Kalinowsky continued (1959, p. 1506), "Post-convulsive excitement is not infrequent and may lead to dangerous aggressiveness, which may last for 15 to 30 minutes." One should not be misled by the use of medical language such as "postconvulsive excitement." The patients are in reality both terrified and enraged. The comment that such an episode lasts 15 to 30 minutes reflects the time it takes for physical force, injected medication, or post-ECT exhaustion to overcome the patient.

In his textbooks (Kalinowsky & Hippius, 1969, p. 201) Kalinowsky more graphically describes the patients' violent response after ECT: "Some patients, particularly males, become dangerously assaultive, develop enormous strength, try to escape, run around and injure themselves, and may strike anyone who attempts to control them."

In a 1978 interview (McDonald), Kalinowsky admitted that the patient was actually trying to fight his way to freedom. But he called this self-defensive response "neurotic," much as he had labeled complaints about memory loss:

> The patient wakes up in a strange environment with people
> around him whom he doesn't recognize, and he fears that he is
> threatened by something. Some patients fight; they try to fight
> their way out. . . . Most of the patients who have neurotic traits
> fight. . . . (serial dots in original)

Giamartino (1974) was critical of Kalinowsky's interpretation that fears of ECT are "psychopathological." He pointed out that the treatment had "questionable clinical reliability," "the possibility of physiological damage to the brain," and "accompanying unpleasant psychological effects." Therefore he suggested it would be "psychopathological" *not* to fear ECT.

The same may be said about *resistance* to ECT. It is "neurotic" only in the sense that it is typically futile and may encourage the administration of still more ECT in order to overcome the patient's alleged irrationality. Sagebiel (1961), for example, stated that the patient's "fear" and "violent resistance" to intensive ECT was "unconsciously motivated" by his "psychosis." This so-called "anxiety phase" of the treatment was "shortened by increasing the intensity of the treatment, i.e., by giving multiple EST's daily." Indeed, if the patient so much as complained about persisting "amnesia" after treatment "it was obvious the treatment had not been successful. This was an indication for the resumption of treatment."

Whereas Sagebiel believes that the patient's psychosis causes him to complain about amnesia and to fear or to resist the treatment, Kalinowsky and his co-authors over the years have repeatedly observed that the "neurotic" patient, and *not* the psychotic one, makes the worst complaints and puts up the most resistance. Given that psychotics by definition are less rational and less in touch with reality, it would be expected that so-called "neurotics" would be more willing and able to express resentment over the loss of their mental faculties. Dropping diagnostic labels altogether, we can simply confirm that the more rational, competent, or able the person, the more he is likely to fear, to resent, and to resist destructive interventions into his mind. This was confirmed by

Pollack and Fink (1961), who found that patients who refused ECT were better educated, more skilled, and less rigid and authoritarian in their personality type than patients who accepted it.

It would not be surprising if patients already suffering from inner terror and self-hate felt themselves pushed to suicide by the threat of ECT. Bennett (1949) warned that patients on wards in which ECT was given indiscriminately might turn to suicide. Lowinger and Huddleson (1946), after reviewing evidence for brain damage from ECT, suggested that the treatment itself might make depressed people "more prone to self-destruction." They also warned, "Some patients resist shocking and will elope."

Pollack and Fink (1961) found that "there were many expressions of a negative attitude toward convulsive therapy long before the referral for convulsive therapy had been made."

> One patient, in treatment for several years prior to her current hospital admission, terminated treatment and transferred to another psychiatrist on each occasion when convulsive therapy was recommended. Another patient asked to sign the voluntary certification form on admission, appended the following note. "P.S., If I am given shock treatment I'll either kill myself or leave the hospital."

Ironically, this study, which acknowledges that some patients threaten suicide, change psychiatrists, or run away rather than submit to ECT, also openly acknowledges that patients were sometimes referred for ECT for reasons "associated with problems of management, *e.g.,* disturbing the ward or eloping from the hospital. . . ." Thus, the potential ECT patient is placed in a dilemma. If he balks at the suggestion of ECT and threatens to take drastic action in order to avoid it, he may place himself in still greater jeopardy, for his resistance is used as one more indication for the treatment.

Clinical Experience with Fear of ECT

My own clinical experiences with modified ECT confirms that *most* patients are extremely afraid of ECT even before they receive it. The hospital grapevine, gossip among the patients, quickly informs individual patients that ECT is a dangerous treatment. Often various ward psychiatrists will have reputations as "shock doctors" and patients will try to avoid or to placate them. The three patients in my six cases who could remember enough of their hospitalization reported such concerns, and I myself frequently had similar worries brought to my attention by patients during my hospital training. More poignantly, some patients grow to fear ECT from directly witnessing its effects on patients in the wards. And finally, as the advocates of ECT admit, most patients grow afraid of the treatments as they undergo it, regardless of their previous convictions about it.

In my five clinical cases with available hospital records, four of five are recorded in the charts as resenting or resisting the treatment, and the fifth patient was put into solitary confinement because of resistance to the treatment. At certain intervals, however, some of these patients became sufficiently apathetic or euphoric so that they stopped resenting or resisting the ECT. This is documented in detail in the chart of one of the six cases. This individual resisted agreeing to ECT despite the persistent efforts of the doctors, who even noted in the chart that they were making extensive efforts directly and through other people to pressure the patient into accepting the treatment. Once the treatment was begun, the patient experienced its awesome effects, and begged to be relieved of it. The chart notes that the doctors reassured the spouse of the patient that all the effects were temporary, again applying pressure to see that the treatment was maintained against the will of the patient—although the patient was supposed to be voluntary. Toward the end of the short course of ECT, the patient became euphoric for a brief time, and in the midst of a severe acute organic brain syndrome, existed on a "high" for several days. Soon the high dissipated, and the patient again deeply resented being forced to continue with the treatment. This patient is the one with brain damage documented on the brain scan, the EEG, neurological examination, and psychological tests.

Following ECT, each of these six patients decided never to subject themselves voluntarily to the treatment. They also decided, partly or wholly because of ECT, to stay away from any psychiatrist who might conceivably subject them to it again. Because several of them were considered "improved" by their psychiatrists after the treatment, they may be listed in some follow-up study as long-term successes who never again returned for treatment.

Considering how terrorized patients are by ECT, it is surprising that studies by ECT advocates do not show a much higher rate of discharge immediately or soon after treatment. The answer in part is contained in the dozens of articles already cited concerning the brain-damaging effect of ECT. As frightened as they may be about the treatment, the patients have been rendered helpless and impotent through the combined impact of memory loss, global intellectual impairment, and apathy or euphoria. They are literally *unable* to leave the hospital any sooner than they do!

For patients who witness these events without themselves undergoing ECT, the effect of ECT is nonetheless intimidating. They do everything in their power to cooperate in order to avoid a similar fate. I described this for the first time in the medical literature when I wrote in the *AMA Archives of General Psychiatry* in 1964:

> Electroconvulsive therapy is a more potent means of coercion. In my own experience, most patients have terror of the treatment. Those few who have requested the treatment, still expressed a great fear of it. . . . In summary, the patient learns, soon after admission, that his voluntary status leaves him vulnerable to certain eventualities, the most disturbing being involuntary electroconvulsive therapy and certification to a larger state hospital. He also tries to find out what kind of behavior will cause these threats to materialize, so that he can modify his behavior accordingly.

Psychological Reactions to Memory Loss

Psychological reactions to retrograde amnesia are very profound. In my six cases, I described the helplessness and frustration experienced when they could not find their way around their own home or their own town following ECT, when they failed to recognize well-known friends and family, or when their vocational skills were obliterated. Brody (1944) described very similar reactions among his patients, and throughout the literature we have found references to the helplessness and dependence produced by memory loss. I have already documented that many psychiatrists advocate using the post-ECT period to take advantage of the patient's dependence and suggestibility, some of which is a reaction to memory loss as well as to other mental disabilities.

Although it is difficult to disentangle the importance of the memory defect from other mental dysfunction following ECT, it is possible to focus on one very crucial result of the severe retrograde amnesia. The patient's memory gaps may make it difficult for him or her to confront or to contend with the psychiatrist. One of my six patients had dearly wished to be freed from the hospital, but the hospital chart shows that when told by his psychiatrist that he had been "dangerous to his parents" before ECT, he felt guilty and questioned his right to be released. The psychiatrist's report about his dangerousness was secondhand and vastly exaggerated, but the amnesic patient had no way of knowing this at the time. In another case a patient protested ECT treatment after release from the hospital and was told by the psychiatrist, "You were suicidal." A careful check of all records, as well as interviews with family members, disclosed no evidence for this allegation. I am not suggesting that dangerousness or suicidal acts might have justified ECT treatment. The point is that the memory loss associated with ECT made it easy for the psychiatrist retrospectively to exaggerate the patient's problems in order to convince the patient of his or her need for the treatment.

There is grave reason to doubt if memory loss brings about any sense of "relief" or other beneficial effects. As Janis (1948) noted, many patients feel they cannot recall "what was bothering me" after ECT; but despite this, few psychiatrists have promoted memory loss *per se* as the therapeutic agent in ECT. Advocates of ECT have been unwilling to take this position because they wish to deny any permanent memory loss (see Kalinowsky and Hippius, 1969, p. 205) and because the patients so obviously feel appalled by their losses. Even an advocate of the brain-disabling hypothesis such as Fink maintains that the complaint of memory loss is unjustified (Fink, 1977) and that memory loss plays no significant role in the patient's changing conduct or outlook.

Occasionally remarks are found in the literature supporting the viewpoint that memory loss is of beneficial effect. Bennett (1949) commented, "It is surprising how many previously important issues disappear or no longer disturb the patient after shock therapy." Alexander and Rosen (1956) advocated ECT for depression on the grounds that, "where the issue is guilt, oblivion is helpful. . . ." On the other hand, Braatoy (1948), with his characteristic directness, dismissed the value of oblivion, noting that such mental dysfunction "casts a veil over the factors that created the background for depression."

> The therapist and the patient may, in some cases, be at first impressed by the immediate result. But this impression is perhaps based merely upon the same form of optimism that we know of old from cases of impairment of the cerebral cortex with the oblivion due to intoxication.

As the Group for the Advancement of Psychiatry reports indicated (1947), many psychotherapeutically oriented psychiatrists feel that the memory loss resulting from ECT makes it difficult for the patient ever again to come to grips with his problems. I have found that post-ECT patients sometimes do have grave difficulties in benefiting from any insight-oriented encounter with a therapist. Although they may succeed in making gains, they are hampered by the blanks their memories, which are often greatest for the time of greatest emotional difficulty leading up to their ECT treatment. They have lost recall for the period of time that may be most pertinent to their problems. They may also distrust the ability of their minds ever again to function at top efficiency, and of course this frightens and frustrates them. Furthermore, their experience with ECT makes them understandably fearful and resentful toward all psychiatrists, even those who have explicitly rejected ECT.

If the post-ECT individual also has a continuing tendency to avoid taking responsibility for his personal affairs, any ECT-induced mental difficulties may give him an all-too-understandable excuse for indulging this tendency. In this regard I want to reemphasize what I said in the preface—many individuals have overcome brain disabilities suffered from ECT and other trauma, and have gone on to lead responsible, happy, and self-fulfilling lives. Nonetheless personal recollections and interpretations of the past heavily determine our current and future conduct, as well as our ethical viewpoint of ourselves and others, and our overall sense of identity. It is obvious that with or without other psychological or physical complications, amnesia for significant segments of the past will make it more difficult for an individual to take responsibility for his or her life after ECT.

Concerned about the tendency to denigrate the importance of memory in modern life, Richard Weaver (1978) has said:

> The human being must live in a present that is enriched and sustained by a past; it is his experience stored up in the form of memory which enables him to be something more than an automaton responding to sensory impingements.
>
> It is equally true that a man's personality is a product in large part of the memory of things he has done, decisions he has made, with their consequences, and so on. Personality cannot be the creation of a moment. . . .
>
> By the same token, without this faculty of memory there can be no such thing as conscience. Conscience is essentially a recollection or pulling together of our ideas of what we are, what things we deal with are, and the structure of values to which we have in our inmost feelings subscribed. It is present awareness of things which no longer have present existence. Thus, when an individual consults his conscience, he refers to a complex of remembered facts, insights, and ideas of obligation —all of which by their very nature cannot be manufactured out of a present moment.

By robbing a person of his memory, we rob him of himself.

Euphoria and Apathy as Psychological Reactions

It is difficult at times to separate direct physical effects on the brain from psychological reactions to these effects. Although there are somewhat predictable patterns in response to brain damage (Goldstein, 1975), the individual's personal tendencies must always be taken into account. As already described, most individuals respond passively to the terror induced by ECT, but some react with open hostility and physical violence. Most patients respond apathetically to brain damage, but a large number also respond euphorically. The alternatives of apathy and euphoria are psychological reactions to the primary physical dysfunction; they can be found in reaction to almost any severe physical or emotional trauma. Apathy is a passive surrender to helplessness. Euphoria, or feeling high, may be seen as an act of denial in which the individual fabricates feeling "great" or "perfect" or "invulnerable" in the face of overwhelming physical or mental stress. Laymen recognize this as an unrealistic and therefore self-defeating reaction. Neurologists see it as a possible sign of severe underlying brain damage. Certain psychiatrists, however look forward to this response in patients, calling it the key element in it "improvement," as we shall see in Chapter 12.

Other Psychological Reactions to ECT

Psychological reactions to ECT are as varied as the human imagination. Many of them have been summarized in the psychiatric literature in sources such as Miller's (1967) "Psychological Theories of ECT: A Review." Some patients who receive ECT may feel that at last they have been punished in proportion to their crimes; perhaps this affords some self-hating individuals a measure of relief from their guilt. Those occasional patients I have seen who have actively sought a repeat ECT treatment have been very guilt-ridden people bent on self-destructiveness. Not merely the relief of guilt, but suicidal wishes may have motivated their desire for ECT.

The desire to give up moral responsibility and self-determination may be another reason why individual patients occasionally seek out and feel grateful for ECT. These individuals do not want to face their difficult life situations or themselves, and prefer to give up authority over themselves in favor of psychiatric authority. They want to have "biological problems" rather than personal ones, and they find psychiatrists who are willing to use a treatment that defines their problems as physical in origin and in solution. In such a person the helplessness and dependence experienced after ECT even may be somewhat gratifying. It may approximate the state of utter irresponsibility that the individual has previously sought to create by more psychological methods (Breggin, 1971b, 1977a, 1977c). This desire to give up authority over oneself may be closely related to the so-called placebo effect; the individual knows that something "potent" and something "medical" has been done to him. He may get a morale boost out of this, especially if he becomes euphoric and denies that his brain and mind have been severely impaired.

Often the brain dysfunction associated with ECT is confused with "mental illness," and patient, family, and psychiatrist alike find themselves confirmed in their suspicions that the patient is "crazy" when he or she acts in a bizarre fashion during and after treatment. This confirmation of the role "mental patient" may assuage the guilt of the patient's family and psychiatrist concerning their treatment of the patient, and even may make a relatively irresponsible patient feel somewhat more secure in a clearly defined role of "cripple" or "mental patient."

The variety of psychological responses to ECT, as I have said, is limited only by the human imagination. But I believe that the reactions I have just enumerated are of relatively little importance in evaluating the effect of ECT, especially during the first weeks after treatment. Such complex or subtle reactions as the relief of guilt are lost amid more devastating and global reactions such as apathy and euphoria, fear, and enforced helplessness and dependence. Indeed, during and soon after ECT, it is practically impossible for any sophisticated mental process to flourish. The patient instead is dominated by the overriding reality of severe mental dysfunction.

12

The Brain-Disabling Hypothesis: An Overview

Brain-disabling therapies invariably produce a variety of complicated and variable effects on the human being. Because the brain is thoroughly integrated in its anatomy and physiology, even relatively local damage to the higher centers that govern emotion and reason will produce widespread physiological and psychological repercussions. When the trauma is diffuse and general, as in ECT, these effects will be still more global. Within this broad spectrum of effects there will be individual differences. Some differences will relate to chance factors influencing the degree of damage in one part of the brain or another. Others will relate to the uniqueness of every individual's psychological response to trauma. Just as individuals will react differently to the same brain disease or to the same emotional shock, individuals will differ in their responses to brain-disabling therapy. This wide variation has helped to keep the effect of the treatment wrapped in mystery. But despite the complexity of the individual's response to ECT, it can be understood as a reaction to the disruption of *normal brain function*.

Fink's "Unified Theory of the Action of Physiodynamic Therapies"

We have already found that many of the original advocates of the somatic therapies espoused the brain-damage-is-good theory of treatment. They openly acknowledged that ECT produces central nervous system

178

pathology, and they credited this pathology with the cure, but these pioneers did not develop their theories in a sophisticated manner. Although Freeman and Watts (1944) related "clinical improvement" to the development of a variety of mental dysfunctions, including indifference to self and to others, loss of abstract reasoning, and diminished initiative and spontaneity, even they did not elaborate the brain- and mind-disabling hypothesis in any coherent detail. However, Max Fink and his colleagues have for more than two decades been developing a brain-disabling hypothesis in sophisticated but guarded terms. That Fink may be replacing Kalinowsky as the best-known advocate of ECT makes his hypothesis particularly pertinent.

In his review paper, "A Unified Theory of the Action of Physiodynamic Therapies" (1957), Fink picked out two neurological indicators of brain dysfunction—pathological brain waves and an increase in seizure incidence—as evidence of an alteration in brain function common to lobotomy, insulin coma, the major tranquilizers, and ECT. Fink summarizied his views as follows:

> 1. The neurophysiologic and clinical neurologic aspects of convulsive therapy, "tranquilizers," insulin coma and lobotomy, are reviewed.
> 2. The efficacy of each therapy in the treatment of psychoses is related to the ability to induce a persistent change in cerebral function, of which a delta shift in the EEG spectrum and an increase in incidence of seizures are two indices.
> 3. Alteration in cerebral function is an essential prerequisite of behavioral change with each of these therapies. Such alteration is neither a "complication," nor an "untoward effect," but is the *sine qua non* of the mode of action of these therapies.
> 4. No evidence has been educed in these studies that the physiodynamic therapies are specific agents for the relief of psychoses; nor do they affect a specific segment of the nervous system; nor do they induce specific behavioral changes.
> 5. The therapeutic process of convulsive therapy, insulin coma, lobotomy and tranquilizers may be ascribed to the induction of a persistent alteration in cerebral function which provides the milieu for a change in adaptation of the subject to his environment.

Fink's hypothesis adheres closely to mine in several important aspects. Brain dysfunction is not seen as a side effect or complication of the treatment, but as its essential mode of action. The treatment does not ameliorate psychoses, nor does it affect particular parts of the brain. Instead, the treatment produces a nonspecific general brain dysfunction, which Fink evaluates as an "improvement."

Fink, Kahn, and Green (1958) specifically stated, "Alteration of brain function is the central effect of electroshock therapy, and is a pre-requisite to behavioral change." That they meant marked brain dysfunc-tion is established by their criteria for "altered brain function," which included a severely abnormal EEG, an acute brain syndrome with diso-rientation and confabulation, and the utilization of denial and euphoria as defense mechanisms. They found that 90 percent of the "improved" patients had developed markedly abnormal EEG records during the treatment, compared to only 20 percent of the "unimproved." They also found that improvement correlated with the use of denial and euphoria as defense mechanisms. Patients with high denial ratings were clinically evaluated as follows: 58 percent clinically "much improved," 38 percent "improved," and only 4 percent "unimproved." By contrast, patients with low denial ratings were randomly distributed among the three categories.

In addition to the presence of severe brain dysfunction and a tend-ency for the patient to use euphoria or denial, Fink et al. cited the expec-tations of the family and the therapists as variables influencing whether the patient was rated as improved.

> Behavioral change in electroshock is dependent upon an alteration in brain function as evidenced by serial changes in delta activity in the electroencephalogram and disorientation and confabulation with intravenous amobarbital.[1]
>
> The pattern of behavioral alteration is shown to vary markedly, depending upon the degree of induced cerebral dys-function, the personality of the subject and the environmental situation.
>
> "Improvement" ratings are seen as a special case of be-havioral change dependent upon the type of adaptation elicited, the expectation of the therapist, administrator and family, and the tolerance of the milieu.

More specifically, the patient was labeled "improved" if a brain-damaged, euphoric patient denied brain dysfunction and psychological problems, and if this denial were accepted by the patient's therapists and family as an "improvement":

> When a depressed patient, who had been withdrawn, crying, and had expressed suicidal thoughts, no longer is seclusive,

---

1. *Amobarbitol* is a sedative that injected intravenously produces a rapid clouding of consciousness. When post-ECT patients respond to amobarbitol with "disorientation" and "confabulation," Fink uses this as an indicator that they have already suffered a degree of brain dysfunction, which is further brought out during the added insult of sedation.

and is jovial, friendly and euphoric, denies his problems and sees his previous thoughts of suicide as "silly," a rating of "much improved" is made.

In another 1958 article Fink dropped the euphemism of "altered brain function" and declared outright, "From the data available, it is probable that the biochemical basis for convulsive therapy is similar to that of craniocerebral trauma." Fink's associates, Weinstein, Linn, and Kahn (1952), had been equally if not more direct in comparing ECT in its effects to lobotomy, prolonged sedation, metrazol convulsions, and even self-inflicted gunshot wounds. Weinstein and Kahn (1959) also declared that patients were most often rated as "improved" when they displayed an organic brain syndrome characterized by "language patterns such as denial, reduplication, changes in tense and person, clichés, and stereotyped expressions," as well as "evasion and withdrawal."

In 1974 Fink reviewed his theoretical model for ECT effects. The main points were more disguised than before within a matrix of hints about possible underlying biochemical mechanisms. But the basic point remained the same: patients who were rated most improved by friends, relatives, and therapists were patients who showed the most severe brain damage on EEG and psychological studies, and who tended to display denial and euphoria persistently as mechanisms of defense. Indeed, Fink admitted that the presumed cure was actually a persisting increase in these rigid defenses following trauma to the brain:

> Patients exhibiting the euphoric-hypomanic mode were more often rated as much improved and recovered. . . . In part, this view is consistent with the temporary nature of many of the treatments—the patients "recovering" for the period of maximum physiologic effect alone; and with the continuing effects in some individuals, those with a psychologic organization described in the experimental studies [denial and euphoria], which allows some subjects to persist in their use of exaggerated defense mechanisms.

Pollack and Fink (1961) also studied the background and personality type of patients who have an accepting attitude toward ECT and who are also rated as improved following the treatment. Compared to individuals who resisted ECT, and who did poorly after treatment, they were more often foreign born, older, less skilled, and more rigid and authoritarian in personality type. They were less psychologically oriented and had less often been exposed to psychotherapy. This group would certainly be easier to "sell" on the idea of a treatment that produces brain dysfunction and damage. They are obviously less sophisticated and more ready to respond to the authority of the doctor. Whether they will actually feel more tolerant toward induced brain dysfunction after they have experienced it is a difficult point to evaluate; but they will certainly be less able to understand and to verbalize their difficulties. They will also be less willing to confront their psychiatrists. Perhaps most important, *other people,* such as psychiatrists, ward staff, and relatives, will be more willing to overlook the effects of brain damage and dysfunction in these patients than in patients who are American born, younger, more skilled, less rigidly authoritarian, and more psychologically oriented.

Undoubtedly because of Fink's influence as a Task Force member and because of his growing authority in the field, the brain-disabling hypothesis actually finds its way into the official Task Force report on ECT by the American Psychiatric Association (1978). Correlations are mentioned between improvement from ECT and "explicit verbal denial as a defense mechanism," disruption of physiological functions associated with the hypothalamus (appetite, weight, menses, libido, and mood), increased EEG slow wave activity, and other indicators of brain dysfunction (pp. 124–125). The Task Force falls short of endorsing Fink's conclusions, however, and while cataloging how ECT disrupts a vast array of central nervous system functions, it denies that any explanation for its effect is now available.

My main disagreement with Fink lies not in his data or his hypothesis but in his attitude toward them. Fink has advocated brain damage as therapy, and has tried to make it scientifically palatable with intricate discussions of the possible "underlying biochemical mechanisms," while admitting that these biochemical mechanisms are identical to those in *any form of severe trauma,* including head injuries. Fink is also mistaken in his emphasis on denial and euphoria as the main traits that psychiatrists value in their patients. ECT advocates value most of the disabilities produced by ECT, including the apathy, docility, suggestibility, and helplessness that so often follow brain damage, as well as the tendency to hide symptoms and complaints.

The Disruption of Normal Brain Function

Occasionally advocates of the somatic therapies have argued that one or another somatic therapy does disable or destroy certain portions of the brain but that these portions are *diseased* or *malfunctioning.* Hoff (1959), for example, has taken the position that insulin coma kills malfunctioning cells, and some psychosurgeons have held this view in regard to their various interventions. The brain-disabling hypothesis proposes the opposite view—that *normal brain function* is under assault.

The integrated anatomy and function of higher levels of the central nervous system do not permit the selective destruction of one area or region without affecting widespread anatomical regions and functions (Breggin, 1979). It is of course possible to disrupt limited areas of the brain, such as those controlling motor activities of the hand or arm, without necessarily disrupting the higher centers (frontal lobes and limbic system) that control reason and emotion or thinking and feeling. But an intervention aimed at modifying motor control or simple neurologic reflexes would not be "psychiatric" in origin or intention. A psychiatric intervention *must* compromise those functions with which psychiatrists deal—thought and feeling as they generate action.

Empirically, the major somatic interventions now in use—including the phenothiazines—produce generalized impairment of the capacity to think, to feel, and to act, and can be considered mind-disabling in general regardless of the differences among them (Breggin, 1979). ECT, despite its unique impact on memory, produces very severe general damage and dysfunction in its acute phase, and, as I have documented extensively, it can suppress overall mental function, creating a relatively apathetic, docile hospital inmate.

Regardless of whether a psychiatrist believes he or she is treating a "mental illness" or even a bona fide neurological disease, ECT does disrupt and even destroy brain function and mental function. Specifically, the brain-disabling hypothesis states that the somatic therapies disrupt normal brain function *regardless of the presence or absence of abnormal brain function.* Indeed, the somatic therapies not only disrupt the operation of the normal brain, they add to the malfunction of any already abnormally functioning brain tissue.

This point is particularly important because the brain-disabling hypothesis undoubtedly will be misunderstood and criticized on the grounds that its author does not "believe in mental illness." This argument wholly misses the point. Many traditional psychiatrists, from Walter Freeman to Max Fink, have believed in both mental illness and brain-damaging therapeutics. The brain-disabling hypothesis says nothing about what is wrong with the patient. It is specific and narrow in its scope and is not dependent on any concept of how and why patients are undergoing psychiatric treatment. The patient may be a criminal or a model citizen; a paragon of rationality or a madman. As we have seen, the patient may be a "Practicing Psychiatrist." The point is that any one of the major somatic therapies given to *any individual* will disrupt or damage whatever normal brain function that individual possesses, while further disrupting or damaging any already diseased portions of the brain.

A patient being given ECT might possibly have a serious brain disease such as a tumor or atherosclerosis. The impact of ECT on such a person will be *qualitatively* the same as on any individual; it will produce an acute organic brain syndrome with confusion, disorientation, memory loss, intellectual disabilities, and emotional instability. However, the impact may be *quantitatively more severe* because the already malfunctioning brain has less reserve capacity with which to absorb the trauma. It is clinically well known that an especially severe reaction to ECT sometimes indicates an underlying brain disease (Chapter 5). Even if a subtle chemical imbalance were responsible for a patient's problem, ECT would only *increase* the amount of physiological disability; because ECT disrupts just about every measurable chemical process in the brain, it can be assumed that ECT would further disrupt the already aberrant chemical process. ECT would certainly add an acute organic brain syndrome, and perhaps some permanent disabilities, to the already existing physiological disorder.

That ECT produces physiological and psychological malfunction in normal brain tissue, regardless of the presence or absence of brain disease or psychiatric disorder, has been confirmed by many observations presented in this book, as well as by common sense. To summarize, ECT affects all people, regardless of their psychiatric diagnosis, in much the same way; the damage done to the brain, as shown in autopsies, EEG studies, or memory tests, is not specific to any diagnostic category, nor does the acute organic brain syndrome differ from one diagnostic category to another. Spontaneous convulsions in epileptics with no other known brain disease, or in epileptics with specific epileptogenic foci, produce similar effects to ECT, including an acute organic brain syndrome and memory loss followed by apathy. ECT affects *animals* in much the same way it affects people: animals, too, develop an acute organic brain syndrome including memory loss, and with repeated treatments they too become more passive and apathetic. Finally, electrical current even disrupts biochemical function in tissue preparations.

The nonspecific leveling effect of ECT on all people is also verified by its once-commonplace use in state mental hospitals regardless of patients' age, sex, or diagnosis (Chapter 10). When given in sufficient intensity, ECT managed to subdue a variety of individuals, from the youthful to the aged and from the retarded to the paranoid, by producing docility, apathy, or euphoric indifference.

In this regard, let me quote my own more picturesque language in another presentation of the brain-disabling hypothesis (1979):

> . . . the hypothesis that the somatic therapies are suppressive of
> normal brain function is wholly independent of the controversy
> concerning the biological nature of mental illness. Put more
> baldly, a blow on the head is blow on the head, regardless of
> the thoughts, feelings, convictions or physical state of the reci-

pient. The only exception has already been examined. The blow
may have a more severe effect if the person already has brain
damage or dysfunction. . . .

If observations on the subjective experience of humans were not
enough to verify the integration of thoughts, feelings and decision-making, physiological and anatomical studies of the brain
confirm the integrated nature of brain function. One cannot
pluck a "thought" or a "feeling" out of the brain as one might
pluck an olive from a tree.

The Specificity of ECT for Psychotic Depression

Even though the case for the efficacy of ECT is wholly unproved, we may
ask ourselves why ECT advocates so often come to the conclusion that
depression, rather than other disorders such as anxiety or paranoid
schizophrenia, is most often helped by the treatment.

First and foremost, depressed people always have been used to
prove the efficacy of various psychiatric treatments simply because they
tend to respond to almost anything that is done to them. Everything from
genuine sympathy to life-threatening trauma will snap a certain number
of depressed people out of their melancholy—temporarily, at least. As a
psychiatric resident I found that the discovery of a "real disease" (e.g., a
benign tumor or an infection) during the admitting physical examination
might immediately cause a depressed person to perk up. This phenomenon is well known among lay people, who are aware that their depressed
friends or family may respond to anything from hard work to a "kick in
the butt." The same common wisdom also leads most people to avoid
interfering in the lives of individuals who are severely anxious or paranoid, for these persons may become more frightened or suspicious if
others interfere. Paranoid people in particular are likely to entrench their
fear and suspicion in response to almost any intervention.

The euphoria commonly encountered following ECT, especially in
the immediate post-ECT period, is much more likely to be interpreted as
a "cure" or as an "improvement" when it arises in aftermath of a depression. It appears to be the "opposite" of the depression, when in fact it is
an irrational denial of the brain damage imposed on the depressed person. On the other hand, euphoria or silliness is likely to seem more like
what it is—a reaction to brain damage—when it suddenly appears in a
person who has not been depressed. Because euphoric people are often
hostile and even paranoid, the paranoid person may even appear worse if
he turns to euphoria in response to his brain damage.

Depressed people are more likely to choose euphoria as a response
to their brain damage, whereas paranoid individuals are more likely to

get more paranoid. This is because depressed people frequently vacillate between lows and highs on their own even without outside encouragement in the form of superimposed brain damage. Therefore, in an equal number of depressed and paranoid people, the "illusion of health" through euphoria is far more likely to develop in previously depressed people.

To whatever extent the specific memory defects following ECT do play a role in the alleged improvement, the effect would be much more noticeable in depressed people. Depressed people are plagued by bad memories. Some, as Alexander and Rosen (1956) suggested, may even seek the oblivion of memory loss. Depressed people also often complain a great deal about unhappy experiences and losses. They beg at times to have a quick cure to wipe away their guilt and their unhappiness. Even if they don't feel good about the retrograde amnesia imposed on them by ECT, they may *seem* better to the casual, biased, or calloused observer who notes that they no longer complain so much about their bad memories. By contrast, paranoid people rarely if ever desire to give up their bad memories. If anything, they store them up as secret proofs or justifications for their paranoid hatred and distrust of those around them. The wiping out of their memory is likely neither to please them nor to remove their major complaints from view.

Depressed people are also less likely to complain about mental impairments following ECT. Some depressed people already feel as if their minds are slow and their memories inadequate. They do not display classic retrograde amnesias, but they do have many vague mental complaints. By contrast, people who choose paranoid defenses often tend to place a great deal of emphasis on their intellectual clarity, and their elaborate delusions can display a high level of intellectual activity. The complaints of depressed persons concerning the acute organic syndrome are less likely to stand out as drastically as the same complaints coming from individuals who have prided themselves on their intellectual acuity.

Anxious people are also likely to make much more of their mental dysfunction following ECT than are depressed people. As already described in regard to fear after ECT (Chapter 11), individuals who are already anxious are more frequently thrown into severe panic states following ECT. The damage done to them is therefore more obvious than the same damage done to depressed people who tend to use denial and to become "high."

The self-destructiveness of depressed individuals is another factor that may make them seem like more suitable candidates for ECT. Depressed people hate and blame themselves, whereas paranoid people hate and blame others. Paranoid people are therefore unsuitable candidates for a treatment such as ECT, which will give them more realistic reasons for hating and blaming others. What was once a delusion—that others are out to get them—becomes a reality following psychiatrically induced brain damage.

So few people actively seek ECT that it cannot generally be looked upon as a sought-after form of punishment or self-destruction, and most of those who do seek it out usually have been reassured by their psychiatrists that it causes no harm whatsoever. But in my own experience those few people who have actively sought ECT have wished to give up responsibility for themselves, and in some cases have had strong self-destructive wishes. Overall, however, even very self-destructive people are usually loathe to go through ECT more than once. Glueck et al. (1957) gave this away when they noted in regard to regressive ECT, "In one case, the course was repeated at the request of the patient himself, who remembered the absence of tension immediately after the treatments." The proud citation of only one patient in their series of 100 cases indicates how rare it is to find anyone who wishes to submit to intensive ECT a second time—even among self-destructive depressed persons. Of the hundreds of thousands subjected to ECT in the United States alone, few have come forward in praise of it. When hearings were held in California concerning legislation to control ECT, many former patients testified concerning its adverse effects, but few could be found to defend it (McDonald, 1977, Part II).

I have already dealt with Kalinowsky's claim that neurotics rather than psychotics complain the most and benefit the least from ECT. His argument is similar to that of Glueck et al., who felt that patients with "intellectual defenses" would complain more about memory loss. It is more valid to observe that people who value their minds are more likely to complain about any mental dysfunction that has been imposed on them. And as I've already noted, so-called neurotics are simply more able and more rational than so-called psychotics, and as such they are more willing and able to complain about mental dysfunction. In effect, the more "sane" the person, the more he is likely to resent ECT. Therefore, ECT is likely to seem a better treatment for psychotic or highly irrational depressed people.

The Specificity of ECT for Women

Why is ECT given more to women than to men? Some advocates of ECT have explained this by claiming that more women develop severe or psychotic depressions. I do not know of any evidence to support this view. But even if it were so, it would not account for those major studies that show that, according to the criteria used by ECT advocates, women respond better than men to ECT (Chapter 9). Indeed, one of the more frequently cited studies showed that men did no better on ECT than on placebo (Clinical Psychiatric Committee, 1965).

I believe that the answer to this question is reflected in the recommendation made so often in the literature that ECT be reserved for individuals who do not require the use of memory and intellect for their livelihood (Chapter 6), as well as in Pollack and Fink's (1961) perception that foreign born, less skilled persons improve more readily with ECT. Such repeated observations immediately suggest why more *women* are given ECT: they are judged to have less need of their brains! I have already commented that this is a cynical statement about human nature, and that the human spirit is demeaned by such a notion. Women are more specifically demeaned, for the "housewife" far more than the "wage earner" will be judged fit to lose a fraction of her mental life.

The situation of many middle-aged depressed women who receive ECT confirms how and why psychiatrists can get away so easily with damaging their brains. Typically, these women have grown frustrated, lonely, and helpless in their roles as housewives by the time they reach the psychiatrist. While their husbands are reaching their peak of satisfaction and accomplishment in the business and professional world, their own careers as mothers and wives are approaching a low ebb. Their children have grown up, their much-valued physical youth is going, and they have little to find hopeful about the future. They may have been taking tranquilizers for some time before they become candidates for ECT, and between the drugs and their own apathy and frustration, they may show little motivation to "use their minds." When brain damage is added to their already existing misery, no one may notice their compounded helplessness. The household tasks simply remain undone as always, and communication with their husbands remains as empty as ever. These women become brain-damaged custodial patients within their own homes. It is hard to imagine a man being kept in a state of chronic dementia in the home with ECT as reported in the case of a housewife (Regestein et al., 1975).

Do I believe that some psychiatrists who use ECT callously choose which patients can sacrifice their brains and which cannot? If we take them at their word there can be no doubt that they do, for they have told us specifically in their publications that individuals who use their minds to earn their living have a greater need and a greater right to maintain the integrity of their minds (Chapter 6). They also have told us that mental function may be "sacrificed" in favor of social adjustment (Chapter 10). But in respect to the great majority of psychiatrists who advocate ECT, a more subtle evaluation may be going on. As psychologist Phyllis Chesler (1972) has argued so cogently, male psychiatrists (and indeed, female psychiatrists!) tend to accept the prevalent social bias that mental incapacity and helpless dependence are far more acceptable in women than in men. As Chesler suggested, psychiatrists actually may value these negative traits in their female patients. Without giving it a moment of conscious consideration, many might find it far easier to subject a woman than a man to brain-damaging treatments.

The brain- and mind-disabling hypothesis easily accounts not only for the so-called effectiveness of ECT, but also for its apparent differential effectiveness with psychotically depressed people, and especially with depressed women.

The Philosophical Context

Because of my desire to adhere as closely as possible to the actual data, I have stayed away from setting my observations within an elaborate philosophical context. Instead, I have *assumed* certain philosophical premises, such as the importance of an intact mind in the life of the individual. I have assumed that the destruction of reason or emotional spontaneity is harmful and even unethical. I have also stayed away from subtle explanations about the relationship between the integrity of one's mind and such political ideals as the right to pursue life, liberty, and happiness. Anyone interested in delving further into these issues might begin with my paper, "Mind-Disabling Therapy: The Common Effects of the Major Tranquilizers, ECT and Psychosurgery" (1979).

In describing the common mode of action of the major tranquilizers, psychosurgery, and ECT in other papers, I have examined some of the broader implications of the brain- and mind-disabling hypothesis (1977b, 1979). In evaluating the resurgence of psychosurgery I have more specifically discussed ethical and political ramifications of brain-damaging therapy (1973a, 1972a, 1973b, 1975a, 1975b). I have placed the somatic therapies in the context of psychiatry's historical role in the politics of the state (1972c, 1974, 1975c), and have proposed an alternative view of how psychotherapy (1971a) and psychiatry (1975d, 1977c) can base themselves on respect for human autonomy and personal freedom.

Despite the rich opportunity this book provides for elaborating on ethical, philosophical, and political themes in regard to electroshock, I have focused on empirical issues related to brain damage and to the brain- and mind-disabling hypothesis. I have wanted to place paramount importance on the evidence that ECT does produce permanent brain damage and irreversible mental dysfunction, and that its clinical effect is achieved by disabling the individual.

Finally, it is important to distinguish between the functions of the brain and the functions of every other organ of the body. In defending the somatic therapies, psychiatrists often observe that other treatments in medicine also impair the functions of various organs. Some heart medications, for example, actually weaken cardiac muscle in the interest of preventing arrhythmias. But there is a grave and all-important difference between the functions of the brain and those of the heart and other organs. The quality of brain function directly affects the quality of the most human functions—thinking, feeling, creating, and decision-making. When these functions are impaired, the *person* is impaired. When a heart or liver is impaired, the person remains the same, provided the impairment has not compromised brain function as well. A liver can be badly scarred, without the person changing in his or her fundamental capacity to experience life. A heart can even be replaced without essentially changing the person. But the death of the brain represents the death of the person, and the impairment of its higher functions means the impairment of the individual as an individual.

A mentally impaired person is also a less free person. Though released from actual confinement after treatment, he is now confined by his relative inability to use his reason and to respond to his emotions. Even to the degree that he may be able to think and to feel, he may be sufficiently impaired to limit his effectiveness in carrying out his wishes. Ultimately, he is less free to know, to experience, and to enjoy his life and the lives of those around him. If he is mildly euphoric, he may seem happy. If he is apathetic, some observers may consider him more even-tempered and calm. In reality he is unfree to live his life for better or worse with the full resources of his mind.

13

Conclusions

Informed Consent

Informed consent is the single most important principle in protecting the rights of individuals subjected to ECT. According to Plotkin (1977),

> . . . informed consent exists when the following three conditions are met: the physician makes a reasonable disclosure to the patient of treatment risks; a voluntary decision is made by the patient based on this disclosure; and the patient is competent to make such a decision. These three elements—disclosure, voluntariness, and competency—clearly apply to a psychiatrist's use of the previously discussed methods of treatment on mental patients [ECT, psychosurgery, psychotropic drugs and behavior therapy].

The question of competence, as Plotkin underscored, is not a medical decision, but a judicial one. The psychiatrist cannot escape his responsibility for providing informed consent by personally declaring the patient to be incompetent. This is a very important point because psychiatrists commonly decide that patients are incompetent to know what is good for them, in effect appointing themselves to the status of legal guardian. Consent becomes a particularly complex problem in regard to ECT because the treatment almost invariably produces sufficient mental disruption in the form of an acute organic brain syndrome to render the patient incompetent by any commonly accepted standard. Typically the psychiatrist makes himself the patient's guardian by deciding to continue the treatment during this period of iatrogenic helplessness.

The degree of disclosure is another important issue that is often obscured by psychiatrists who decide for the patient that knowing the risks of the treatment might be injurious in itself to the patient. "For the patient's own good," the patient will not be informed of the dangers involved in the treatment. Plotkin made it clear that this is not a legally acceptable position:

> It now appears safe to conclude that the modern trend requires the doctor to disclose all information that the "prudent" patient needs in order to consent knowingly to treatment, even if the physician believes that disclosure of the information might be harmful to the patient.

In actual practice, patients are never fully informed of the devastating effects of ECT that they will invariably experience during the acute organic brain syndrome, and they are never fully informed about the possible lasting damage to both memory and overall mental function. As already described in Chapter 1, often they are not given a choice about whether or not they want the treatment (See Beresford, 1971; Asnis et al., 1978). Not only have noted authorities advocated giving ECT without the consent of the patient or even his relative (Kalinowsky & Hoch, 1961; Kalinowsky & Hippius, 1969; see Chapter 1), but over the years strategies have been proposed in the psychiatric literature for controlling the resistive patient with more ECT (see Chapter 10). While forthrightly recognizing the dangers associated with ECT, Impastato (1957) recommended dealing with patients' fears of the treatment by not telling patients that they are about to receive ECT. A well-known advocate of the treatment, Bennett (1949), has suggested holding patients incommunicado during the treatment in order to keep them from fulfilling their desire to end the treatment:

> *Nursing Management:* First, no visiting is the rule. Friends or relatives are not allowed during the active shock therapy treatment. The patient's confusional period makes relatives anxious about his welfare, and visiting during treatment complicates nursing management, destroys rapport between patient and doctor and increases the patient's drive for premature termination of treatment.

In my experience, these attitudes are still prevalent today.

Informed consent is undermined more subtly when the psychiatrist withholds information concerning the potentially damaging effects of the treatment. Strain (1972), for example, notes that many individuals are very afraid of ECT, and he recommends reassuring the family that no permanent memory loss will follow the treatment. The American Psychiatric Association Task Force on ECT took a similar stance in regard to informing patients and relatives about the mental hazards of the treatment, even though the Task Force Report recognized the controversial nature of the treatment, reported that 41 percent of psychiatrists suspect that it causes brain damage, and identified studies indicating that patients frequently complain of long-term memory loss following ECT. The Task Force specifically recommended reassuring the family of the patient that "confusion and memory changes" are "temporary" in nature (p. 110). This is an obvious attempt to keep the patient in treatment during the period of the acute organic brain syndrome when patient and family alike are likely to ask for termination of the treatment. This suggestion to reassure patients is in marked contrast with an appendix to the Task Force report, which presents a model for informed consent, including a warning that "poor memory function" is a "frequent side effect" and that some patients at least continue to complain about poor memory function for "prolonged periods of time." Which is the patient likely to believe—the verbal, face-to-face reassurances of the doctor that the treatment is harmless, or a formal warning tacked on the end of a very lengthy official consent form? Clearly, the Task Force is advising doctors to meet some of the legal requirements on paper while maintaining their traditional posture in clinical situations.

Although withholding information about brain damage and memory loss is routine ECT practice, the degree to which patients are pressured into taking the treatment varies widely from psychiatrist to psychiatrist and institution to institution. In one hospital with which I am familiar, individual staff members usually presented ECT as an option that the patients might reasonably accept or reject; although they were not informed about its hazards, many rejected it. In another hospital the clinical administrator always presented ECT as a dire necessity that the patients must undergo or risk commitment to the frightening, remote state hospital. Almost every patient agreed to ECT under this pressure.

Of the six cases I discussed in Chapter 2, one requested the treatment, one was encouraged to take it, one was systematically pushed into it by several collaborating doctors, and three were forced to take it against their vociferously expressed objections. In all six cases the patients demanded or begged to be taken off the treatment after it had begun. All six thus became involuntary or unwilling subjects of ECT.

Progress in Psychiatric Reform

California is the only state to pass reform legislation specifically protecting the rights of potential ECT patients (McDonald, 1977; Plotkin, 1977). This law requires that a patient be fully informed about the risks and benefits of the treatment, and that any question about his or her capacity to give informed consent must be decided at a court hearing. The court may then decide that the patient is not capable of giving informed consent, and a relative or other individual may be assigned the responsibility. This legislation is considered significant by many reform-minded individuals, but it falls far short of the recommendations I will make, and it remains to be seen if it will actually improve the legal status of psychiatric patients. Other attempts at reform legislation have had little impact over the years (Plotkin, 1977; Ennis and Siegel, 1973; Szasz, 1963). In the absence of strict legal enforcement, the degree to which the legislation actually will reach into the hospitals will be determined largely by the attitudes of psychiatrists; without exception, all official psychiatric organizations fought strongly against the legislation and continue to repudiate it (McDonald, 1977).

Public concern over hospitals using ECT for a large percentage of their admissions also brought about the threat of legislation in Massachusetts, but this was aborted when the Department of Mental Health promulgated new regulations (Dietz, 1972; *Psychiatric News,* 1973). However, the new regulations are very weak, requiring only that psychiatrists obtain additional psychiatric opinions before giving more than 35 ECT to any patient in one calendar year.

There is a gradually changing climate within the law itself, reflected in the California statutes and in efforts to develop similar codes in other states; but it is another matter to effect actual changes within psychiatric practices. New York State has been among the leaders in developing so-called reform legislation in psychiatry over the decades. But as the survey recently conducted in New York City indicates (Asnis et al., 1978), some psychiatrists continue to give ECT against the will of the patient by substituting the signature of a relative on the consent form or by going ahead with the treatment entirely on their own discretion. My own knowledge of psychiatric practice in New York State from 1962 to the present has demonstrated no appreciable improvement in the legal status of mental patients. My more direct and personal experience in the area of Washington, D.C., Maryland, and Virginia confirms that any changes in public attitudes have not reached into the hospitals or into the courts. Reports made to the Center for the Study of Psychiatry from across the nation—and around the world—indicate no significant improvement in the status of mental patients within the last 10 to 15 years. Plotkin's (1977) review of the subject confirms this impression.

Protecting the Vulnerable Patient

Reform-minded critics and commissions (see Plotkin, 1977; National Commission, 1977) typically advocate that informed consent can be obtained from involuntary patients and prisoners, and that in the absence of informed consent with incompetent patients, guardians and review boards may substitute for the individual. I do not believe that this approach provides satisfactory safeguards for especially vulnerable individuals who live under government or parental control, such as involuntary mental patients, prisoners, individuals under guardianship, and children. These vulnerable persons should be protected by an absolute prohibition against being treated with dangerous, mentally disruptive, experimental, or controversial psychiatric treatments. Indeed, even the so-called *voluntary* mental patient is in an extremely vulnerable position, and his consent to any procedure must be greeted with great skepticism and caution.

I will not focus upon the more obvious libertarian right of the individual to *refuse* any treatment. Szasz (1963, 1970, 1974) and I (1971a, b, 1974, 1975c) have thoroughly discussed the basis for the case against involuntary treatment. Briefly, I believe it is the right of every individual to be free of unwanted interferences in his life, except when the individual has broken criminal codes and been found guilty in the criminal courts. No one should be incarcerated "for his own good," and no one should receive treatments, medical or psychiatric, that he does not want. Involuntary treatment is not only a "crime against humanity" (Szasz, 1970), it results in horrible abuses, and seldom if ever helps anyone. The story of electroshock is an egregious example of what happens when psychiatrists are permitted to treat people against their will. Without involuntary treatment, the major psychiatric interventions—tranquilizers, electroshock, and psychosurgery—would never have been developed (Breggin, 1974, 1975c; also see in Chapter 10, the section on "Somatic Treatment and the Mental Hospital"). The most important step in any reform must be the abolition of involuntary psychiatric treatment or hospitalization.

The tough questions arise when the vulnerable patient *wants* or *seems to want* a dangerous, mentally disruptive, experimental, or controversial psychiatric treatment. How can he be protected from the demoralizing pressures and coercion that can make him appear to want a treatment he would never select if he were free of the psychiatric system?

With these concerns in mind, I began in late 1971 what would become an international campaign to alert the public and the medical profession to the resurgence of lobotomy and newer forms of psychosurgery (Trotter, 1973a, b; Breggin, 1979). I encouraged the development of legal actions and federal regulations to protect vulnerable individuals from psychosurgery, and over the ensuing years a number of precedents have been established. I am now proposing that these protections be expanded and applied to electroconvulsive therapy.

One of the most important precedents was set by a three-judge panel in Michigan (Kaimowitz, 1973, also see Breggin, 1973b, 1975a) that was convened to determine if an involuntary state mental hospital patient could give consent to psychosurgery. The Kaimowitz court ruled that the status of such a patient makes voluntary, informed consent an impossibility. The patient had been provided a lay review committee to verify his consent, the patient's parents had also signed permissions for the surgery, and a scientific review committee had approved the project. Yet the court found that the status of involuntary patient placed him in such a vulnerable position that his consent could not be freely given. On questioning in court, it became obvious that the patient gave consent in the hope of gaining release and that he never would have consented to the treatment if he had been free to leave. The court also found that the demoralizing, coercive conditions within the state mental hospital so effectively compromised the patient's identity and self-esteem that he was not psychologically in a position to give consent.

The court also focused its attention on the nature of the treatment being offered to the patient. It found that psychosurgery can have devastating effects on mental function, including irreversible interference with thought processes, blunting of feeling, and impairment of memory. It ruled that the treatment was invasive of the mind, and that the patient should be protected from it on the basis of the constitutional right to privacy and the constitutional right to freedom of speech (and thought). The treatment, the court declared, invaded privacy and destroyed the capacity to exercise freedom of thought and speech. It also ruled that the effects of the treatment were so dangerously unpredictable that the patient could not be truly informed concerning its outcome. The court concluded that an involuntary state mental hospital patient could not give informed consent to psychosurgery and should not be subjected to it under any conditions, even if he requested it.

During the time in which Kaimowitz was developing, I worked closely with a number of congressmen and senators in an effort to place limits on the federal funding of psychosurgery (Breggin, 1975a, 1979; Trotter, 1973a, b). One result was legislation calling for a special committee to investigate psychosurgery as a part of the larger National Commission for the Protection of Human Subjects of Biomedical and Behavioral Research (National Commission, 1977). The psychosurgery committee was dominated by establishment-oriented professionals whose major concern was the protection of psychiatry from criticism rather than the protection of patients from dangerous psychiatric treatments, and it strongly opposed the rulings of the Kaimowitz court. But the committee itself had no power to act. This power was vested in the Secretary of Health, Education and Welfare, and on reviewing the report, Secretary Califano (Califano, 1978) placed limits on the population to which psychosurgery can be administered. His conclusion about psychosurgery itself—that it is not experimental—contradicts Kaimowitz, testimony at the psychosurgery hearings, and his own decision to place controls upon it; but his regulations were built upon Kaimowitz and in part parallel my own proposals. The Secretary stated (Califano, 1978): "These regulations . . . would ban use of the procedures with prisoners, children, involuntarily confined mental patients, legally incompetent patients, and any patient, who, in the judgment of the attending physician, is not competent to give informed consent."

The Secretary used prisoners and children as the prototype of individuals unable because of their condition to give informed consent, and he "banned absolutely" the use of psychosurgery on prisoners or children in Public Health Hospitals or with Department of Health, Education and Welfare funds. He then observed that the problem with incompetent adults was more complex, but concluded that their situation was similar enough to that of children and prisoners. Further citing the "public concern" about psychosurgery, he also banned it "on any patient who, in the judgment of the attending physician, is not, in fact, competent, although he or she may not have been adjudicated."

The Secretary limited the enforcement of his regulations to projects funded through the Department of Health, Education and Welfare, and to patients in Public Health Service facilities. He urged the private sector to adopt the same regulations, but on a voluntary basis. He also failed to prohibit the use of psychosurgery on *voluntary* patients in PHS facilities, and he failed to ban HEW funding of research using human subjects. I would go further than the Secretary. *All psychosurgery in federal facilities should be banned and all federal funding of psychosurgery research involving human subjects should be stopped.* No dangerous, mentally disruptive, experimental, and controversial treatment should be developed, carried out, or promoted in federal or state facilities. Nor should research on human subjects be funded when the treatment is already known to be very damaging, when it has little rational justification, and when all authorities (National Commission, 1978; Kaimowitz, 1973) agree that animal research has not been adequately developed. I would also ban psychosurgery in the private sector in regard to vulnerable individuals who are in effect wards of the state or wholly under the control of authorities. Thus, involuntary mental patients, incompetents, and children would not be permitted to undergo psychosurgery even in the private sector. This extension of the Califano regulations and Kaimowitz precedents would in effect *ban all psychosurgery except psychosurgery on voluntary patients in the private sector.* Only voluntary patients in the private sector are remotely capable of giving voluntary, informed consent, and, as I shall discuss, even their status must be viewed with skepticism.

Extending Psychosurgery Precedents to ECT

It is not a great leap to extend the psychosurgical regulations and precedents to electroshock. When I first began to call for an end to federal funding for psychosurgery, one objection was the difficulty finding a definition for psychosurgery that would not also include electroshock therapy. Both cause brain tissue damage; both are aimed at the control of thoughts, feelings, and actions; and both are applied to persons who have no disease of the brain. The main difference is that psychosurgery usually involves direct contact between an instrument and brain tissue, while electroshock is applied to the outside of the head. But even this distinction is blurred, for one form of psychosurgery, ultrasonic radiation of the brain, involves the boring of button-sized holes in the skull without any direct contact between an instrument and the brain itself. Instead, the frontal lobes are sprayed with sound waves through the burr holes (Breggin, 1972a, 1973a).

Throughout this book we have found comparisons made between the effects of electroconvulsive therapy and the effects of old-fashioned lobotomy. Both traumatize and/or destroy tissue in the fontal lobes of the brain. While the damage from ECT may be less severe in any one area, it is more widespread, and compromises the memory functions of the temporal lobe as well. As previously quoted in Chapter 10, some modern advocates of psychosurgery have justified the technology on the grounds that it is less damaging than intensive courses of ECT (Lehmann, 1972; Pribam, 1974; Scoville, 1972).

The uses to which psychosurgery and electroshock are put are also very similar. Historically, psychosurgery and ECT both developed in the state mental hospital and were given widespread use for the control of unruly, difficult, or uncooperative patients (see Chapter 10; Breggin, 1973a, 1975b). In more modern times, psychosurgery and ECT are sometimes recommended for different diagnostic categories, psychosurgery more frequently for neuroses and ECT more frequently for psychoses. But in actual practice, psychosurgery is usually performed on patients who have already been given ECT (National Commission, 1977). Both treatments are also disproportionately applied to women (Breggin, 1973a; National Commission, 1977).

Psychosurgery and electroshock also share a common lack of scientific or theoretical justification, and the chief advocates of both treatments generally agree that their efforts are "empirical." According to my own formulation (Breggin, 1979), both have their effect by disabling the brain and the mind.

ECT and Involuntary Mental Patients and Prisoners

The Kaimowitz decision focused on the involuntary state mental hospital patient, but involuntary patients in any mental hospital, including the most modern facilities, are subjected to the same elements of coercion and demoralization as state mental hospital patients. In my novel *The Crazy from the Sane* (1971a) and in "Coercion of Voluntary Patients in an Open Hospital" (1964) I have portrayed the conditions under which the typical involuntary mental patient exists in a modern teaching hospital. This individual is literally subject to the whims of his psychiatrist. Typically he will be treated against his will with massive doses of major tranquilizers that place him in a chemical straitjacket by virtue of their neurologically disabling effects, and that further impose a chemical lobotomy by means of their toxic effect upon brain function (Breggin, 1979). If the hospital in which he is incarcerated uses electroshock, he may be subjected to this against his will, typically with the agreement of the nearest relative, who is likely to listen to the psychiatrist's recommendation. If the individual rebels against his treatment, he may also be committed to the state hospital. Every involuntary mental patient lives within the threatening shadow of the state mental hospital (Breggin, 1964, 1971a, 1974).

Even without the threat or actual imposition of the various somatic therapies and commitment to a state mental hospital, the involuntary mental patient is wholly at the mercy of his doctors. When he gets up and when he goes to bed, who may visit with him, what he may read, when he may sit and with whom, what he can do to pass the time away, when he may visit off the ward or outside the hospital, when he will be released—every aspect of his life is under the psychiatrist's control. My legal experience demonstrates that he may frequently be held incommunicado, his mail opened and censored and phone calls prohibited, wholly without lawful process. He cannot feel free to defy authorities with such power over him. He will surely be tempted to "consent" to procedures in order to appease this authority.

Much like the state hospital, the environment of the modern mental hospital is also demeaning to the person's identity and self-esteem. He is diagnosed as suffering from a "mental disease," he is treated as an irresponsible child, isolated from his family and his job, and made dependent upon the good will of others for everything he needs and wants. His confidence in his own judgment will be undermined by these conditions, and his ability to make choices on his own will be compromised.

Although many of his legal rights are better protected, the prisoner is in much the same vulnerable position as the involuntary mental patient. When he is subjected to the additional threat and humiliation of psychiatric treatment in the medical wing of the prison, he is placed in heightened jeopardy. My wife and I (Lundy & Breggin, 1974), and Coleman (1974), have analyzed the situation of the prisoner as especially vulnerable to the dangers of psychiatric treatment. Neither involuntary mental patients nor prisoners can give truly voluntary consent to dangerous, mentally disruptive, experimental, or controversial treatments such as psychosurgery and electroshock. They must be protected by a ban against the use of these technologies on involuntary patients and prisoners.

In coming to a similar conclusion concerning state hospital patients, the Kaimowitz court stressed the dangerous, mentally disruptive, and experimental nature of the treatment in question. I have added the concept of "controversiality." A controversy is a dispute over opposing views, especially a public one. The dispute about electroshock is intense and involves both the public and the profession. The existence of a medical or psychiatric controversy implies that presumably *competent, uncoerced,* and *informed* individuals differ strongly in their evaluation of a treatment. In other words, those individuals best in a position to give informed consent disagree strongly on the merits of the treatment. This suggests that were the involuntary patient or prisoner equally competent, uncoerced, and informed, he or she might also reject the treatment. It also suggests that the involuntary patient or prisoner would not even be exposed to the possibility of the treatment were he or she under the care of a physician who rejected the controversial treatment. Prohibiting the use of a controversial treatment protects the vulnerable person against coercion and also against the chance factor that he is under the care of physicians who happen to favor it. If the treatment in question is dangerous, irreversibly destructive of the mind, and experimental, this increases the individual's need for protection.

The issue of "controversy" is of great concern to those who advocate the treatment, for if the treatment is controversial, then some measure of control or supervision of those who use it may be justified. Throughout its presentation of the issues, the American Psychiatric Association report (1978) on ECT recognized its controversial nature. In describing the history of ECT, it noted that the treatment was greeted "with considerable enthusiasm" in the beginning, but that "in more recent years, considerable controversy has surrounded ECT . . ." (p. 13). Its survey indicated that 32 percent of psychiatrists polled expressed "some opposition" to the treatment, 1 percent were "ambivalent" or "undecided," and 67 percent showed "some degree of favorable attitude." Furthermore, a remarkable 41 percent agreed with the statement: "It is likely that ECT produces slight or subtle brain damage." How many respondents would have agreed with an even stronger statement concerning brain damage must remain unknown because the questionnaire did not include such a statement. It is also very likely that positive views of ECT were disproportionately represented in the 74.1 percent of the questionnaires correctly filled out and fed into the computer. The questionnaire was admittedly very long, which suggests that motivation to fill it out would have greatly affected results. A great deal of publicity about protecting ECT from criticism had been generated in the psychiatric press, and certainly advocates of ECT would have been highly motivated to take the time to answer the questionnaire in a positive manner. Many psychiatrists who never use ECT would have been little motivated to set aside time from busy practices to fill out a form dealing with a treatment they had long ago discarded. The Task Force even admits that some psychiatrists returned their questionnaires without answering the questions because "they had no recent experience with ECT." Had these nonusers filled out their questionnaires, they surely would not have been among the most enthusiastic supporters of the treatment.

Even though the controversial nature of ECT is obvious from the Task Force report, the Task Force disregarded its own data and its own statements when dealing with the *legal* and *legislative* implications of the controversy. It complained about California legislation, which cites "a division of opinion" concerning the value of the treatment. Instead, the Task Force abruptly and without elaboration attempted to discredit critics of ECT "whose credentials and motives have not been subjected to scrutiny." It then came to the conclusion that "this Task Force finds no division of *informed* opinion about the efficacy" of ECT (p. 145; italics in original). By informed opinion, the Task Force means the opinion of those who frequently use the treatment. Obviously, those who frequently use the treatment are unanimous in supporting its usefulness! If they were not, they would appear flagrantly unethical. Such a criterion for determining whether or not a treatment is controversial means that only treatments that have no users are controversial. Indeed, the most obvious forms of quackery will be unanimously supported by those most informed about them—*the frequent users!*

There is a danger in the recommendations that I make establishing classes of vulnerable individuals who are subject to government or parental authority. The extension of such a principle to larger or broader classes of allegedly vulnerable persons would pose a serious threat to political freedom. Indeed, the establishment of any vulnerable classes based on the Kaimowitz and Califano models already further compromises the freedom of these persons, while protecting them.

In a personal communication to me in 1979, Szasz proposed alternative solutions to my categories of vulnerable persons. He believes that prisoners and involuntary mental patients must be treated as wholly separate categories. Prisoners should be allowed to choose any treatments they wish, much as they might elect to take aspirin or seek an abortion. Coercion by means of manipulating the length of sentence would be ruled out in experimental or controversial treatments by the requirement that the prisoner accept the maximum sentence before submitting to these treatments.

Regarding mental patients, Szasz would end all involuntary treatment, without confusing the issue by taking interim steps to protect them from specific therapies. He believes that efforts to protect them from specific therapies are futile and in the long run distract from the primary importance of doing away with involuntary treatment and hospitalization. When involuntary mental hospitalization is abolished, mental patients will not need special protections.

I basically agree with Szasz that the single most important issue is the abolition of involuntary treatment. But I do not agree that all efforts to reform the psychiatric system distract from this fundamental requirement. Indeed, the publicity surrounding the psychosurgery and electroshock controversies has helped educate the public concerning the dangers of involuntary treatment. While the fight against involuntary treatment goes on, we must also make every effort to protect those individuals who remain vulnerable.

Prisoners in my opinion will *always* remain in far too vulnerable a position to permit them to contract for irreversible, physically destructive activities, such as suicide, dangerous or painful medical experimentation, and brain-disabling psychiatric treatments. While such freedoms are essential for ordinary citizens, they too easily become weapons against incarcerated persons. It becomes difficult to imagine a prison system in which the authorities would not be able to drive inmates into self-destructive activities if these activities were available to them. The prisoner's opportunity to choose irreversible, self-destructive alternatives places far too much power in the hands of the authorities who control his life. Szasz's solution also requires that a distinction be made between ordinary activities and those which can only be undertaken when the prisoner has agreed to the maximum sentence. This is already a compromise of the prisoner's freedom, and a severe one at that. Since the compromise must be made, I would make it in a manner that truly protects the prisoner—by prohibiting irreversible, self-destructive alternatives.

ECT and Incompetent Patients

The concept of competence itself raises many complex issues. Typically the determination of incompetence is based not on a neurological evaluation of impaired brain function, but on a psychiatric diagnosis of "mental illness," combined with a psychiatric judgment that the individual is unable to handle his own affairs. Szasz (1974, 1976) and I (1974, 1975c, 1977c) have criticized the concept of "mental illness" as a mixed and self-contradictory metaphor. But surely a person can be neurologically impaired and rendered relatively unable to think and to make judgments. The post-ECT patient exists in such a condition for days, weeks, or longer after the treatment. But psychological incompetence is another matter. It rests not on biological impairment, but on the alleged irrationality of the individual. It is a matter of a difference of opinion—the opinion of the individual being judged and the opinion of the person doing the judging. I would permit such individuals to live their own lives in their own ways. This might mean that some individuals whom I judge to be "irrational" or "self-destructive" might choose to accept treatments, such as ECT, which I think will harm them. Such an alternative, I believe, is preferable to vesting psychiatrists with power over the lives of others.

However, when dealing with an individual who has been declared incompetent, we have created a new problem—an inherently coercive relationship between the incompetent and both his guardian and the state. Regardless of the validity of the concept of incompetence, there can be no doubt that anyone who has been declared incompetent is in an extremely vulnerable position. His role is a mixture of mental patient, prisoner, and child. For this reason I agree with Secretary Califano's conclusion that individuals under guardianship should be banned from receiving psychosurgery, and I would extend this ban to electroshock.

If we also accept the validity of mental incompetence as a concept, then the banning of dangerous, mentally destructive, experimental, or controversial treatments becomes even more imperative. The concept of "controversiality" applies here even more obviously than in the case of the involuntary patient or prisoner, for it can be assumed that if the incompetent were to gain competence, or if he were to be assigned to different physicians, he and his physicians might choose to reject the controversial treatment. Therefore, he should be protected from hazardous, controversial treatments during his incompetence, regardless of his guardian's opinions.

Children are in a role that combines the vulnerability of mental patient, prisoner, and incompetent, and for this reason, I would ban electroshock for them as well, regardless of their parents' opinions.

ECT and Voluntary Mental Patients

In 1964 I elaborated for the first time in the psychiatric literature the reality that voluntary patients are not truly voluntary. In most states (Ennis and Siegel, 1973), the patient is voluntary only in regard to entering the hospital. Once within the hospital, the individual typically cannot leave without giving notice. Depending upon the state, the physician may then hold the patient against his or her will for a sufficient period of time in which to begin commitment proceedings. Often the patient does not realize this when signing into the hospital, and may only discover it upon trying to leave. In my experience, this is so intimidating that the individual will usually withdraw the request to leave rather than face the possibility of commitment (Breggin, 1964). If the person decides to fight commitment, he may be given little more than a two- or three-minute perfunctory hearing in which the judge in effect puts a routine stamp of approval on the psychiatrist's recommendations. In some states, the patient may even be excluded from the hearing if his psychiatrists believe it to be in his best interest. Since it is routine practice to force medications on voluntary patients, the patient may be so stupified and neurologically impaired as to be incapable of defending himself. His drugged condition may also be falsely attributed to "mental illness" by his psychiatrists and the judge.

Some states have now built protections into the commitment proceedings, including the presence of a legal advocate for the patient. However, psychiatric hospitalization and the threat of commitment are so humiliating and demoralizing that the patient continues to have little chance against his psychiatrists. Since the patient is frequently at odds with his family, he may be faced with the combined forces of his psychiatrists and his family, with no one willing to back him up (Breggin, 1971a).

Until the law and psychiatric practice change so that voluntary patients cannot be treated against their will or subjected to commitment proceedings, the status of voluntary patient will remain a myth. For this reason, I have been tempted in the past to say that voluntary private patients should be prevented from receiving treatments such as psychosurgery and electroshock, even if they seem to desire them. However, this borders on arbitrarily constricting the rights of seemingly free persons. Instead of making it impossible for so-called voluntary adult patients in the private sector to select hazardous and controversial treatments for themselves, I would urge the courts to take into consideration the vulnerable position of so-called voluntary patients when considering whether or not their consent has been freely given. It should be presumed that the consent may have been coerced, and it should be up to those prescribing the treatment to demonstrate that the patient freely and knowingly chose the therapy. The recommendations that I will make concerning the criteria for informed consent for electroshock should be strictly adhered to.

Why Consent Is Rarely Voluntary during ECT

Even if it were possible to give voluntary, informed consent during a patient's stay in a mental hospital, and even if ECT advocates made its hazards known beforehand, electroshock presents a special problem that effectively rules out consent in most or all cases. Despite giving initial consent to the treatment, the patient typically tries to reject it when he begins to experience the onset of an acute organic brain syndrome. His fear and outrage are always ignored, and often he is drugged, isolated and/or given extended ECT treatments until rendered unable to protest with any strength or coherence. As the patient passes from abject terror to incoherence, his psychiatrist may use his growing mental incompetence to justify further treatment on the grounds that the patient is too irrational to know what is good for him. I have never seen, or heard, or read of a single individual whose ECT was prematurely terminated on the grounds that he had changed his mind after experiencing the treatment and no longer wanted it. Most so-called voluntary ECT patients, therefore, become truly involuntary as soon as they experience its devastating effects. At first they are involuntary because their protests are ignored. Later they become involuntary because they are too brain-damaged to protest their worsening condition.

It may be argued that many medical and surgical treatments, once begun, render the patient unable to protest. Most obviously this is true when medical or surgical procedures interfere with brain function. However, if the medical patient at any time *protests* the procedure, it will be terminated. The same standard should be applied to psychiatric treatment. If the originally willing ECT patient protests his treatment once he or she experiences its devastating effects, the treatment should be stopped. To continue the treatment until the patient is unable to protest should constitute malpractice, and assault and battery.

Why ECT Patients Have Been Unable to Seek Legal Redress

The question naturally arises, "How has such a situation persisted without severe legal repercussions in the form of multiple malpractice suits?" Much of the answer to this lies in the material with which I developed the brain- and mind-disabling hypothesis. Patients are often so demoralized and intimidated by the ECT experience that they wish to have nothing more to do with the psychiatrist or, if they do continue to relate to him, they wish to placate him at all costs. Patients are also profoundly confused by the experience. They cannot recall many of the details surrounding the treatment, or even surrounding admission to the hospital. They do not know if they wanted the treatment, or if it was forced on them. They do not recall what they were told about it beforehand. Furthermore, they have difficulty determining whether the mental dysfunction and memory loss they experience is part of their "craziness" and "problems," or if it was caused by the ECT. They are typically so ashamed of the memory loss and mental dysfunction that they wish to hide it from themselves and from others. With good reason, they are also likely to fear that their physician or relatives will think they are "still mentally ill" if they complain about memory loss, nightmares, fatigue or other sequelae of the treatment.

Many patients face grave difficulties if they attempt to elicit the help of relatives in seeking legal satisfaction. They may have been making life very difficult for their relatives—as well as for themselves—shortly before being given ECT. The relatives may have encouraged the patients to accept ECT, and may have signed the consent form in their stead. Their guilt will now interfere with any help they may wish to offer; it seems in their best interest to act as if the treatment were reasonable and legitimate. In addition, the families may have been kept away from the patients on doctor's orders during the treatment time, wholly misleading them into believing that the ECT effects were nothing more than the progression of "mental illness" during the hospitalization. If they did see the patients during the acute organic brain syndrome, they may have been told outright that the patients were just "upset."

If a patient decides to seek consultation with a lawyer, he or she will be met with incredulity. I know of one lawyer who could not believe that a wealthy client could have been given more than 100 ECT in a respected private hospital while being held incommunicado. Furthermore, the lawyer is likely to doubt a patient's honest explanation that he or she has lost much of his or her memory. If the patient outwardly seems "mentally sound," the lawyer may become convinced that the alleged memory loss is a ruse or fabrication. If the lawyer requests the hospital records and is met with an explanation that it "might not be good for the patient's mental health to get involved in a legal action," the psychiatrically unsophisticated, well-meaning lawyer may drop the case "in the patient's best interest."

In legal actions in which I have participated as an expert witness or consultant, I have seen all the above factors play a role. In those suits that have come to deposition or trial other factors have acted against the patient. It is usually impossible to find a psychiatrist from the community who is willing to testify against one of his colleagues. Expert witnesses must be brought in from out of town, and this is not likely to impress a judge or jury. In a case in which a young man fresh out of high school was given almost 100 ECT against his will on the grounds that he was "paranoid because he didn't trust his doctors," no physician in a medium-size city could be found to testify against the psychiatrists. If expert witnesses are sought from outside the community, they may be disqualified in certain states, such as my neighboring Virginia, on the grounds that they lack the familiarity to testify about local "community practice."

The standard of "community practice," which still prevails in some states, is a major obstacle to any psychiatric malpractice suit, but especially to those involving ECT. In many cities electroshock is practiced by a close-knit group of highly dedicated ECT advocates who believe that the treatment is utterly harmless when given to anyone of any age in any number. This group establishes the standards of "community practice" and makes it impossible for their members to lose malpractice suits.

Bringing in an expert from outside the community to testify on "national standards" is fraught with difficulties. With the exception of those who advocate ECT, very few psychiatrists know anything about its use or its hazards. They do not feel prepared to withstand a vigorous cross-examination by lawyers carefully prepared by pro-ECT psychiatrists. Even if "national standards" rather than community standards are used in the jurisdiction, it will be hard for the expert witness to establish standards that place any limits on the use of ECT. Typically, Kalinowsky's books will be cited, and sometimes Kalinowsky himself will be asked to give a deposition or to testify. The standards he has established are so broad that they make it virtually impossible for a psychiatrist to be faulted in a malpractice suit.

There is still another reason why post-ECT patients will not fare well in court. To whatever extent a patient suffers from obvious brain damage, a jury is likely to be put off or dismayed by his or her conduct. The jury will grow to dislike a patient who is angry and hostile. If a patient is apathetic or euphoric, the jury's sympathy will not be aroused as it would, let us say, by a grief-stricken widow who has lost her husband by a surgeon's error. Few people who have endured ECT-induced brain damage will make good witnesses on their own behalf.

Criteria for Informed Consent

The patient electing to receive ECT should be informed about and should understand the following six points:

1. The treatment frequently produces severe brain damage when tested on animals, and this damage is permanent in a significant number of cases. Human autopsy and brain wave studies also show permanent brain damage in many cases.
2. In some studies the treatment has a mortality rate of 1:1,000 among all patients given the treatment, and a much higher rate in high-risk populations such as older individuals and individuals with cardiovascular, respiratory, or central nervous system disease.
3. Early in the treatment the patient will experience the loss of all his mental faculties, and typically endure grave fear and emotional upset. Severe headaches and nightmares may persist.
4. The treatment causes some permanent memory loss in all cases, especially for the period surrounding the treatment, and many research studies and case reports demonstrate that most patients experience a significant permanent memory loss for past personal events. In many cases severe losses may extend back months or years, and other forms of mental dysfunction may become permanent.
5. Despite 40 years or more of usage, the efficacy of the treatment has not been established for any psychiatric disorder or for suicide.
6. Despite this lengthy period of usage, the treatment remains highly controversial, so that many psychiatrists and psychiatric hospitals never resort to it.

Malpractice suits may involve ECT carried out years earlier, because the statute of limitations may not start to run until the patient has a guardian appointed or until he or she is discharged from the hospital and becomes able to bring a legal action. ECT also may be included in a suit as a part of a long history of various treatments. It is therefore important to establish a time in the historical development of ECT after which any potential ECT patient should have been informed about its many hazards. The answer to this question depends in part on the requirements of consent in general at any given time in history. I wish to bypass that difficult legal issue, and instead focus on the more medical question: at what point in the history of ECT should psychiatrists have become aware of its typical hazards? A reasonable psychiatrist should have anticipated most of its hazards *before the time it was first used by Cerletti.* Psychiatrists were well aware that ECT was closely related to Metrazol shock treatment and insulin coma treatment, both of which produced severe brain damage and dysfunction as well as great fear (see Kennedy, 1940; Jessner & Ryan, 1941). Moreover, Bini and Cerletti had already demonstrated severe, irreversible brain damage in dogs subjected to ECT. Thus the early pioneers of ECT should have informed their patients that it was experimental and highly dangerous.

By the publication of Jessner and Ryan's standard *Shock Treatment in Psychiatry* in 1941, many of the dangers of ECT were recognized in the profession as a whole, including brain damage in animals and memory disturbances in humans. With the publication of the critical *Shock Therapy* report by the Group for the Advancement of Psychiatry in 1947, establishment psychiatry in the United States fully recognized that ECT was highly controversial and that it was frequently abused even by the standards of many of its advocates. Certainly any patient subjected to ECT after 1947 deserved to know about its highly controversial nature as well as its many hazards.

If the standards I propose mean that no reasonable person acting in his own self-interest would have consented to the treatment at any time in its history, this reflects upon the treatment itself.

Recommendations

1. Individual psychiatrists should stop using ECT, and should make their positions known professionally and publicly.
2. Private psychiatric hospitals and clinics should independently refuse to permit the use of ECT, but

should not be *legally* prohibited from giving it to
voluntary patients.

3. The government should ban ECT in federal and state
facilities and should stop supporting it through
grants or promotional publications.

4. Medical and psychiatric organizations such as the
American Psychiatric Association should stop defending and promoting ECT.

5. Individuals who have been harmed by ECT may
seek legal redress through malpractice suits if they
believe the facts of their cases justify such actions.

6. Injunctions to stop ECT may be sought when there
is cause to believe that inmates are being subjected
to the treatment without informed consent. A precedent for this has been established in a successful
attempt to prohibit the use of psychosurgery in
Michigan state hospitals (Kaimowitz, 1973; Breggin, 1973b, 1975a).

7. Federal and state regulations and legal precedents
should protect certain vulnerable groups from electroconvulsive therapy: involuntary mental patients,
prisoners, children, and individuals under guardianship. Even if persons in these groups appear to desire ECT, physicians should be prohibited from administering it to them. In addition, it should be
recognized that even so-called voluntary mental patients in private hospitals do not enjoy a truly voluntary status, and that their consent to dangerous,
mentally disruptive, experimental, or controversial
treatments, such as ECT, should be viewed with
great skepticism by the courts.

8. Federal and state legislation should be enacted af-
firming the right of *every* individual to refuse *any*
and *all* psychiatric treatment. Brain-damaging therapies such as psychosurgery, the major tranquilizers, and ECT provide inroads for the initiation of
such legislation.

There are a number of courses of action I specifically recommend
against. I recommend against any call for "more research" into the
effects of ECT if this research involves subjecting human beings to the
treatment. Typically psychiatry has reacted to criticism of its methods

by asking for more money to improve and test its methods. Enough is already known about the damaging effects of ECT to make it unethical to subject humans to it even on an experimental basis.

In my effort to discourage a resurgence of psychosurgery, I successfully called for the establishment of a federal commission to investigate psychosurgery (Trotter, 1973a, b; National Commission, 1977). I now believe that it is usually futile to involve the government in this manner. When government commissions or agencies are formed, they are typically dominated by "recognized authorities"—individuals with strong vested interests in the issue. Even if such authorities dislike one or another practice, they will not oppose it in principle, exposing themselves to censure from their colleagues and tarnishing the image of their profession. Instead, these authorities invariably call for greater federal investments in establishment practices (National Commission, 1977).

I am now against seeking a government ban on electroshock or any other treatments in the private sector. When the government gets into the business of outlawing treatments, it usually sets itself on the side of establishment medicine and against innovative or noninstitutional medicine. Under the guise of controlling medical practice it prevents individuals from seeking personally chosen methods of treatment on the grounds that the authorities do not approve of them.

From a practical viewpoint I am therefore against the involvement of government in policing private, voluntary medical practices. But I am also against it in principle. The government should not have the right to dictate to ordinary citizens what they may or may not seek for themselves as a treatment. Nor should it have the right to dictate to physicians what treatments they may provide to them. As I believe I have made clear, we are a long way from creating a judicial climate in which even voluntary private patients can receive justice. But impatience with legal process should not cause us to ask for the complete outlawing of any treatment. The "cure" of government control in this case is indeed worse than the disease; we lose still more of our individual rights in our efforts to protect our well-being. The best protection against abusive therapies is the right of the individual to reject any therapy, combined with the right to understand the effects of any therapy he or she chooses.

It is crucial to distinguish between what is ethical and what is legal. I believe that it is unethical for a person to seek ECT as a method of treatment for himself because in doing so he risks sacrificing his highest mental functions. But unless the individual is an involuntary patient, prisoner, incompetent, or child, I believe it should be his legal right to do so in a private facility. I believe it is even more unethical for any physician to administer ECT to any patient for any reason, and yet I also believe that it should be his legal right to do so, provided that the patient is in a position to make a choice and has been informed of the consequences.

There may be some disappointment among critics of ECT that I have not provided a strategy that can lead immediately to its complete abolition, even though I wish to see it totally abandoned. I have observed that most government interventions do more harm than good, and have carefully circumscribed the kinds of governmental action that I consider philosophically and practically sound. There are no easy strategies for stopping a treatment that has the active support of a strong minority of the psychiatric profession and the tacit support of many others. If we believe in human freedom, there is no substitute for patient, well-documented discourse as a method for influencing human affairs.

It is with great reluctance and caution that I call for a total, legislative ban on ECT in federal and state hospitals, for such a ban in effect limits freedom of choice from those citizens who voluntarily enter these facilities, and I fear and distrust government regulation. I call for a ban on ECT in government facilities because the government, state and federal, must be prevented from using its power to develop and promote dangerous, mentally disruptive, and experimental psychiatric treatments. In my utopia (Breggin, 1974, 1975c), the government would not provide or support *any* form of psychiatric treatment, and *all involuntary treatment* would be banned. Under these conditions, truly *voluntary* private psychiatric facilities might develop, for the patients in them would no longer be intimidated by the threat of involuntary commitment. Informed, voluntary consent might then become a reality; patients could decide for themselves if they want ECT. With the courts enforcing the criteria of informed consent that I have outlined, I believe that few patients would seek such a treatment for themselves.

What Will Replace ECT?

The critic of psychiatric treatments is often called on to suggest an alternative therapy. There is an inherent fallacy in this approach. If a physician makes a criticism of a quack cancer cure, the public and the profession do not challenge him to come up with a better one. People realize that cancer is a reality that may or may not be amenable to medical cure at the present time. But the critic who suggests that severely depressed or suicidal people should not be given ECT is expected to find another solution. This is because psychiatry plays a political role in our society. The psychiatrist is potentially responsible for institutionalizing and controlling any and all individuals who come under his or her care. Having assumed or accepted this role, the psychiatrist is then expected to make up a solution if no valid one is otherwise available (Breggin, 1974, 1975a; Szasz, 1963, 1974).

Fortunately, however, the problem of replacing ECT does not raise complex and dire consequences. This is because it already has been widely replaced by many other approaches in psychiatry, except among those staunch advocates who continue to administer the treatment regularly. Because many individual psychiatrists and many hospitals, both large and small, already do without ECT, ECT advocates cannot legitimately raise the specter of thousands of needy patients languishing or even dying of suicide in the absence of ECT. Nor is ECT typically used as a last-resort therapy by those who most frequently administer it. Instead it is administered in cases in which other psychiatrists *would* find alternatives. The doctor and the institution, not the patient's problems or diagnosis, determine if and when ECT will be prescribed.

If ECT were banished from the earth tomorrow, there would be no increase in human misery in the form of depression and suicide. Most psychiatrists and hospitals would go about their business as usual.

The Current Status of ECT Criticism

Only a few authoritative sources in psychiatry even hint at the data suggested in this book. In the United States one textbook (Gregory, 1968) has suggested the possibility of permanent brain damage following ECT:

> In spite of the fact that intensive electroshock treatments produce recognizable brain damage (e.g., diffuse punctate hemorrhages) in experimental animals, and that patients show some permanent residual amnesia (which is maximal for the period of several months immediately preceding and during treatment), some advocates of this method claim that there is little or no permanent impairment of intellectual function.

In a similar vein a Russian textbook (Portnov & Fedotov, 1969, in English translation) has also warned about the dangers of ECT:

> Until recently electro-convulsive therapy was used on a fairly wide scale. The method, however, involves gross interference in bodily functions and entails pin-point hemorrhages in the

brain tissue. Its application is, therefore, restricted to cases where all other methods of treatment have failed.

A course of convulsive therapy is followed by a memory loss of the type of retrograde or anterograde amnesia, which is a clinical manifestation of both the functional and organic changes occurring in the brain due to the electric shock.

Despite such occasional cautions, it is difficult to find a criticism of ECT *in principle* in the medical literature. Giamartino (1974) did take a moral stand against ECT:

> The moral and ethical considerations surrounding the practice of electroconvulsive therapy have virtually been ignored. Most research has been devoted to noting this treatment's efficacy but conclusive empirical evidence in favor of it does not, as such, exist. The argument that psychiatrists use electroconvulsive therapy solely to prevent harm to the patient is examined and rejected. The illusion of treatment implies that psychiatrists may have ulterior motives in turning to this mode of therapy. If these ulterior motives influence a psychiatrist's choice of treatment, the treatment may be considered morally wrong.

But while Giamartino was critical of psychiatrists who use ECT for "ulterior motives," he left open the possibility of using it for allegedly good motives.

Ironically, the inventor of ECT, Cerletti, is posthumously credited as one of the few psychiatrists to call for its abolition. In an obituary for Cerletti in *Psychosomatics,* psychiatrist Frank Ayd (1963) praised him as an "inspiring friend," "a humanist of many interests," and one of "the leading men of science in the twentieth century." He cited Cerletti as saying, "When I saw the patient's reaction, I thought to myself: 'This ought to be abolished!' Ever since I have looked forward to the time when another treatment would replace electroshock." But in all his writing, Cerletti sought praise for his invention of ECT, and in his later papers (1950) he downplayed any ill effects of the treatment and showed resentment that his colleague Bini had been credited with helping develop it.

In the last few years criticism of ECT has been generated on a national level by ex-psychiatric inmates like Leonard Frank (1978), who have affected both public opinion and legislation; by reporters such as Jean Dietz (1972, 1975); by a few psychiatrists, including myself (1977) and Lee Coleman (1978), and most courageously by neurologist John Friedberg (1975, 1976, 1977a, b). Another neurologist, Robert Grimm (1976, 1978), has also subjected ECT to criticism, although he has not called for its abolition.

Psychiatrist Thomas Szasz (1971) has examined Cerletti's own account of the first ECT treatment, and has characterized it as a combination of "force and fraud." Szasz believes that the somatic treatments perpetrate the fiction that legitimate medical treatments are being used to treat real patients, when in reality methods of torture are being applied to prisoners. According to Szasz, the cost of maintaining this fiction is high: "it requires the sacrifice of the patient as a person; of the psychiatrist as a critical thinker and moral agent; and of the legal system as a protector of the citizen from the abuse of state power."

Electroshock not only harms the patients upon whom it is inflicted; it corrupts the profession that countenances and advocates it. Throughout the world each year tens of thousands of patients are subjected to severe brain damage and irreversible mental dysfunction. Psychiatry is a profession that often laments its inability to cure or to prevent diseases, but it has in its power the capacity to prevent thousands of cases of brain damage. It can do so by abolishing its own use of electroconvulsive therapy.

Bibliography _____

Abrams R: Multiple ECT: What have we learned?, in *Psychobiology of Convulsive Therapy*. Edited by Fink M, Kety S, McGaugh J, Williams T. New York, Wiley, 1974

Abrams R, Taylor MA: Anterior bifrontal ECT: a clinical trial. *Br J Psychiatry* **122**: 587-590, 1974

Abrams R, Taylor MA: Diencephalic stimulation and the effects of ECT in endogenous depression. *Br J Psychiatry* **129**:482-485, 1976

Aird RB, Strait LA, Pace JW, et al: Current pathway and neurophysiologic effects of electrically induced convulsions. *J Nerv Ment Dis* **123**:505-512, 1956

Aleksandrovskaya MM, Kruglikov RI: Influence of electroshock on memory function and glial-neuronal relationship in rat brain. *Proc Acad Sci USSR* **197**:1216-1218, 1971

Alexander L, Lowenbach H: Experimental studies on electro-shock treatment. *J Neuropathol Exp Neurol* **3**:139-171, 1944

Alexander L, Rosen IM: Management of psychological issues in conjunction with physical treatment. *Confin Neurol* **16**:154-156, 1956

Alexander SP, Gahagan LH, Lewis WH: Deaths following electrotherapy. *JAMA* **161**:577-581, 1956

Allen IM: Cerebral injury with electric shock treatment. *NZ Med J* **50**:356-364, 1951

Allen IM: Cerebral lesions from electric shock treatment. *NZ Med J* **58**:369-377, 1959

Allen MR: Electroconvulsive therapy: an old question, new answers. *Psychiatric Annals* **8**:47-65, 1978

Alpers BJ: The brain changes associated with electrical shock treatment: A critical review. *J Lancet* **66**:363-369, 1946

Alpers BJ, Hughes J: Changes in the brain after electrically induced convulsions in cats. *Arch Neurol Psychiatry* **47**:385-398, 1942a

Alpers BJ, Hughes J: The brain changes in electrically induced convulsions in the human. *J Neuropathol Exp Neurol* **1**:173-186, 1942b

American Psychiatric Association: Task Force on Electroconvulsive Therapy (ECT), 12-page untitled questionnaire on the effects of ECT sent to a sample of members of the Association with an accompanying letter dated November 15, 1976

American Psychiatric Association: Task Force Report 14: Electroconvulsive Therapy. Washington, D.C., A.P.A., September, 1978

Andersen R: Differences in the course of learning as measured by various memory tasks after amygdalotomy in man, in *Psychosurgery*. Ed Hitchcock E, Laitinen L, Vaernet K. Springfield, Ill, Charles C. Thomas, 1972

Anderson EW: Mental disease: Physical methods of treatment, in *The Medical Annual*. Ed Tidy H, Short AR. Baltimore, Williams & Wilkins, 1951

Anderson EW: Mental disease: physical methods of treatment, in *The Medical Annual*. Ed Tidy H, Short AR. Baltimore, Williams & Wilkins, 1952

Anderson WAD: *Pathology*. St. Louis, Mosby, 1971

Anonymous: Memory defects following shock treatments. Letter to *JAMA* **136**:289, 1948

Arieti S: Histopathologic changes in experimental Metrazol convulsions in monkeys. *Am J Psychiatry* **98**:70-76, 1941

Arieti S: Histopathologic changes in experimental Metrazol convulsions in mon-

Arnold HO, Hoff H: Intensive therapy of psychoses in a university hospital, in *Current Therapies in Psychiatry: 1961*. Ed Masserman JH. New York, Grune & Stratton, 1961

Arnot R: Observations on the effects of electric convulsive treatment in man— psychological. *Dis Nerv Sys* **36**:499-502, 1975

Ashton R, Hess N: Amnesia for random shapes following unilateral and bilateral electroconvulsive shock therapy. *Percept Mot Skills* **42**:669-670, 1976

Asnis GM, Fink M, Saferstein S: ECT in metropolitan New York hospitals: A survey of practice, 1975-1976. *Am J Psychiatry* **135**:479-482, 1978

Assael MI, Halperin B, Alpern S: Centrencephalic epilepsy induced by electrical convulsive treatment. *Electroencephalogr Clin Neurophysiol* **23**:195, 1967

Avery D, Winokur G: Mortality in depressed patients treated with electroconvulsive therapy and antidepressants. *Arch Gen Psychiatry* **33**(9):1029-1037, 1976

Ayd FJ Jr: Guest editorial: Ugo Cerletti, MD, 1877-1963. *Psychomatics* **4**:A-6–A-7, 1963

Bagchi BK, Howell RW, Schmale HT: The electroencephalogram and clinical effects of electrically induced convulsions in the treatment of mental disorders. *Am J Psychiatry* **102**:49-60, 1945

Barker JC, Baker AA: Deaths associated with electroplexy. *J Ment Sci* **105**:339-348, 1959

Barrera S, Lewis N, Pacella B, et al: Brain changes associated with electrically induced seizures. *Trans Amer Neurol Assoc.* Richmond, Va, William Byrd Press, 1942, pp 31-35

Bayles S, Busse EW, Ebaugh FG: Square waves (BST) versus sine waves in electroconvulsive therapy. *Am J Psychiatry* **107**:34-41, 1950

Bazan NG Jr, Rakowski H: Increased levels of brain free fatty acids after electroconvulsive shock. *Life Sci* **9**:501-507, 1970

Bennett AE: Evaluation of progress in established physiochemical treatments in neuropsychiatry. III. The use of electroshock in the total psychiatric program. *Dis Nerv Syst* **10**:195-206, 1949

Berent S, Cohen BD, Silverman AJ: Changes in verbal and non-verbal learning following a single left or right unilateral electroconvulsive treatment. *Biol Psychiatry* **10**:95-100, 1975

Beresford HR: Legal issues relating to electroconvulsive therapy. *Arch Gen Psychiatry* **25**:100-102, 1971

Berkwitz NJ: Faradic shock treatment of "functional" psychoses: preliminary report. *J Lancet* **59**:351-355, 1939

Bersot MH: Auto-observation d'électro-choc. *Ann Med Psychol* **101**:488-489, 1943

Bidder TG, Strain JJ, Brunschwig L: Bilateral and unilateral ECT: follow-up study and critique. *Am J Psychiatry* **127**:737-745, 1970

Bigelow N: The involutional psychoses, in *American Handbook of Psychiatry, I.* Ed Arieti S. New York, Basic Books, 1959

Bini L: Experimental researches on epileptic attacks induced by the electric current. *Am J Psychiatry* 172-174, 1938 (supp)

Blachly PH, Gowing D: Multiple monitored electroconvulsive treatments. *Compr Psychiatry* **7**:100-109, 1966

Bockoven SJ: *Moral Treatment in America.* New York, Springer, 1963

Bowman KM: Review of psychiatric progress 1941: alcoholism, neurosyphilis, shock therapy and geriatrics. *Am J Psychiatry* **98**:589-591, 1942

Braatoy T: Indications for shock treatment in psychiatry. *Am J Psychiatry* **104**:573-575, 1948

Breggin PR: Coercion of voluntary patients in an open hospital. *Arch Gen Psychiatry* **10**:173-181, 1964

Breggin PR: *The Crazy from the Sane.* New York, Lyle Stuart, 1971a

Breggin PR: Psychotherapy as applied ethics. *Psychiatry* **34**:59-75, 1971b

Breggin PR: Lobotomy is still bad medicine. *Medical Opinion* **8**:32-36, 1972a

Breggin PR: The politics of therapy. *M/H (Mental Health)* **56**:9-13, 1972b

Breggin PR: The return of lobotomy and psychosurgery. *Congressional Record,* Feb 24, 1972, E1602-E1612. Reprinted in *Quality of Health Care—Human Experimentation,* Hearings before Senator Edward Kennedy's Subcommittee on Health, US Senate. Washington, DC, US Government Printing Office, 1973a

Breggin PR: Testimony given in *Kaimowitz v Department of Mental Health,* Civil No. 73-19, 434-AW (Cir Ct Wayne Co., Michigan, July 10, 1973b)

Breggin PR: The second wave of psychosurgery. *M/H (Mental Health)* **57**:10-13, 1973c. Reprinted in French in *La Folie II.* Ed Verdiglione A. Paris,

Union Generale D'Editions, 1976

Breggin PR: Therapy as applied utopian politics. *Ment Health Soc* **1**:129-146, 1974

Breggin PR: Psychosurgery for political purposes. *Duquesne Law Rev* **13**:841-862, 1975a

Breggin PR: Psychosurgery for the control of violence: A critical review, in *Neural Bases of Violence and Aggression,* Ch IV. Ed Fields W, Sweet W. St Louis, Warren H Green, 1975b

Breggin PR: Psychiatry and psychotherapy as political processes. *Am J Psychother* **29**:369-382, 1975c

Breggin PR: Needed: voluntaristic psychiatry. *Reason,* Sept 1975d, p 7

Breggin PR: Why we consent to oppression. *Reason,* Sept 1977a, p 28

Breggin PR: If psychosurgery is wrong in principle? *Psychiatric Opinion* **14**:Nov/Dec 1977b, p 23

Breggin PR: Madness is a failure of free will; therapy too often encourages it, in *La Folie Dans La Psychanalyse.* Ed Verdiglione A. Paris, Payot, 1977c. In French

Breggin PR: Mind-disabling therapy: the common effects of the major tranquilizers, ECT and psychosurgery, in *The Psychosurgery Debate: A Model for Policy Makers in Mental Health.* Ed Valenstein E. New York, WH Freeman, 1979 (in press)

Brengelman JC: *The Effect of Repeated Electroshock on Learning in Depressives.* Berlin, Springer, 1959

Bridenbaugh RH, Drake FR, O'Regan TJ: Multiple monitored electroconvulsive treatment of schizophrenia. *Compr Psychiatry* **13**:9-17, 1972

Brill HE, Crumpton S, Eiduson HM, et al: Relative effectiveness of various components of electroconvulsive therapy. *Arch Neurol Psychiatr* **81**:627-635, 1959

Broderson P, Paulson OB, Bolwig TG, et al: Cerebral hyperemia in electrically induced epileptic seizures. *Arch Neurol* **28**:334-338, 1973

Brody MP: Prolonged memory defects following electrotherapy. *J Ment Sci* **90**:777-779, 1944

Brosin HW: Psychiatric conditions following head injuries, in *American Handbook of Psychiatry, II.* Ed Arieti S. New York, Basic Books, 1959

Brunschwig L, Strain J, Bidder TG: Issues in the assessment of post-ECT memory changes. *Br J Psychiatry* **119**:73-74, 1971

Brussel JA, Schneider J: The B.E.S.T. in treatment and control of chronically disturbed mental patients—a preliminary report. *Psychiatric Q Supp* **25**:55-64, 1951

Califano JA: Determination of the secretary regarding the recommendation on psychosurgery of the national commission for the protection of human subjects of biomedical and behavioral research. *Federal Register* V. 43, no.221, November 15, 1978, pp. 53242-53245

Cameron DE, Pande SK: Treatment of the chronic paranoid schizophrenic patient. *Can Med Assoc J* **78**:92-95, 1958

Cammer L: Electrotherapy (ECT): An invaluable therapeutic modality. *Psychiatric Opinion,* Jan 1978, p 24

Cannicott SM: Unilateral electroconvulsive therapy. *Postgrad Med J* 38:451-459, 1962

Cannicott SM, Waggoner RW: Comparative study of unilateral and bilateral electroconvulsive therapy. *Arch Gen Psychiatry* 16:229-232, 1967

Cerletti U: Old and new information about electroshock. *Am J Psychiatry* 107:87-94, 1950

Cerletti U: Electroshock therapy. *J Clin Exper Psychopath* 15:191-217, 1954

Cerletti U: Electroshock therapy, in *The Great Physiodynamic Therapies in Psychiatry: An Historical Reappraisal.* Ed Sackle AM, et al. New York, Hoeber-Harper, 1956. Reprinted in *The Age of Madness.* Ed Szasz TS. Garden City, NY, Anchor Press/Doubleday, 1973

Cerletti U, Bini L: L'electroshock: le alterazioni istopatologiche del sistema nervoso in sequito all'. *E S Riv Sper Freniatr ecc* 64, 1940

Chesler P: *Women and Madness.* Garden City, NY, Doubleday, 1972

Chevalier JA: Permanence of amnesia after a single post-trial electroconvulsive seizure. *J Comp Physiol Psychol* 59:125-127, 1965

Chusid JG, Pacella BL: The electroencephalogram in the electric shock therapies. *J Nerv Ment Dis* 116:95-107, 1952

Clark M, Lubenow GC: Attack on electroshock. *Newsweek,* March 17, 1975, p 86

Clinical Psychiatric Committee: Clinical trial of the treatment of depressive illness: report to the Medical Research Council. *Br Med J* 5438:881-886, 1965

Clinical Psychiatry News: Group forms to answer critics of electroconvulsive therapy. November 1975, p 3

Cobb S: Review of neuropsychiatry for 1938. *Arch Intern Med* 62:883-889, 1938

Coleman L: Prisons: the crime of treatment. *Psychiatric Opinion,* June 1974, p 5

Coleman L: Introduction, in *The History of Shock Treatment.* Ed Frank LR. Revised and expanded edition published by LR Frank, 2300 Webster St, San Francisco, CA 94115, 1978

Colon EJ, Notermans SLH: A long-term study of the effects of electro-convulsions on the structure of the cerbral cortex. *Acta Neuropathol* 32:21-25, 1975

Cook LC: Convulsion therapy. *J Ment Sci* 90:435-464, 1944

Corsellis JM, Meyer A: Histological changes in the brain after uncomplicated electroconvulsant treatments. *J Ment Sci* 100:375-383, 1954

Costello CG, Belton GP, Abra JC, et al: The amnesic and therapeutic effects of bilateral and unilateral ECT. *Br J Psychiatry* 116:69-78, 1970

Cowen P: Mental health department probes hospital's shock treatment. *Boston Globe,* Dec 6, 1972

Cronholm B: Post ECT amnesia, in *The Pathology of Memory.* Ed Talland GA, Waugh NE. New York, Academic Press, 1969

Cronholm B, Molander L: Memory disturbances after electroconvulsive therapy: 5 conditions one month after a series of treatments. *Acta Psychiatr Neurol Scand* 40:211-216, 1964

Cronholm B, Ottosson JO: Experimental studies of the therapeutic action of electroconvulsive therapy in endogenous depression: The role of the electric stimulation and the seizure studied by variation of the stimulus intensity and modification by lidocaine of seizure discharge. *Acta Psychiatr Neurol Scand* (Supp 35), 69-96, 1960

Cronholm B, Ottosson JO: Memory functions in endogenous depression before and after electroconvulsive therapy. *Arch Gen Psychiatry* **5**:193-199, 1961

Cronholm B, Ottosson JO: The experience of memory function after electroconvulsive therapy. *Br J Psychiatry* **109**:251-258, 1963a

Cronholm B, Ottosson JO: Ultrabrief stimulus technique in electroconvulsive therapy: I. Influence on retrograde amnesia of treatments with the Elther ES electroshock apparatus, Siemens Konvulsator III and of lidocaine-modified treatment. *J Nerv Ment Dis* **137**:117-123, 1963b

Cronin D, Bodley P, Potts L, et al: Unilateral and bilateral ECT: A study of memory disturbance and relief from depression. *J Neurol Neurosurg Psychiatry* **33**:705-713, 1970

Cunningham ML: Uses and abuses of electrotherapy. *Med J Aust* **1**: 175-176, 1975

Davies RK, Detre TP, Egger MD, et al: Electroconvulsive therapy instruments: Should they be reevaluated? *Arch Gen Psychiatry* **25**:97-99, 1971

Dedichen HH: A comparison of 1459 shock-treated and 969 non-shock-treated psychoses in Norwegian hospitals. *Acta Psychiatr Neurol Scand* (Supp) 37, 1946

d'Elia G: Unilateral electroconvulsive therapy, in *Psychobiology of Convulsive Therapy.* Ed Fink M, Kety S, McGaugh J, et al. New York, Wiley, 1974

d'Elia G, Raotma H: Is unilateral ECT less effective than bilateral ECT? *Br J Psychiatry* **126**:83-89, 1975

Deutsch A: *The Shame of the States.* New York , Harcourt, Brace, 1948

Deutsch A: *The Mentally Ill in America,* 2nd Ed. New York, Columbia University, 1949

Diethelm O: Fear as a therapeutic agent. *Arch Neurol Psychiatry* **40**:414-416, 1938

Diethelm O: An historical view on somatic treatment in psychiatry. *Am J Psychiatry* **95**:1165-1179, 1939

Dietz J: Shock therapy lacks scientific study, law. *Boston Globe,* July 25, 1972, p 1

Dietz J: ECT study reveals disparity between public and private units. *Psychiatric News,* Aug 6, 1975, p 1

Dolenz BJ: Unilateral ECT. *Am J Psychiatry* **120**:1133, 1964

Dornbush RL, Williams M: Memory and ECT, in *Psychobiology of Convulsive Therapy.* Ed Fink M, Kety S, McGaugh J, et al. New York, Wiley, 1974

Dunn A, Giuditta A, Wilson JE, et al: The effect of electroshock on brain RNA and protein synthesis and its possible relationship to behavioral effects, in *Psychobiology of Convulsive Therapy.* Ed Fink M, Kety S, McGaugh J, et al. New York, Wiley, 1974

Eastwood MR, Peacocke J: Seasonal patterns of suicide, depression and electro-convulsive therapy. *Br J Psychiatry* **129**:472-475, 1976

Ebaugh F, Barnacle C, Neuburger K: Fatalities following electroconvulsive therapy. *Trans Am Neurol Assoc,* Richmond VA, 1942, pp 36-41

Ebaugh F, Barnacle C, Neuburger K: Fatalities following electric convulsive therapy. *Arch Neurol Psychiatry* **49**:107-117, 1943

Echlin FA: Vasospasm and forced cerebral ischemia. *Arch Neurol Psychiatry* **47**:77-96, 1942

Elmore JL, Sugerman AA: Precipitation of psychosis during electroshock therapy. *Dis Nerv Syst* **36**:115-117, 1975

Ennis B, Siegel L: *The Rights of Mental Patients: The Basic ACLU Guide to a Mental Patient's Rights,* New York, Avon, 1973

Essman WB: Electroshock-induced retrograde amnesia in seizure-protected mice. *Psychol Rep* **22**:929-935, 1968

Essman WB: *Neurochemistry of Cerebral Electroshock.* New York, Wiley, 1973.

Essman WB: Effects of electroconvulsive shock on cerebral protein synthesis, in *Psychobiology of Convulsive Therapy.* Ed Fink M, Kety S, McGaugh J, et al. New York, Wiley, 1974

Exner J, Murillo L: Effectiveness of regressive ECT with process schizophrenia. *Dis Nerv Syst* **34**:44-48, 1973

Eyman EV, Morris HH Jr: Deaths associated with electric shock therapy. *Arch Neurol Psychiatry* **64**:263-265, 1950

Faden V: Personal communication describing survey techniques used in gathering data for memorandum # 16, Electric shock therapy in selected inpatient psychiatric settings, May 11, 1978 (see Taube & Faden, 1977)

Ferraro A, Roizen L: Cerebral morphologic changes in monkeys subjected to a large number of electrically induced convulsions. *Am J Psychiatry* **106**:278-284, 1949

Ferraro A, Roizen L, Helford M: Morphologic changes in the brain of monkeys following electrically induced convulsions. *J Neuropathol Exp Neurol* **5**:285-308, 1946

Fink M: A unified theory of the action of the physiodynamic therapies. *J Hillside Hosp* **6**:197-206, 1957

Fink M: Effect of anticholinergic agent, diethazine, on EEG and behavior: Significance for theory of convulsive therapy. *Arch Neurol Psychiatry* **80**:380-386, 1958

Fink M: Introduction. *Seminars in Psychiatry* **4**:1-2, 1972

Fink M: Induced seizures and human behavior, in *Psychobiology of Convulsive Therapy.* Ed Fink M, Kety S, McGaugh J, et al. New York, Wiley, 1974

Fink M: Myths of "shock therapy." *Am J Psychiatry* **134**:991-996, 1977

Fink M, Abrams R: Answers to questions frequently asked about ECT, *Seminars in Psychiatry* **4**:33-38, 1972

Fink M, Kahn RL, Green M: Experimental studies of the electroshock process. *Dis Nerv Syst* **19**:113-118, 1958

Fink M, Kety S, McGaugh J, et al., Eds: *Psychobiology of Convulsive Therapy.*
New York, Wiley, 1974

Fisher KJ, Greiner A: Acute lethal catatonia treated by hypothermia. *Can Med
Assoc J* 82:8630-8634, 1960

Frank LR, Ed: *The History of Shock Treatment.* San Francisco, Network
Against Psychiatric Assault (NAPA), 1975. Revised and expanded edition
published by LR Frank, 2300 Webster St, San Francisco, CA 94115, 1978

Frankel F: Electro-convulsive therapy in Massachussetts: A task force report.
Mass Ment Health J 4:3-29, 1973

Frankel F: Current perspectives on ECT: A discussion. *Am J Psychiatry*
134:1014-1019, 1977

Freeman W: Editorial comment: Brain damaging therapeutics. *Dis Nerv Syst*
2:83, 1941

Freeman W: Adolescents in distress—therapeutic possibilities of lobotomy. *Dis
Nerv Syst* 22:555-558, 1961

Freeman W, Watts JW: Physiological psychology. *Annu Rev Psychol* 6:517-542,
1944

Freeman W, Watts JW: *Psychosurgery.* Springfield, Ill, Charles C. Thomas,
1950

Friedberg J: Electroshock therapy: Let's stop blasting the brain. *Psychol Today*
9:18-23, 1975

Friedberg J: *Shock Treatment Is Not Good for Your Brain.* San Francisco, Glide
Publications, 1976

Friedberg J: ECT as a neurologic injury. *Psychiatric Opinion,* Jan/Feb 1977a, p
17

Friedberg J: Shock treatment, brain damage, and memory loss: A neurological
perspective. *Am J Psychiatry* 134:1010-1014, 1977b

Fromholt A, Christensen L, Stromgren LS: The effects of unilateral and bilateral
electroconvulsive therapy on memory. *Acta Psychiatr Neurol Scand*
49:466-478, 1973

Frontiers in Psychiatry (Roche Report): From couch to coffee shop: A new
personality via "psychosynthesis." Nov 1, 1972a, p 1

Frontiers in Psychiatry (Roche Report): Electroshock: Key element in personality change therapy. Nov 15, 1972b, p 1

Gaitz CM, Pokorny AD, Mills M: Death following electroconvulsive therapy.
Arch Neurol Psychiatry 75:493-499, 1956

Gallinek A: Fear and anxiety in the course of electroshock therapy. *Am J Psychiatry* 113:428-434, 1956

Geoghegan JJ, Stevenson GH: Prophylactic electroshock. *Am J Psychiatry*
105:494-496, 1949

Giamartino GA: Electroconvulsive therapy and the illusion of treatment. *Psychol
Rep* 35:1127-1131, 1974

Globus JH, Van Harreueld A, Wiersma CAG: The influence of electric current
application on the structure of the brain of dogs. *J Neuropathol Exp Neurol*
2:263-276, 1943

Glueck BC Jr, Reiss H, Bernard LE: Regressive electric shock therapy. *Psychiatr Q* 31:117-136, 1957

Goffman, E: *Asylums, Essays on the Social Situation of Mental Patients and Other Inmates.* Garden City, NY, Anchor Books, 1961

Goldman D: Historical aspects of electroshock therapy, electrical current modification, treatment technique, and some electroencephalographic observations. *J Neuropsychiatry* 3:210-215, 1961

Goldman D, Murray M: Studies on the use of refrigeration therapy in mental disease with report of 16 cases. *J Nerv Ment Dis* 97:152-165, 1943

Goldman H, Gomer FE, Templer D: Long-term effects of electroconvulsive therapy upon memory and perceptual-motor performance. *J Clin Psychol* 28:32-34, 1972

Goldstein K: Functional disturbances in brain damage, in *American Handbook of Psychiatry,* 2nd Ed, Vol IV. Ed Arieti S. New York, Basic Books, 1975

Gomez J: Death after ECT. *Br Med J* 2:45, 1974

Gomez J: Subjective side-effects of ECT. *Br J Psychiatry* 127:609-611, 1975

Gordon M: Fifty shock therapy theories. *Milit Surg* 103:397-401, 1948

Graber HK, McHugh RB: Regressive electroshock therapy in chronic schizophrenia, a controlled study (preliminary report). *J Lancet* 80:24-27, 1960

Grahn AR, Gehrich JL, Couvillon LA, Moench LG: *A Study of Safety and Performance Requirements for Electroconvulsive Therapy Devices.* Utah Biomedical Test Laboratory, University of Utah Research Institute, Salt Lake City, December 15, 1977

Gralnick A: Fatalities associated with electric shock treatment of psychoses. *Arch Neurol Psychiatry* 51:397-402, 1944

Greenblatt M: Efficacy of ECT in affective and schizophrenic illness. *Am J Psychiatry* 134:1001-1005, 1977

Greenblatt M, Freeman H, Meshorer E, et al: Comparative efficacy of antidepressant drugs and placebo in relation to electric shock treatment, in *Biological Treatment in Psychiatry.* Ed Rinkel M. New York, LC Page, 1966

Greenblatt M, Grosser G, Wechsler H: Differential response to somatic therapy. *Am J Psychiatry* 120:935-943, 1964

Greenough WT, Schwitzgebel RL, Fulcher JK: Permanence of ECS-produced amnesia as a function of test conditions. *J Comp Physiol Psychol* 66:554-556, 1968

Gregory I: *Fundamentals of Psychiatry.* Philadelphia, Saunders, 1968

Grimm RJ: Brain control in a democratic society, in *Issues in Brain/Behavior Control.* Ed Smith WL, Kling A. New York, Spectrum, 1976

Grimm RJ: Convulsions as therapy: The outer shadows. *Psychiatric Opinion,* Jan 1978, p 30

Grinker RR, Sr., Sahs AL: *Neurology,* 6th Ed. Springfield, Ill, Charles C Thomas, 1966

Grosser GH, Pearsall DT, Fisher CL, et al: The regulation of electro-convulsive treatment in Massachusetts: A follow-up. Departmental report by The Department of Mental Health of the State of Massachusetts, 1974

Group for the Advancement of Psychiatry: *Report No. 1: Shock Therapy.* New

York, Group for the Advancement of Psychiatry, 1947

Group for the Advancement of Psychiatry: *Report No. 15: Revised Electro-shock Therapy Report*. New York, Group for the Advancement of Psychiatry, 1950

Guido JA, Jones J: 'Placebo' (simulation) electroconvulsive therapy. *Am J Psychiatry* **117**:838-839, 1961

Halliday AM, Davison K, Browne MW, et al: A comparison of the effects on depression and memory of bilateral ECT and unilateral ECT to the dominant and non-dominant hemispheres. *Br J Psychiatry* **114**:997-1012, 1968

Halpern L, Peyser E: The effect of various convulsive procedures on the cranial vessels of the dog angiographically visualized. *J Neuropathol Exp Neurol* **12**:277-282, 1953

Hargreaves WA, Fischer A, Elashoff RM, et al: Delayed onset of impairment following electrically induced convulsions. *Acta Psychiatr Neurol Scand* **48**:69-77, 1972

Harms E: The origin and early history of electrotherapy and electroshock. *Am J Psychiatry* **111**:933-934, 1955

Harper RG, Wiens AM: Electroconvulsive therapy and memory. *J Nerv Ment Dis* **161**:245-254, 1975

Harris A: Wiswall Hospital: Shock therapy abuse. *Boston Phoenix*, Nov 14, 1972, p 1

Hartelius H: Cerebral changes following electrically induced convulsions. *Acta Psychiatr Neurol Scand* **77**(supp): 1-128, 1952

Hassin GB: Changes in the brain in legal electrocution. *Arch Neurol Psychiatry* **30**:1046-1060, 1933

Hayes KJ: Current path in electric convulsive shock. *Arch Neurol Psychiatry* **63**:102-109, 1950

Heilbrunn G: Prevention of hemorrhages in the brain in experimental electric shock. *Arch Neurol Psychiatry* **50**:450-455, 1943

Heilbrunn G, Liebert E: Biopsies of the brain following artifically produced convulsions. *Arch Neurol Psychiatry* **46**:548-550, 1941

Heilbrunn G, Weil A: Pathologic changes in the central nervous system in experimental electric shock. *Arch Neurol Psychiatry* **47**:918-927, 1942

Henry AF, Short JF: *Suicide and Homicide*. Glencoe, Ill, Free Press, 1954

Himwich HE, Alexander FAD, Lipetz B: Effect of acute anoxia produced by breathing nitrogen on the course of schizophrenia. *Proc Soc Exp Biol Med* **39**:367-369, 1938

Himwich HE, Kalinowsky L, Stone WE: Effect of shock therapy on the brain. *Biology of Mental Health and Disease*, Ch 33. New York, Hoeber, 1952

Hirsch CS, Martin DL: Unexpected death in young epileptics. *Neurology* **21**:682-690, 1971

Hoch P: Discussion and concluding remarks. *J Pers* **17**:48-51, 1948

Hoen TI, Morello A, O'Neil FG: Hypothermia (cold narcosis) in the treatment of schizophrenia, *Psychiatr Q* **31**:696-702, 1957

Hoff H: History of organic treatment of schizophrenia, in *Insulin Treatment in*

Psychiatry. Ed Rinkel M, Himwich H. New York, Philosophic Library, 1959

Holt WL Jr: Intensive maintenance EST: A clinical note concerning two unusual cases. *Int J Neuropsychiat* 1:391-394, 1965

Hunt HF: Electroconvulsive shock and learning. *Trans NY Acad Sci* 27:923-945, 1965

Hurwitz TD: Electroconvulsive therapy: A review. *Compr Psychiatry* 15:303-314, 1974

Huston P, Locher L: Manic-depressive psychoses: Course when treated and untreated with electric shock. *Arch Neurol Psychiatry* 6:37-48, 1948

Huston P, Strother CR: The effect of electric shock on mental efficiency. *Am J Psychiatry* 104:707-712, 1948

Impastato D: Prevention of fatalities in electroshock therapy. *Dis Nerv Syst* 18(Sec 2):34-75, 1957

Impastato D, Karliner W: Control of memory impairment in EST by unilateral stimulation of the non-dominant hemisphere. *Dis Nerv Syst* 27:183-188, 1966

Jacobs JSL, Gibson WE. Treatment of schizophrenia with intensive electric convulsive therapy. *Wis Med J* 45:395-397, 1946

Jaffe J, Fink M, Kahn RL: Changes in verbal transactions with induced altered brain function. *J Nerv Ment Dis* 130:235-239, 1960

Janis IL: Memory loss following electric convulsive treatments. *J Pers* 17:29-32, 1948

Janis IL: Psychological effects of electric convulsive treatments. *J Nerv Ment Dis* 111:359-382, 383-397, 469-489, 1950

Janis IL, Astrachan M: The effect of electroconvulsive treatments on memory efficiency. *J Abnorm Psychol* 46:501-511, 1951

Jessner L, Ryan VG: *Shock Treatment in Psychiatry.* New York, Grune & Stratton, 1941

Jones JE: Non-ECT. *World Medicine,* Sept 1974, p 24

Kafi A, Dennis M, Todd R: Indoklon and electric convulsive therapy. *Behav Neuropsychiatry* 1:25-30, 1969

Kaimowitz v. Department of Mental Health, Civil No. 73-19434-AW, Circuit Court for the County of Wayne, State of Michigan, July 10, 1973

Kalinowsky L: Organic psychotic syndromes occurring during electric convulsive therapy. *Arch Neurol Psychiatry* 53:269-273, 1945

Kalinowsky L: The danger of various types of medication during electric convulsive therapy. *Am J Psychiatry* 112:745-746, 1956

Kalinowsky L: Problems of psychotherapy and transference in shock treatments and psychosurgery. *Psychosom Med* 18:399, 1957

Kalinowsky L: Convulsive shock treatment, in *American Handbook of Psychiatry,* Vol II. Ed Arieti S. New York, Basic Books, 1959

Kalinowsky L: Electroshock treatment—who needs it? (Questions and answers). *JAMA* **217**:1112, 1971

Kalinowsky L: Electric and other convulsive treatments, in *American Handbook of Psychiatry,* Vol V. Ed Arieti S. New York, Basic Books, 1975a

Kalinowsky L: The convulsive therapies, in *Comprehensive Textbook of Psychiatry.* Ed Freedman AM, Kaplan HI, Sadock BJ. Baltimore, Williams & Wilkins, 1975b

Kalinowsky L, Hippius H: *Pharmacological, Convulsive and Other Somatic Treatments in Psychiatry.* New York, Grune & Stratton, 1969

Kalinowsky L, Hoch P: *Somatic Treatments in Psychiatry.* New York, Grune & Stratton, 1946, 1961

Kennedy A: Critical review of the treatment of mental disorders by induced convulsions. *J Neurol Psychiatry* **3**:49-82, 1940

Kennedy CJC, Anchel D: Regressive electric-shock in schizophrenics refractory to other shock therapies. *Psychiatr Q* **22**:317-320, 1948

Klotz M: Serial electroencephalographic changes due to electrotherapy. *Dis Nerv Syst* **16**:120-121, 1955

Kolb L: *Modern Clinical Psychiatry,* 9th Ed. Philadelphia, Saunders, 1977

Kolb L, Vogel VH: The use of shock therapy in 305 mental hospitals. *Am J Psychiatry* **99**:90-100, 1942

Kraepelin E: *One Hundred Years of Psychiatry.* New York, Citadel Press, 1962

Langworthy OR: Nerve cell injuries in cases of human electrocution. *JAMA* **95**:107-108, 1930

Larsen E, Vraa-Jensen G: Ischaemic changes in the brain following electroshock therapy. *Acta Psychiatr Neurol Scand* **28**:75-80, 1953

Laurell B, Ed: Flurothyl convulsive therapy. *Acta Psychiatr Scand* **46** (supp 213): 1-79, 1970

Lee JC, Olszewski J: Increased cerebrovascular permeability after repeated electroshocks. *Neurology* **11**:515-519, 1961

Leflar RB, Wolfe SM: *Proposed Classification of Neurological Devices: Electroshock Devices* (Comments of Public Citizen Health Research Group to Food and Drug Administration). Health Research Group, Washington, D.C., January 29, 1979

Lehmann H: *Perspectives in Psychosurgery.* Presented at Hahnemann Medical College, Philadelphia, June 1972

Levy NA, Serota HM, Grinker RR: Disturbances in brain function following convulsive shock therapy. *Arch Neurol Psychiatry* **47**:1009-1029, 1942

Levy R: The clinical evaluation of unilateral ECT. *Br J Psychiatry* **114**:459-463, 1968

Liban E, Halpern L, Rozanski J: Vascular changes in the brain in a fatality following electroshock. *J Neuropathol Exp Neurol* **10**:309-318, 1951

Liberson WT: Brief stimulus therapy, physiological and clinical observations. *Am J Psychiatry* **105**:28-39, 1948

Liberson WT: Review of psychiatric progress, 1948, electroencephalography. *Am J Psychiatry* **105**:503-505, 1949

Lidbeck WL: Pathologic changes in the brain after electric shock. *J Neuropathol Exp Neurol* **3**:81-85, 1944

Lovell R: Some neurochemical aspects of convulsions, in *Handbook of Neurochemistry*, Vol VI. Ed Lajtha A. New York, Plenum, 1971

Lovett Doust JW, Barchha R, Lee RSY, et al: Acute effects of ECT on the cerebral circulation in man. *Eur Neurol* **12**:47-62, 1974

Lowenbach H, Stainbrook EJ: Observations on mental patients after electroshock. *Am J Psychiatry* **98**:828-833, 1942

Lowinger L, Huddleson J: Complications of electric shock therapy. *Am J Psychiatry* **102**:594-598, 1946

Lundy PJ, Breggin PR: Psychiatric oppression of prisoners. *Psychiatric Opinion,* June, 1974, p 30

Madow L: Brain changes in electroshock therapy. *Am J Psychiatry* **113**:337-347, 1956

Marshall TJ, Dobbs D: Treatment technique and apnea in electroshock. *Dis Nerv Syst* **20**:582-583, 1959

Martin PA: Convulsive therapies: review of 511 cases at Pontiac State Hospital. *J Nerv Ment Dis* **109**:142-157, 1949

Martin WL, Ford HF, McDanald EC, et al: Clinical evaluation of unilateral EST. *Am J Psychiatry* **121**:1087-1090, 1965

Masserman JH, Jacques MG: Effects of cerebral electroshock on experimental neuroses in cats. *Am J Psychiatry* **104**:92-99, 1947

Mather NJ de V: Psychoneurosis treated with electrical convulsions (correspondence). *Lancet* **2**:615, 1946

Matsuba T, Kawai S, Kurosawa M, et al: Circulatory dynamics during electric convulsion therapy. *Folia Psychiatr Neurol Jap* **22**:333-346, 1968

Matsuda Y: Characteristics of slow wave EEG accompanying electroconvulsive shock treatment in typical and atypical schizophrenia. *Bull Osaka Med Sch* **14**:1-14, 1968

Matthew JR, Constan E: Complications following ECT over a three year period in a state institution. *Am J Psychiatry* **120**:1119-1120, 1964

Mayer-Gross W: Retrograde amnesia. *Lancet* **245**:603-605, 1943

Mayer-Gross W, Slater E, Roth M: *Clinical Psychiatry*. Baltimore, Williams & Wilkins, 1955

McDonald MC: The regulation of ECT. *Psychiatric News,* Jan 21, 1977 (Part I) and Feb 4, 1977 (Part II), p 1

McDonald MC: ECT: Lothar Kalinowsky remembers (an interview). *Psychiatric News,* May 5, 1978, p 1

McGaugh JL: Electroconvulsive shock: Effects on learning and memory in animals, in *Psychobiology of Convulsive Therapy*. Ed Fink M, Kety S, McGaugh J, et al. New York, Wiley, 1974

McGaugh JL, Alpern HP: Effects of electroshock on memory: Amnesia without convulsions. *Science* **152**:665-666, 1966

McGaugh JL, Williams TA: Neurophysiological and behavioral effects of convulsive phenomena, in *Psychobiology of Convulsive Therapy*. Ed Fink M, Kety S, McGaugh J, et al. New York, Wiley, 1974

McKegney FP, Panzetta AF: An unusual fatal outcome of electro-convulsive therapy. *Am J Psychiatry* **120**:398-400, 1963

Medlicott RW: Convulsive therapy. Results and complications in four hundred cases. *NZ Med J* **47**:338-348, 1948

Meduna LJ: The convulsive treatment. A reappraisal. *J Clin Exp Psychopath* **15**:219-233, 1954

Meduna LJ, Friedman E: The convulsive-irritative therapy of psychoses. *JAMA* **112**:501-509, 1939

Merritt HH: *A Textbook of Neurology*. Philadelphia, Lea & Febiger, 1973

Meyer A, Teare D: Cerebral fat embolism after electrical convulsion therapy. *Br Med J* **2**:42-44, 1945

Meyer JS, Ericsson AD: Cerebral circulation and metabolism in neurological disorders, in *Pharmacology of Cerebral Stimulation*, Vol I. Ed Carpi A. Oxford, Pergamon Press, 1972

Miller DH, Clancy J: A comparison between unidirectional current nonconvulsive electrical stimulation given with Reiter's Machine, standard alternating current electroshock (Cerletti Method), and pentothal in chronic schizophrenia. *Am J Psychiatry* **109**:617-620, 1953

Miller, E: Psychological theories of ECT: A review. *Br J Psychiatry* **113**:301-311, 1967

Millet JAP, Mosse EP: On certain psychological aspects of electroshock therapy. *Psychosom Med* **6**:226-236, 1944

Misurec J: Electroencephalogram of therapeutic electroshock. *Activ Nerv Sup* (Praha) **7**:198-199, 1965

Mitford J: *Kind and Usual Punishment*. New York, Knopf, 1973

Miura T, Okada M, Okamoto M: Retrograde amnesia provoked by electroconvulsive therapy. *Dis Nerv Syst* **21**:649-650, 1960

Moore MT: Electrocerebral shock therapy. *Arch Neurol Psychiatry* **57**:693-711, 1947

Moriarty JD, Siemens JC: Electroencephalographic study of electric shock therapy. *Arch Neurol Psychiatry* **57**:712-718, 1947

Morrissey JP, Burton NM, Steadman HJ: *Developing an Empirical Base for Psycho-legal Policy Analyses of ECT: A New York State Survey*. Bureau of Special Projects Research, New York Department of Mental Hygiene, January 1979

Morrison LR, Weeks A, Cobb S: Histopathology of different types of electric shock on mammalian brains. *J Industrial Hyg* **12**:324-337, 364-380, 1930

Mosovich A, Katzenelbogen S: Electroshock therapy, clinical and electroencephalographic studies. *J Nerv Ment Dis* **107**:517-530, 1948

Moss-Herjanik B: Prolonged unconsciousness following electroconvulsive therapy. *Am J Psychiatry* **124**:74-76, 1967

National Commission for the Protection of Human Subjects of Biomedical and Behavioral Research: *Report and Recommendations on Psychosurgery*.

DHEW Publication No. (OS)77-0001, U.S. Government Printing Office, Washington, D.C. 20402, 1977

National Institute of Mental Health: *Facts about Electroshock Therapy*. DHEW Publication No. (HSM) 72-9152, Rockville, Maryland, 1972

Neuburger K, Whitehead RW, Rutledge K, et al: Pathologic changes in the brains of dogs given repeated electric shocks. *Am J Med Sci* **204**:381-387, 1942

Novello JR, Ed: *A Practical Handbook of Psychiatry*. Springfield, Ill, Charles C Thomas, 1974

Noyes A: Symposium: Complications of and contraindications to electric shock therapy. *Arch Neurol Psychiatry* **49**:788-791, 1943

Noyes A: *Modern Clinical Psychiatry*, 3rd Ed. Philadelphia, Saunders, 1948

Noyes A, Kolb L: *Modern Clinical Psychiatry*, 8th Ed. Philadelphia, Saunders, 1973

Osgood CW: Unusual reactions to electroshock. *J Nerv Ment Dis* **100**:343-351, 1944

Ottosson JO: Electroconvulsive therapy—electrostimulatory or convulsive therapy. *J Neuropsychiatry* **3**:216–220, 1961

Ottosson JO: Systemic effects of ECT, in *Psychobiology of Convulsive Therapy*. Ed Fink M, Kety S, McGaugh J, et al. New York, Wiley, 1974

Pacella BL: Sequelae and complications of convulsive shock therapy. *Bull NY Acad Med* **20**:575-585, 1944

Pacella BL, Barrera SE, Kalinowsky L: Variations in electroencephalogram associated with electric shock therapy of patients with mental disorders. *Arch Neurol Psychiatry* **47**:367-384, 1942

Pacella BL, Impastato DJ: Focal stimulation therapy. *Am J Psychiatry* **110**:576-578, 1954

Pacella BL, Piotrowski Z, Lewis N: The effects of electric convulsive therapy on certain personality traits in psychiatric patients. *Am J Psychiatry* **104**:883-891, 1947

Page JD: Studies in electrically induced convulsions in rats. *Psychol Bull* **37**:485-486, 1940

Paulson GW: Exacerbation of organic brain disease by electroconvulsive treatment. *N Carolina Med J* **28**:328-331, 1967

Peck, RE: *The Miracle of Shock Treatment*. Jericho, NY, Exposition Press, 1974

Penfield W, Mathieson G: Memory: Autopsy findings and comments on the role of hippocampus in experiential recall. *Arch Neurol* **31**:145-154, 1974

Perlson J: Case of schizophrenia treated with 248 electric shock treatments. *Arch Neurol Psychiatry* **54**:409-411, 1945

Perlson J: Shock therapy (correspondence). *Playboy*, Aug 1970, pp 50-51

Pitts FN: Medical aspects of ECT. *Semin Psychiatry* **4**:27-32, 1972

Plotkin R: Limiting the therapeutic orgy: mental patients' right to refuse treatment. *Northwestern Univ Law Rev* **72**:461-525, 1977

Pollack M, Fink M: Sociopsychological characteristics of patients who refuse convulsive therapy. *J Nerv Ment Dis* **132**:153-157, 1961

Portnov A, Fedotov D: *Psychiatry*. Moscow, MIR, 1969

Posner JB, Plum F, Van Poznak A: Cerebral metabolism during electrically induced seizures in man. *Arch Neurol* **20**:388-395, 1969

Practising Psychiatrist: The experience of electroconvulsive therapy. *Br J Psychiatry* **111**:365-367, 1965

Pribam K: Interview—lobotomy to physics to Freud. *Am Psychol Assoc Monitor* **5**:9-10, 1974

Proctor LD, Goodwin JE: Comparative electroencephalographic observations following electroshock therapy using raw 60 cycle alternating and unidirectional fluctuating current. *Am J Psychiatry* **99**:525-533, 1943

Proctor LD, Goodwin JE: Clinical and electrophysiological observations following electroshock. *Am J Psychiatry* **101**:797-800, 1945

Pryor GT, Otis LS: Brain biochemical and behavioral effects of 1, 2, 4 or 8 weeks electroshock treatment. *Life Sci* **8**:387-399, 1969

Psychiatric News: Closer regulation of electric shock equipment urged. Sept 15, 1971, p 17

Psychiatric News: State to regulate ECT following report of abuse. June 20, 1973, p 1

Psychiatric News: California enacts rigid shock therapy controls. Feb 5, 1975a, p 1

Psychiatric News: Society organizes to defend ECT. Nov 19, 1975b, p 1

Psychiatric News: California area branches draft ECT guidelines. Feb 6, 1976, p 1

Psychiatric News: Insurance Committee hears ECT surcharge protest. Apr 7, 1978a, p 33

Psychiatric News: Members' Insurance to have new coverages, limits. Apr 7, 1978b, p 40

Pulver SE: The first electroconvulsive treatment given in the United States. *Am J Psychiatry* **117**:845-846, 1961

Pulver S, Jacobs E: Effect of nonconvulsive electrostimulation upon some side effects of ECT. *Dis Nerv Syst* **22**:382-388, 1961

Quandt J, Sommer H: Zur Frage der Hirngewebsschadigungen nach electrischer Krampfbehandlung. *Ztschr. Neurol u Psychiat* **34**:513, 1966

Rabin A I: Persons who received more than 100 electric shock treatments. *J Pers* **17**:42-47, 1948

Regestein QR, Murawski BJ, Engle RP: A case of prolonged reversible dementia associated with abuse of electroconvulsive therapy. *J Nerv Ment Dis* **161**:200-203, 1975

Reinhart MJ: Profound regression following two electroconvulsive treatments. *Can Psychiatr Assoc J* **12**:426-428, 1967

Riese W: Report of two new cases of sudden death after electroshock with histopathological findings in the central nervous system. *J Neuropathol Exp Neurol* **7**:98-99, 1948

Riese W, Fultz GS: Electric shock treatment succeeded by complete flaccid paralysis, hallucinations and sudden death. *Am J Psychiatry* **106**:206-211, 1949

Robitscher JB: Psychosurgery and other somatic means of altering behavior. *Bull
Am Acad Psychiatry Law* **11**:7-33, 1974

Rosenblatt S, Chanley JD, Sobotka H, et al: Interrelationships between electroshock, the blood-brain barrier, and catecholamines. *J Neurochem*
5:172-176, 1960

Roth M, Garside R: Some characteristics common to electroconvulsive therapy
and prefrontal leucotomy and their bearing on the mode of action of the two
treatments. *J Neuropsychiatry* **3**:221-230, 1962

Rothchild D, Van Gordon DJ, Varjabedian A: Regressive shock therapy in
schizophrenia. *Dis Nerv Syst* **11**:147-150, 1951

Roubicek J, Volavka J, Abrams R, et al: Lateralized EEG changes after induced
convulsions. *Electroencephalogr Clin Neurophysiol* **29**:324, 1970

Routtenberg A, Kay KE: Effect of one electroconvulsive seizure on rat behavior. *J
Comp Physiol Psychol* **59**:285-288, 1965

Rush B: *Medical Inquiries and Observations upon the Diseases of the Mind,* 5th
Ed. Philadelphia, Grigg & Elliott, 1835

Rush B: Deception and terror as cures for madness, in *The Age of Madness.* Ed
Szasz T. Garden City, NY, Anchor Books, 1973

Russell RW: Contributions of research on infrahuman animals to the under-
standing of electric convulsive shock phenomena. *J Pers* **17**:17-28, 1947

Sagebiel JL: Regressive convulsive therapy and lobotomy in the treatment of
mental disorders. *Dis Nerv Syst* **22**:193-220, 1961

Sakel M: The nature and origin of the hypoglycemic treatment of psychoses. *Am
J. Psychiatry* **94** (supp): 24-40, 1938

Salzman C: ECT and ethical psychiatry. *Am J Psychiatry* **134**:1006-1009, 1977

Salzman C, Konikov W, Relyea R: Modifications of electroshock therapy by
succinylcholine chloride. *Dis Nerv Syst* **16**:153-156, 1955

Sanford JL: Electric and convulsive treatments in psychiatry. *Dis Nerv Syst*
27:333-338, 1966

Schulz H, Müller J, Roth B, et al: Changes in the passive EEG during convulsive
treatment. *Electroencephalogr Clin Neurophysiol* **26**:227-228, 1969

Schwartzman AE, Termansen PE: Intensive electroconvulsive therapy: A follow-up study. *Can Psychiatr Assoc J* **12**:217-218, 1967

Science News Letter: Shocks of many kinds are useful against mental ills. May
21, 1938, p 337

Scoville W: Psychosurgery and other lesions of the brain affecting human behavior, in *Psychosurgery.* Ed Hitchcock E, Laitinen L, Vaernet K. Springfield,
Ill, Charles C Thomas, 1972

Seltzer B, Benson F: The temporal pattern of retrograde amnesia in Korsakoff's
disease. *Neurol* **24**:527-530, 1974

Sharp LI, Gabriel AR, Impastato DJ: Management of the acutely disturbed
patient by sedative electroshock therapy. *Dis Nerv Syst* **14**:21-23, 1953

Sherman L, Mergener J, Levitin D: Effect of convulsive therapy on memory. *Am
J Psychiatry* **98**:401-403, 1941

Shoor M, Adams FH: The intensive electric shock therapy of chronic disturbed psychiatric patients. *Am J Psychiatry* **107**:279-282, 1950

Siekert RG, Williams CS, Windle WF: Histologic study of the brains of monkeys after experimental electric shock. *Arch Neurol Psychiatry* **63**:79-86, 1950

Simon A, Yeager CL, Bowman KM: Studies in electronarcosis therapy, IV. Electroencephalographic investigations. *J Nerv Ment Dis* **118**:131-143, 1953

Slater E, Roth M: *Clinical Psychiatry*, 3rd Ed. Baltimore, Williams & Wilkins, 1969

Small IF: Inhalant convulsive therapy, in *Psychobiology of Convulsive Therapy.* Ed Fink M, Kety S, McGaugh J, et al. New York, Wiley, 1974

Small JG: EEG and neurophysiological studies of convulsive therapies, in *Psychobiology of Convulsive Therapy.* Ed Fink M, Kety S, McGaugh J, et al. New York, Wiley, 1974

Small IF, Sharpley P, Small JG: Influences of cyclert upon memory changes with ECT. *Am J Psychiatry* **125**:837-840, 1968

Small IF, Small JG, Milstein V, et al: Neuropsychological observation with psychosis and somatic treatment. *J Nerv Ment Dis* **155**:6-13, 1972

Small JG, Small IF, Perez HC, et al: Electroencephalographic and neurophysiological studies of electrically induced seizures. *J Nerv Ment Dis* **150**:479-489, 1970

Smith K, Biddy RL: Shock treatment, in *Progress in Neurology and Psychiatry.* Ed Spiegel EA. New York, Grune & Stratton, 1964

Spiegel-Adolf M, Wilcox PH, Spiegel EA: Cerebrospinal fluid changes in electroshock treatment of psychoses. *Am J Psychiatry* **104**:697-706, 1948

Spradly JB, Martin-Foucher MH: New treatment in psychiatric disorders. *Dis Nerv Syst* **10**:235-238, 1949

Sprague DW, Taylor RC: The complications of electric shock therapy with a case study. *Ohio State Med J* **44**:51-54, 1948

Squire LR: Amnesia for remote events following electroconvulsive therapy. *Behav Biol* **12**:119-125, 1974

Squire LR: A stable impairment in remote memory following electroconvulsive therapy. *Neuropsychologia* **13**:51-58, 1975

Squire LR: ECT and memory loss. *Am J Psychiatry* **134**:997-1001, 1977

Squire LR, Chace PM: Memory functions six to nine months after electroconvulsive therapy. *Arch Gen Psychiatry* **32**:1557-1564, 1975

Squire LR, Chace PM, Slater PC: Retrograde amnesia following electroconvulsive therapy. *Nature* **266**:775-777, 1976

Squire LR, Slater PC, Chace PM: Retrograde amnesia: Temporal gradient in very long term memory following electroconvulsive therapy. *Science* **187**:77-79, 1975

Squire LR, Slater PC, Chace PM: Anterograde amnesia following electroconvulsive therapy: No evidence for state-dependent learning. *Behav Biol* **17**:31-41, 1976

Stainbrook EJ: Shock therapy: Psychologic theory and research. *Psychol Bull* **43**:21-60, 1946

Stein J, Schulz H, Müller J, et al: A polygraphic study of electroconvulsive treatment in psychotics under general anesthesia and muscular relaxation. *Electroencephalogr Clin Neurophysiol* **26**:227, 1969

Stengel E: Intensive ECT. *J Ment Sci* **97**:139-142, 1951

Stieper DR, Williams M, Duncan CP: Changes in impersonal and personal memory following electro-convulsive therapy. *J Clin Psychol* **7**:361-366, 1951

Stone CP: Losses and gains in cognitive functions as related to electroconvulsive shocks. *J Abnorm Psychol* **42**:206-214, 1947

Stones MJ: Electroconvulsive treatment and short term memory. *Br J Psychiatry* **122**:591-594, 1973

Strain JJ: ECT: A classic approach takes new forms. In *Psychiatry 1972,* a special edition of *Medical World News.* New York, McGraw-Hill, 1972

Strain JJ, Bidder TG: Transient cerebral complications associated with multiple monitored electroconvulsive therapy. *Dis Nerv Syst* **32**:95-100, 1971

Strain JJ, Brunschwig L, Duffy JP, et al: Comparison of therapeutic effects and memory changes with bilateral and unilateral ECT. *Am J Psychiatry* **125**:294-304, 1968

Strauss J: Epileptic disorders, in *American Handbook of Psychiatry,* Vol. II, Ed Arieti S. New York, Basic Books, 1959

Stromgren LS: Unilateral versus bilateral electroconvulsive therapy. *Acta Psychiatr Neurol Scand* (supp) 240, 1973

Sutherland EM, Oliver JE, Knight DR: E.E.G., memory and confusion in dominant, non-dominant and bi-temporal E.C.T. *Br J Psychiatry* **115**:1059-1064, 1969

Sutherland JM, Tait H, Eadie MJ: *The Epilepsies.* London, Churchill Livingston, 1974

Symonds C: Disorders of memory. *Brain* **89**:625-644, 1966

Szasz TS: *Law, Liberty and Psychiatry.* New York, Macmillan, 1963

Szasz TS: Involuntary mental hospitalization: A crime against humanity, in *Ideology and Insanity.* New York, Anchor Books, 1970

Szasz TS: From the slaughterhouse to the madhouse. *Psychother: Theory, Research and Practice* **8**:64-67, 1971

Szasz TS: *The Myth of Mental Illness,* Rev Ed. New York, Harper & Row, 1974

Talbott, JH, Tillotson KJ: The effects of cold on mental disorders; a study of 10 patients suffering from schizophrenia and treated with hypothermia. *Dis Nerv Syst* **2**:116-126, 1941

Taube C, Faden V: *Electric Shock Therapy in Selected Inpatient Psychiatric Settings (Memorandum # 16).* Rockville, MD, Survey and Reports Branch, National Institute of Mental Health, September 16, 1977

Taylor RM, Pacella BL: The significance of abnormal electroencephalograms prior to electroconvulsive therapy. *J Nerv Ment Dis* **107**:220-227, 1948

Templer DI, Ruff CF, Armstrong G: Cognitive functioning and degree of psychosis in schizophrenics given many electroconvulsive treatments. *Br J Psychiatry* **123**:441-443, 1973

Teuber H, Corkin S, Twitchell TE: A study of cingulotomy in man. Published in the Appendix to *The Report on Psychosurgery of the National Commission for the Protection of Human Subjects of Biomedical and Behavioral Research,* US Dept HEW, DHEW Publication No. (OS) 77-0002, Washington, D.C. 1977

Tien HC: Editorial: 100 questions and answers in ELT. *World J. Psychosynthesis* 6:31-39, 1974

Tien HC: Return of electrotherapy in Michigan. *Mich Med* 74:251-257, 1975

Tooth G, Blackburn JM: Disturbances of memory after convulsive treatment. *Lancet* 237:17-20, 1939

Tow PM: *Personality Changes Following Frontal Leucotomy.* London, Oxford U. Press, 1955

Trotter R: Psychosurgery, the courts and Congress. *Sci News,* May 12, 1973a, p 310

Trotter R: Peter Breggin's private war. *Human Behavior,* Nov 1973b, p 50

Turek IS: EEG correlates of electroconvulsive treatment. *Dis Nerv Syst* 33:584-589, 1972

Tyler EA, Lowenbach H: Polydiurnal electric shock treatment in mental disorders. *NC Med J* 8:577-582, 1947

Ulett G, Smith K, Gleser G: Evaluation of convulsive and subconvulsive shock therapies utilizing a control group. *Am J Psychiatry* 112:795-802, 1956

Valentine M, Keddie KMG, Dunne D: A comparison of techniques in electroconvulsive therapy. *Br J Psychiatry* 114:989-996, 1968

Volavka J: Neurophysiology of ECT. *Semin Psychiatry* 4:55-66, 1972

Volavka J, Feldstein S, Abrams R, et al: EEG and clinical changes after bilateral and unilateral electroconvulsive therapy. *Electroencephalogr Clin Neurophysiol* 32:631-369, 1972

Voris H: Craniocerebral trauma, in *Clinical Neurology.* Ed Baker AB. New York, Hoeber-Harper, 1962

Watkins C, Stainbrook EJ, Lowenbach H: Report on subconvulsive reaction to electric shock and its sequelae in normal subject. *Psychiatr Q* 15:724-729, 1941

Weaver L, Williams R, Rush S: Current density in bilateral and unilateral ECT. *Biol Psychiatry* 11:303-312, 1976

Weaver RM: Individuality and modernity, in *Essays on Individuality.* Ed by Morley F. Indianapolis, Liberty Press, 1978

Weil A, Brinegar WC: Electroencephalographic studies following electric shock therapy. *Arch Neurol Psychiatry* 57:719-729, 1947

Weinstein EA, Kahn RL: Symbolic reorganization in brain injuries, in *American Handbook of Psychiatry,* Vol I. Ed Arieti S. New York, Basic Books, 1959

Weinstein EA, Linn L, Kahn RL: Psychosis during electroshock therapy: Its relation to the theory of shock therapy, *Am J Psychiatry* 109:22-26, 1952

White RH, Shea JJ, Jonas MA: Multiple monitored electroconvulsive therapy. *Am J Psychiatry* 125:622-626, 1968

Whitty CWM, Zangwill MA, Eds: *Amnesia.* London, Butterworths, 1966

Wilcox KW: The pattern of cognitive reorientation following loss of consciousness. *Papers of the Mich Acad Sci, Arts and Letters* **41**:357-366, 1955

Wilcox PH: Brain facilitation not destruction the aim of electroshock therapy. *Dis Nerv Syst* **7**:201-207, 1946

Wilcox PH: Electroshock therapy: A review of over 23,000 treatments using unidirectional currents. *Am J Psychiatry* **104**:100-112, 1947

Will OA, Rehfeldt FL, Newmann MH: A fatality in electroshock therapy: Report of a case and review of certain previously described cases. *J Nerv Ment Dis* **107**:105-126, 1948

Williams M: Errors in picture recognition after ECT. *Neuropsychologia* **11**:429-436, 1973

Winkelman NW, Moore M: Neurohistologic findings in experimental electric shock treatment. *J Neuropathol Exp Neurol* **3**:199-209, 1944

Wortis J: Review of psychiatric progress 1942, physiological treatment of the psychoses. *Am J Psychiatry* **97**:602-603, 1943

Zamora EN, Kaebling R: Memory and electroconvulsive therapy. *Am J Psychiatry* **122**:546-554, 1965

Zinkin S, Birtchnell J: Unilateral electroconvulsive therapy: Its effects on memory and its therapeutic efficacy. *Br J Psychiatry* **114**:973-988, 1968

Ziskind E, Somerfeld-Ziskind E, Ziskind L: Metrazol and electric convulsive therapy of the affective psychoses. *Arch Neurol Psychiatry* **53**:212-217, 1945

Zornetzer S: Retrograde amnesia and brain seizures in rodents: Electrophysiological and neuroanatomical analyses, in *Psychobiology of Convulsive Therapy*. Ed Fink M, Kety S, McGaugh J, et al. New York, Wiley, 1974

Zubin J: Memory functioning in patients treated with electric shock therapy. *J Pers* **17**:33-41, 1948

Zubin J, Barrera SE: Effect of electric convulsive therapy on memory. *Proc Soc Exp Biol Med* **48**:596-597, 1941

Zung WW, Rogers J, Krugman A: Effect of electroconvulsive therapy in memory in depressive disorders. *Recent Adv Biol Psychiatry* **10**:160-178, 1968

Index _____

Note: Page numbers in italics refer to definitions of terms.